VEGETABLE HARVEST

VEGETABLE HARVEST

⇒ *Vegetables at the Center of the Plate* ⇐

PATRICIA WELLS

wm

WILLIAM MORROW

An Imprint of HarperCollins*Publishers*

HarperCollins books may be purchased for educational, business, or sales promotional use. For information please write: Special Markets Department, HarperCollins Publishers, 10 East 53rd Street, New York, NY 10022.

FIRST EDITION

Photographs © 2007 by Patricia Wells

Library of Congress Cataloging-in-Publication Data

Wells, Patricia.
   Vegetable harvest / Patricia Wells.
     p. cm.
   Includes index.
   ISBN 978-0-06-075244-6
   ISBN-10: 0-06-075244-0
   1. Cookery (Vegetables)   I. Title.

TX801.W42 2007
641.6'5—dc22

2006043723

07 08 09 10 11 IM 10 9 8 7 6 5 4 3 2 1

For Jean-Paul Boyer and his crew (and especially René),
with thanks for past, present, and future vegetable harvests.
Thank you for helping to perfect my paradise.

CONTENTS

Acknowledgments   ix

Introduction   x

Appetizers, Starters, and First Courses   1
Les Amuse-Bouche, les Hors-d'Oeuvres et les Entrées

Salads   21
Les Salades

Soups   47
Les Soupes et les Potages

Fish and Shellfish   75
Les Poissons, Coquillages et Fruits de Mer

Poultry and Meats   107
Les Volailles et les Viandes

Pasta, Rice, Beans, and Grains   135
Les Pâtes, Riz, Légumes Sec et Céréales

Vegetables   155
Les Légumes

Potatoes   221
Les Pommes de Terre

Eggs, Cheese, and Friends   233
Les Oeufs, les Fromages et leurs Amis

Breads   247
Les Pains

Desserts   267
Les Desserts

The Pantry   293
Au Garde-Manger

Index   315

☙ACKNOWLEDGMENTS☙

This book owes its greatest debt of gratitude to the farmers who work so hard to produce the vegetables that grace my table. When I look at the calendar and think of how each week—in some seasons, almost each day—brings a new seasonal awareness, the year is filled with new joys and rediscoveries, from the first-of-season asparagus in February to the first-of-season black truffle in November.

In Paris, I must thank Joël Thiebault for the glorious vegetables delivered to my door on Fridays or selected at his stand at the President Wilson market each Wednesday and Saturday. In Provence, it's the small growers at our Tuesday and Saturday farmers' market in Vaison-la-Romaine who have my thanks, as well as Josiane and Corinne Méliani at Les Gourmandines.

I want to thank too our friends who are always willing to experiment with us at table, including Rita and Yale Kramer, Susan Herrmann-Loomis, Steven Rothfeld, Andrew Axilrod and Alyson de Groot, Johanne Killeen and George Germon, Devon Fredericks and Eli Zabar, Ina and Jeffrey Garten, and Dorie and Michael Greenspan. Thank you, Juan Sanchez, for enriching my life in so many ways, especially on the road to wine inspiration.

Thanks to the friends and restaurateurs who have shared so many recipes, including Guy and Tina Julien at La Beaugravière, Flora and Raoul Reichrath at Le Grand Pré, Marlies and Johannes Sailers at Les Abeilles, and the many other chefs who have inspired so many recipes in this book.

Thanks to Heather Mallory for her careful vegetable research, to Marie-Agnes Lo Casico for helping with vegetable history and food expressions, to Janyne Kizer for the recipe testing. Thank you, Amanda Urban, my friend and super-efficient agent, who always gets back to me in a millisecond, no matter where she may be. Thank you, Elisabeth Hopkins, for careful attention to the manuscript. Thanks to Lucy Baker at William Morrow for keeping tabs on everything and of course to my friend and editor Harriet Bell, for making the entire experience so smooth and painless. Thank you all.

Special thanks also to all of my students, many of whom inspired recipes in the book and helped to improve them in so many ways.

⊱INTRODUCTION⊰

It was an August morning of abundant Provençal sunshine, and I was putting the finishing touches on my last book—*The Provence Cookbook*. I had spent the morning testing a quartet of vegetable recipes, and as I placed the completed dishes on the table under the oak tree for lunch, a lightbulb went on. The dishes all looked so natural and so perfect, and I had so enjoyed creating them that I simply knew vegetables would be the topic of my next book.

Every book changes an author in some ways. But *Vegetable Harvest* has totally altered the way I look at markets, menus and seasons, and the role of vegetables in the diet and in the menu. Rather than creating a meal around the fish, the poultry, or the meat, I found that I began putting the vegetables first.

With vegetables no longer afterthoughts, I began trying to see how many I could pack into our diet each day. Even classic combinations were altered to give vegetables a bigger role. So beef with carrots became carrots and beef, and a newly created spring lamb couscous soon found its way to our dinner table as a generous blend of zucchini, chickpeas, and couscous. Flanked of course by tender morsels of *gigot*. Instead of meat or poultry or fish and a side of vegetables, I tripled the number of vegetables in each meal.

As cooks, we all get stuck in a rut. Asparagus is cooked one way, zucchini another, eggplant another. To break out, I tried to find all the ways of serving a single vegetable and to include not just one but three different preparations of zucchini (or green beans or eggplant) in a single meal. Likewise, we tend to steam, braise, roast, blanch vegetables the same way time and again. Again, the routine became a challenge to experiment, looking for the best-tasting and most wholesome way of cooking each ingredient. I found there was always a better or even a best way.

The students in my cooking classes, in both Paris and Provence, responded with enthusiasm, happy to go back home knowing how delicious steamed peas with herbs could taste or to know that the stem of the artichoke is one of the tenderest, most delicious parts of that regal vegetable.

As I photographed in markets, I also found myself more and more connected to each and every vegetable. They were not just food to me, but little wonders of life. I marveled over the veins of the perfect winter cabbage, noticed the colors of the soil that clung to the carrots fresh from the earth, sighed with pleasure at the kaleidoscope of colors of the heirloom tomatoes in my garden, smiled as I spied through the lens the classic color-wheel pairing of vegetables side by side: The French almost make a ritual of it, with deep purple beets and wintergreen mâche always teamed up, as are alabaster cauliflower and ruby radishes. And is there anything more beautiful than first-of-season white or green or purple-tipped asparagus, gently gnarled fava beans, or the pert honeycomb of a perfect spring morel?

With each season, vegetables seem to speak of hope. Their colors, the aromas as they cook, the intense flavors, are all there as simple, pure pleasures.

In this book I have chosen to include nutritional information for each recipe. Not to make us slaves to calories or fat, protein, or carbohydrates. But to let us know what we are consuming. As well as pleasure, food is fuel, so let's put the best fuel we can into our bodies. As one who cooks and eats for a living, I find that I need to pay careful attention to portion size as well as nutritional balance. I want every bit of my food to count, so there is simply no room for empty calories or food that is more caloric than need be. So as one who values flavor above all, I have worked hard to make the food as tasty and nutritious as it can be.

As cooks today, we are all looking for shortcuts and convenience. To me, shopping every day is not just a necessity but a joy. But like everyone, I have days without much time to think about the dinner table, and on those days I do appreciate some convenience. Prewashed and packaged greens, frozen peas, and canned chickpeas or artichoke hearts are a godsend.

In *Vegetable Harvest* I have taken a very personal approach to defining the vegetable world. The ingredients here include nuts and seeds as well as fruits we consider vegetables, like tomatoes and avocado. In truth, I decided to include anything that would grow in my garden in Provence. That's very personal indeed.

The greatest character of a vegetable is that it gives so much of itself while asking so little of us who prepare it. For example, some of the recipes here that I find most sublime are the simplest ones, like steamed creamy cabbage, cauliflower purée, and heirloom tomato broth with fresh tarragon. These are dishes that come together on their own, as the French say, *se mangent tout seul,* meaning they go down easily, with no need of embellishment.

Finally, this book brings a fervent wish: May all our tables be forever laden with fresh, gorgeous, fragrant vegetables!

APPETIZERS, STARTERS, AND FIRST COURSES

*Les Amuse-Bouche, les Hors-d'Oeuvres
et les Entrées*

❖

TOASTED, SEASONED PUMPKIN SEEDS

Graines de Courge Grillées

I confess to an addiction to these savory toasted seeds, for they offer everything I look for in a snack: crunch, saltiness, a haunting flavor that one cannot immediately identify. Around five in the afternoon I can often be found in my office with a little bowl of these irresistible treats at the ready. I like to put them in bread dough—like the Pumpkin Bread with Toasted Pumpkin Seeds (page 254)—and always carry a little bag of them in my purse, should hunger call. 2 cups

EQUIPMENT: A rimmed baking sheet.

2 cups (8 ounces) hulled pumpkin or squash seeds
1 teaspoon sesame-seasoned sea salt (gomasio) or ½ teaspoon fine sea salt
2 tablespoons tamari or other Japanese soy sauce

1. Preheat the oven to 425 degrees F.

2. In a large bowl, combine the seeds with the sesame-seasoned sea salt and the tamari, tossing to evenly coat the seeds. Spread the seeds in a single layer on the baking sheet. Place in the oven and toast, shaking the pan from time to time, until the seeds change color from a steel-gray to a toasty brown, begin to pop and puff up, and are crisp and golden, about 12 minutes. The seeds can be stored in an airtight container for up to two weeks.

19 calories per tablespoon ⁖ 1 g fat ⁖ 1 g protein ⁖ 2 g carbohydrates

✣Variation: Combine 2 cups sunflower seeds, 2 tablespoons flax seeds, and 2 tablespoons sesame seeds with the same quantity of tamari and sesame-seasoned salt. Toast in the same manner.

✣c 53 calories per tablespoon ❄ 5 g fat ❄ 2 g protein ❄ 1 g carbohydrates

Tip: Tongs are a most useful piece of equipment in the kitchen. I always have several sets hanging from the front of my stove. I find them especially helpful for pulling hard-to-reach items, such as baking sheets, out of the oven.

SMOKED SALMON WITH DILL-MUSTARD SAUCE

Saumon Fumé, Sauce Moutarde à la Menthe

A sip of white wine, a thin silken slice of top-quality smoked salmon, and a touch of this sauce—light, delicious, and perky—and one's appetite is opened for the treats to come. 10 servings

EQUIPMENT: 10 chilled dinner plates.

1 tablespoon freshly squeezed lemon juice
3 tablespoons imported French mustard
1/2 teaspoon fine sea salt
1/4 cup extra-virgin olive oil
2 tablespoons *crème fraîche* or sour cream
3 tablespoons finely minced fresh dill or wild fennel fronds
20 thin slices (about 2 pounds) smoked salmon

1. In a medium bowl, whisk together the lemon juice, mustard, and salt. Whisking, slowly add the oil in a thin, steady stream. Add the *crème fraîche,* stirring until well combined. Stir in the minced herbs. Taste for seasoning.

2. Arrange 2 slices of smoked salmon on each of 10 chilled dinner plates and drizzle with about 1 tablespoon of the sauce. Serve.

160 calories per serving ◦ 10 g fat ◦ 16 g protein ◦ trace of carbohydrates

Wine Suggestion

The intense flavors of smoked salmon can present challenges for wine matching. Look for a wine with lots of character, one that is dry and pungent: an Alsatian Pinot Gris (anything from the house of Zind-Humbrecht), a vintage champagne (a J. Lassalle *blanc de blancs*), or a Chablis Grand Cru (from Domaine François Raveneau) with lots of minerality.

EVERGREEN TOMATO COOLER

Jus de Tomates Vertes

The bright green Evergreen tomato is a favorite in my garden. When I have a bumper crop, I turn to this quick and delicious appetizer drink. There is no need to peel the tomatoes when you prepare this: the skin adds extra flavor, texture, and nutrients. 4 servings

EQUIPMENT: A food processor or a blender.

4 garden-fresh Evergreen tomatoes (about 10 ounces), cored and quartered (do not peel)
Zesty Lemon Salt (page 310)
Fresh cilantro leaves for garnish

In a food processor or a blender, purée the tomatoes. Season to taste with lemon salt. Chill thoroughly before serving. Serve in small, clear glasses as a refreshing aperitif, garnishing with fresh cilantro leaves at the last minute.

16 calories per serving ⁕ trace of fat ⁕ 1 g protein ⁕ 3 g carbohydrates

SAVORY MIXED HERB AND
GOAT CHEESE SORBET

Sorbet au Chèvre Frais et aux Herbes Aromatiques

This unusual sorbet can wear many hats. I like to serve it in little ice-cream bowls as a surprise appetizer on a warm summer's night, and often swirl it into a chilled vegetable soup as part of a first course. Variations are endless, using a single herb or several, according to your mood and tastes. 8 servings

EQUIPMENT: A food processor or a blender; an ice-cream maker.

8 ounces soft fresh goat's milk cheese
1 cup buttermilk, shaken to blend
1/3 cup minced fresh herb leaves, such as chives, tarragon, parsley, and mint
1/2 cup light cream
1/2 teaspoon fine sea salt

In a food processor or a blender, combine the cheese, buttermilk, herbs, light cream, and salt. Process until the mixture is well blended and the herbs are evenly distributed. Transfer to an ice-cream maker and freeze according to the manufacturer's instructions.

170 calories per serving * 13 g fat * 10 g protein * 3 g carbohydrates

Note: Make sure all ingredients are thoroughly chilled before proceeding.

SPICY POLENTA-CHEESE CRACKERS

Biscuits de Polenta au Poivre de Cayenne

These crunchy, irresistible crackers have just the right amount of spice to wake up your palate and serve as the opening act to a very fine meal. 75 crackers

EQUIPMENT: A food processor or a blender; 2 nonstick baking sheets; a 1¾-inch round biscuit cutter or a glass.

1 cup bread flour
1 cup instant polenta
¾ teaspoon fine sea salt
½ teaspoon baking soda
¼ teaspoon cayenne pepper
½ cup freshly grated Parmigiano-Reggiano cheese
2½ tablespoons cold unsalted butter, cut into ¼-inch pieces
¾ cup buttermilk, shaken to blend

1.   Preheat the oven to 375 degrees F.

2.   In a food processor or a blender, combine the flour, polenta, sea salt, baking soda, cayenne pepper, and cheese. Process to blend. Add the butter and process just until the mixture resembles coarse meal. Add the buttermilk and process until the dough just forms a ball. Transfer the dough to a lightly floured surface and knead for a few seconds. Wrap in plastic wrap and set aside at room temperature for 15 minutes.

3.   Cut the dough into quarters. Set one quarter on a lightly floured surface; cover the remaining pieces with plastic. Roll out the dough ¹⁄₁₆ inch thick. Using a 1¾-inch biscuit cutter or a glass, cut out rounds of dough and arrange them on a nonstick baking sheet. Repeat with the remaining dough. Place the baking sheets in the oven and bake until the crackers are golden and crisp, 12 to 15 minutes. Once cool, transfer to airtight containers. The crackers can be stored in an airtight container for up to two weeks.

27 calories per cracker ⁕ 1 g fat ⁕ 1 g protein ⁕ 4 g carbohydrates

"S'embarquer sans biscuit!" To launch into something with no backup.

SQUID SQUARES STEWED IN TOMATOES AND WHITE WINE

Dés de Calamar à la Tomate

These tender squid are delicious as appetizers. Serve them in a small bowl, with toothpicks. As a variation, I sometimes spear a green olive, then a square of tasty squid, and arrange them on a platter. 40 servings

EQUIPMENT: A large skillet with a lid; toothpicks.

2 tablespoons extra-virgin olive oil
1 pound squid, cleaned and cut into ¾-inch squares
About ½ cup dry white wine
1 pound ripe red tomatoes, cored, peeled, seeded, and chopped (or one 15-ounce can tomatoes in their juices, puréed in a food processor or a blender)
Bouquet garni: several parsley stems, celery leaves, and sprigs of thyme, encased in a wire mesh tea infuser
½ teaspoon fine sea salt
1 small fresh hot pepper or hot red pepper flakes to taste
40 green olives, pitted (optional)

In a large skillet, heat the oil until hot but not smoking. Add the squid squares and sear over high heat, tossing from time to time, for 1 to 2 minutes, until the squid is browned. (Think that you are browning meat!) Slowly add the wine, tomatoes, bouquet garni, salt, and hot pepper. Cover and simmer gently until the squid is tender, about 1 hour, adding more wine or water if the sauce becomes too thick. Taste from time to time to check tenderness. Remove the bouquet garni. Taste for seasoning. Serve in a small bowl, with toothpicks.

27 calories per serving ◦ 1 g fat ◦ 2 g protein ◦ 1 g carbohydrates

CHORIZO WITH SHERRY VINEGAR AND THYME

Chorizo au Thym et au Vinaigre de Xérès

Color, spice, a touch of vinegar, a hint of thyme, all perfect for the starting lineup to a special meal. A sip of champagne, anyone? 48 servings

EQUIPMENT: A large skillet; toothpicks.

12 slices (about 8 ounces) dried chorizo (each about 2 inches in diameter, cut ⅓ inch thick)
1 tablespoon best-quality sherry-wine vinegar
1 teaspoon fresh or dried thyme leaves

Heat a large skillet over moderate heat. Add the sausage and brown on one side, about 30 seconds. Turn and brown on the other side, about 30 seconds more. Drizzle with the vinegar. Remove from the heat and cut each slice of chorizo into 4 pie-shaped wedges. Transfer to a serving platter. Sprinkle with thyme. Serve immediately, offering guests skewers or toothpicks and cocktail napkins.

✵c 22 calories per serving ❀ 2 g fat ❀ 1 g protein ❀ trace of carbohydrates

---

A Menu for March

Chorizo with Sherry Vinegar and Thyme
Steamed Leeks in Mustard and Caper Vinaigrette (page 188)
Lamb Couscous with Chickpeas and Zucchini (page 124)
Pumpkin Flan with Lemon Sauce (page 287)

TOMATO AND STRAWBERRY GAZPACHO

Gaspacho à la Fraise

As cooks as well as diners, we often need to make a leap of faith. I have an instinctive dislike for mixing fruits and vegetables on the same plate or in the same glass. But I saw enough of this combination and was quite curious, so I took the plunge. So should you; you'll fall in love. 8 servings

EQUIPMENT: A food processor or a blender.

1 pound garden-fresh tomatoes, rinsed, cored, and quartered (do not peel)
1 pound fresh strawberries, rinsed and stemmed
1 teaspoon balsamic vinegar

In a food processor or a blender, purée the tomatoes and the strawberries. Add the vinegar and blend again. Taste for seasoning. Chill thoroughly before serving. Serve in small, clear glasses as a refreshing aperitif.

27 calories per serving ❋ trace of fat ❋ 1 g protein ❋ 6 g carbohydrates

Origins: The tomato was first cultivated by the Incas and was imported to Europe in the sixteenth century. It was at first considered an aphrodisiac, while in the north of France it was thought to be a poison.

CHUNKY EGGPLANT-CUMIN SPREAD

Caviar d'Aubergine au Cumin

In the summer months, I make this eggplant dip at least once a week, keeping it on hand for sampling with thin homemade toasts and a predinner sip of wine. I like to keep this "caviar" a bit chunky so you know that you are eating earthy eggplant. So please do not process to a smooth purée. 3 cups

EQUIPMENT: A baking sheet; a small skillet; a food processor or a blender.

4 small, firm eggplants (each about 8 ounces), rinsed and dried
2 teaspoons cumin seeds
2 plump, moist cloves garlic, peeled, halved, green germ removed
1 tablespoon tahini (sesame paste)
1 tablespoon freshly squeezed lemon juice
½ teaspoon fine sea salt

1. Preheat the oven to 450 degrees F.

2. With a meat fork, prick the eggplants all over. Place the eggplants directly on an oven rack placed in the center of the oven. (Placing the eggplants directly on the rack allows the air to circulate as the eggplants cook. The eggplants will roast rather than steam.) Place a baking sheet on another rack beneath the eggplants to collect any juices. Roast until the eggplants are soft and collapsed, about 25 minutes. There is no need to turn them.

3. Remove the rack with the eggplants from the oven. Place the eggplants on a clean work surface and, with a sharp knife, trim off the stem ends and discard. Cut the eggplants lengthwise in half. With a small spoon, scrape out the eggplant pulp, discarding the skin.

4. Toast the cumin: Place the cumin in a small skillet over moderate heat. Shake the pan regularly until the seeds are fragrant and evenly toasted, about 2 minutes. Watch carefully! They can burn quickly. Transfer the cumin to a large plate to cool. Set aside. Once cool, grind to a fine powder in a spice grinder.

5. In a food processor or a blender, combine the garlic, tahini, lemon juice, and salt and process to blend. Add the eggplant and process just for a few seconds, to blend the ingredients. Transfer to a bowl and mix once again with 2 forks. Stir in the cumin. Taste for seasoning. Store in an airtight container in the refrigerator for up to two days. Stir again at serving time, serving slightly chilled or at room temperature.

11 calories per tablespoon ⁕ trace of fat ⁕ trace of protein ⁕ 2 g carbohydrates

BEET TARTARE WITH CAPERS, MUSTARD, AND SHALLOTS

Tartare de Betterave aux Câpres, Moutarde et Échalotes

Early one September my friend Steven Rothfeld and I toured Burgundy in search of spectacular photos, good meals, and a few recipes. We sampled this delightful appetizer at a small family restaurant in the Mâcon region. I like to spoon the tartare onto leaves of Belgian endive and pass a platter at aperitif time. 30 servings

EQUIPMENT: A food processor or a blender.

2 shallots, trimmed, peeled, and cut into thin rings
½ cup cornichons
¼ cup drained capers in vinegar
½ cup fresh parsley leaves
1 pound cooked beets, trimmed and peeled
1 teaspoon Worcestershire sauce
¼ cup imported French mustard
1 plump, moist clove garlic, peeled, halved, green germ removed, minced
1 large egg yolk
Tabasco sauce to taste
About 30 Belgian endive leaves

In a food processor or a blender, combine the shallots, cornichons, capers, and parsley and process to chop coarsely. Add the remaining ingredients except the endive and process, keeping the mixture fairly coarse. Taste for seasoning. Serve immediately, as an appetizer, on individual leaves of Belgian endive.

19 calories per serving ⁕ trace of fat ⁕ 1 g protein ⁕ 4 g carbohydrates

Origins: Red beets were introduced to France from Italy at the end of the fifteenth century. By the nineteenth century beets were well known, sold as a baked delicacy on the streets of Marseille.

CHICKPEA AND BASIL PURÉE

Tartinade de Pois Chiches au Basilic

On Friday, the last day of class in my Provençal cooking school, we do a lot of improvisation. We always take all the leftover bits of cheese from the week and create soufflés or use them to stuff zucchini blossoms or to mix with herbs as part of the final cheese course. One Friday in July I assigned two students to create varied mixtures for the freshly picked squash blossoms we stuff and roast. They suggested mixing some freshly cooked chickpeas with some Light Basil Purée. At first I made a face, fearful that the mixture would turn out a dull, unappetizing gray. Then I changed my mind and said, "Oh, just go for it!" They did, and to our delight the mixture was a pale golden color, flecked nicely with green. Better yet, the combination was alive, electric, full of great summer flavors. 2¼ cups

EQUIPMENT: A food processor or a blender.

2 cups canned chickpeas, drained (reserve liquid) and rinsed
About ¼ cup Light Basil Purée (page 301), or to taste

Combine the chickpeas and basil purée in a food processor or a blender. Blend until smooth, adding some of the reserved liquid if necessary. The mixture can be used as a dip for crackers or raw vegetables or as a stuffing for squash or zucchini blossoms. Store in an airtight container in the refrigerator for up to two days.

49 calories per tablespoon ❋ 2 g fat ❋ 1 g protein ❋ 7 g carbohydrates

---

Origins: The ancient Greeks and Romans thought basil would grow only if you screamed wild curses and shouted unintelligibly while sowing the seeds. They also believed that if you left a basil leaf under a pot, it would turn into a scorpion.

CHICKPEA DIP WITH FRESH CILANTRO

Purée de Pois Chiches à la Coriandre

One of the greatest advantages of having a fertile garden is that one can create new tastes at the drop of a hat. One day guests were coming up the hill, and I didn't have enough appetizers to get the meal going. I grabbed a handful of fresh cilantro from the courtyard garden, puréed it with a can of drained chickpeas and the zest of the lemons on hand, and *voilà,* we were ready to uncork the champagne and begin the feast. 2¼ cups

EQUIPMENT: A food processor or a blender.

2 cups canned chickpeas, drained (reserve liquid) and rinsed
1 tablespoon freshly squeezed lemon juice
Grated zest of 1 lemon, preferably organic
½ teaspoon fine sea salt
2 plump, moist cloves garlic, peeled, halved, green germ removed, minced
1 cup fresh cilantro leaves, several leaves reserved for garnish

In a food processor or a blender, combine the chickpeas, lemon juice, lemon zest, salt, garlic, and most of the cilantro leaves. Blend until smooth, adding 5 to 6 tablespoons of the reserved liquid if necessary. Taste for seasoning. Store in an airtight container in the refrigerator for up to two days. At serving time, garnish with fresh cilantro leaves.

16 calories per tablespoon ⁕ trace of fat ⁕ 1 g protein ⁕ 3 g carbohydrates

ARTICHOKE AND WHITE BEAN DIP

Purée d'Artichaut et de Haricots Blancs

This clean-flavored dip is a quick pantry special, one that can be whipped up in seconds and garnished with parsley and mint at the last minute. 2¼ cups

EQUIPMENT: A food processor or a blender.

5 drained canned artichoke hearts
2 cups canned white beans, drained and rinsed
Grated zest of 1 lemon, preferably organic
1 tablespoon freshly squeezed lemon juice
¼ cup flat-leaf parsley leaves, finely minced
¼ cup fresh mint leaves, finely minced

In a food processor or a blender, combine the artichokes, beans, lemon zest, and lemon juice and purée. Add half of the parsley and mint and purée again. Store in an airtight container in the refrigerator for up to two days. At serving time, transfer to a large bowl and garnish with the remaining herbs.

44 calories per tablespoon ∗ trace of fat ∗ 3 g protein ∗ 9 g carbohydrates

"Avoir un coeur d'artichaut." To be fickle in love.

Folklore: To find out what your little girl will be when she grows up, place three wild artichokes beneath her crib. Label each one: Single, Married, Nun. The one that opens first is the response to your question.

SALADS

Les Salades

◈

BISTROT PAUL BERT'S WATERCRESS SALAD WITH CREAMY BACON AND POACHED EGG

La Salade de Cresson du Bistrot Paul Bert

One chilly December evening we made our first visit to the lively Bistrot Paul Bert, in Paris's eleventh *arrondissement*. The jam-packed, classic old-time bistro took the phrase *elbow to elbow* to new heights. We were so tightly squeezed that Walter was seated next to a pole, and the only possible way for him to eat was to wrap his arm around the pole to cut his meat! We forgave all because the food was just so delicious. I ordered this updated version of the bistro classic *frisée aux lardons,* usually curly endive showered with big chunks of bacon and topped with a poached egg. I immediately warmed to the idea of replacing the endive with watercress. And bathing the bacon in cream results in a smoked flavor with each and every bite. Since then, it's become a lunchtime favorite. 4 servings

EQUIPMENT: A large skillet; 4 ramekins; a large, deep skillet with a lid.

5 ounces smoked bacon, rind removed, cut into ¼-inch cubes (1½ cups)
1 cup Creamy Lemon-Chive Dressing (page 299)
2 bunches of watercress (about 1 pound), rinsed, dried, and stemmed
1 tablespoon distilled vinegar
4 ultra-fresh large eggs
¼ cup finely chopped fresh chives
Freshly ground black pepper

1. In a large, dry skillet, brown the bacon over moderate heat until crisp and golden, about 5 minutes. With a slotted spoon, transfer the bacon to several layers of paper towel to absorb the fat. Blot the top of the bacon with several layers of paper towel to absorb any remaining fat.

2. In a large, shallow salad bowl, combine the bacon and the dressing and toss to blend. Add the watercress and toss to evenly coat the greens. Divide the salad among 4 large dinner plates.

3. In a large, deep skillet, bring 2 inches of water to a boil. Reduce the heat to maintain a simmer and add the vinegar. Break the eggs into the ramekins and, one by one, carefully lower the lip of the ramekin ½ inch into the water. Let the eggs flow out. Immediately cover the skillet. Poach the eggs until the whites are firm but the yolks are still runny and are covered with a thin translucent layer of white, about 3 minutes for medium-firm eggs and 5 minutes for firm yolks. With a slotted spoon, carefully lift the eggs from

the water, drain, and place on the dressed greens. Season with chives and plenty of black pepper. Serve immediately.

✢ᴄ 342 calories per serving ❂ 28 g fat ❂ 19 g protein ❂ 5 g carbohydrates

That Extra Touch: This is a simple recipe but takes careful organization. Make sure the eggs are at their peak of freshness (older eggs tend to spread out in the water) and are poached at the very last minute and served warm. I add vinegar to help the eggs hold their shape and allow the whites to coagulate faster.

Folklore: Salad is an aphrodisiac, so always grow a variety of lettuces and greens in your garden to assure fertility.

RADISH AND BUTTER LETTUCE SALAD
WITH RADISH SANDWICHES

Salade de Laitue et Radis, Accompagnée de Canapés aux Radis

The French *understand* radishes! All year long, in each market, one finds bunches of varied red radishes, their leaves fresh and alive. My students always notice them as we wander through markets and, more often than not, beg me to include them in the week's menu. This is one salad they particularly love. It can be made all year round but seems most perfect in the early days of spring. 4 servings

1 head of butter lettuce
1 bunch of radishes (about 30), washed and trimmed, the freshest leaves reserved
2 tablespoons unsalted butter, at room temperature
Zest of 1 lemon, preferably organic
4 slices dark rye bread, such as dense Swedish rye
Coarse sea salt
1/4 cup Creamy Lemon-Chive Dressing (page 299)
Fleur de sel

1.   Trim the lettuce, discarding the outer leaves. Wash and dry the leaves and tear into bite-sized pieces. Place in a salad bowl. Set aside.

2.   Slice the radishes into thin rounds. Reserve about one quarter of the radishes. Cut those rounds into narrow strips. Finely chop the leaves. Transfer the strips of radish and the leaves to paper towels to absorb any excess moisture.

3.   On a small plate, use a fork to mash together the butter and lemon zest. Add the drained radish strips and chopped radish leaves and mash to blend. Taste for seasoning. Spread on slices of dark rye bread. Season with coarse sea salt.

4.   Add the radish rounds to the lettuce in the salad bowl. Add just enough dressing to lightly coat the greens. Season with *fleur de sel*. Divide evenly among 4 salad plates. Place a slice of the open-faced radish sandwich at the edge of the plate.

❖ 179 calories per serving ❖ 9 g fat ❖ 9 g protein ❖ 21 g carbohydrates

CUCUMBER, SPRING ONION, AND GOAT CHEESE SALAD LE CINQ-MARS

La Salade de Concombre au Chèvre Frais du Cinq-Mars

Le Cinq-Mars is an adorable Parisian Left Bank bistro around the corner from the Musée d'Orsay. It was here that I first sampled a version of this salad one chilly day in February. It brought a nice, light touch of sunshine into my life, with a promise that spring was not too far away. 4 servings

EQUIPMENT: A grapefruit spoon; a mandoline or a very sharp knife.

2 European or hothouse cucumbers (about 1 pound each), scrubbed and trimmed
3 spring onions (or 6 scallions), trimmed and peeled
Several tablespoons Creamy Lemon-Chive Dressing (page 299)
2 *crottins de Chavignol* goat's milk cheeses, halved crosswise

1.   With a fork, score the skin of the cucumbers all along the length of the vegetable. (This will make for a more attractive presentation once cut.) Cut the cucumber lengthwise in half. With a grapefruit spoon, carve out and discard the seeds. Cut each half into 1/2-inch-thick slices. Place in a large bowl.

2.   With a mandoline or a very sharp knife, cut the onions crosswise into paper-thin slices. Separate into rings and drop into the bowl. Add just enough dressing to lightly coat the cucumbers and onions.

3.   Arrange the salad on individual salad plates. Place a disc of fresh goat's milk cheese on top of each salad. Serve.

150 calories per serving ◦ 10 g fat ◦ 7 g protein ◦ 10 g carbohydrates

Wine Suggestion

I can't imagine eating the delicate goat's milk cheese without a few sips of flinty white Sancerre, one of the finest Sauvignon Blancs in the world.

What I Learned: Grapefruit spoons are good for more than eating grapefruit! I find all sorts of uses for the slightly jagged–edged spoons. They're great for scraping the hairy choke from an artichoke, as well as ridding the cucumber of its seeds.

"Il me rend chèvre!" He's driving me crazy!

CUCUMBER AND DILL SALAD

Salade de Concombre à l'Aneth

This is a quintessential summer salad, a classic combination of fresh dill and refreshing cucumbers, seasoned with just a touch of vinegar and sugar, for a delicate sweet-and-sour blend. Make it part of every summer buffet. 4 servings

EQUIPMENT: A mandoline or a very sharp knife.

1 European or hothouse cucumber (about 1 pound), scrubbed and trimmed
1½ teaspoons coarse sea salt
¼ cup Champagne vinegar
¼ cup finely chopped fresh dill
1½ tablespoons sugar

1.   With a fork, score the skin of the cucumber all along the length of the vegetable. (This will make for a more attractive presentation once cut.) Using a mandoline or a very sharp knife, slice the cucumber very thinly. Place the cucumber slices in a colander set over a bowl. Sprinkle with the salt. Toss to evenly coat the cucumber slices with the salt. Let stand at room temperature for 15 minutes, tossing occasionally.

2.   In a medium bowl, combine the vinegar, dill, and sugar. Stir to dissolve the sugar.

3.   Drain the cucumber well and pat dry with a clean towel. Add the cucumber to the dressing and toss to blend. Refrigerate for at least 15 minutes and up to 2 hours. Serve chilled.

*c 24 calories per serving * trace of fat * 1 g protein * 6 g carbohydrates

FRÉDÉRIC ANTON'S HEIRLOOM TOMATO SALAD

La Salade de Tomates de Frédéric Anton

It takes a large measure of confidence for a chef to simply label his dish *La Tomate* and then present diners with a plate of perfect sliced heirloom tomatoes, anointed with the surprise of vanilla-flecked dressing, a touch of lime zest, freshly ground black pepper, and *fleur de sel*. This dish is on the menu at the elegant, excellent Le Pré Catelan in Paris, where Frédéric Anton works magic in the kitchen. 4 servings

EQUIPMENT: 2 small jars with lids; 4 chilled dinner plates.

2 plump, moist vanilla beans
2 limes, preferably organic
¼ cup extra-virgin olive oil
Fine sea salt
3 (about 2 pounds) large, firm ripe red heirloom tomatoes
Fleur de sel
Freshly ground black pepper

1.   One day before serving the salad, prepare the vanilla dressing: Flatten the vanilla beans and cut in half lengthwise. With a small spoon, scrape out the seeds and place them in a jar. (Reserve the pods for another use.) Zest the limes, reserving the zest in another small covered jar. Juice the limes and add, along with the oil and the salt, to the jar with the vanilla seeds. Shake to blend. Cover and refrigerate.

2.   At serving time, rinse, core, and peel the tomatoes. Cut them crosswise into ½-inch-thick slices. Drizzle each of the 4 chilled plates with a touch of the vanilla dressing. Arrange the tomato slices side by side on the plates. Drizzle with more vanilla dressing. Sprinkle with the lime zest, *fleur de sel*, and pepper. Serve.

  170 calories per serving ⁕ 14 g fat ⁕ 2 g protein ⁕ 11 g carbohydrates

CHERRY TOMATO AND BLACK OLIVE SALAD

Salade de Tomates-Cerises et Olives Noires

Come August, our vegetable garden is brimming with all manner of tiny tomatoes—round ones, oval ones, varieties shaped like a pear, and even like a pigeon heart, the *coeur de pigeon* variety. That's when this salad is a godsend, for when the crop is in, it must be consumed. This is also a good way to use up any leftover bits of soft cheese: sometimes I combine crumbed blue cheese, goat's milk cheese, and soft sheep's milk cheese. 6 servings

4 cups cherry tomatoes, preferably a mix of red, yellow, and green varieties
3 ounces fresh goat's milk cheese, cubed
20 ripe black olives, pitted and halved
¼ cup fresh basil leaves, cut into chiffonade
2 tablespoons freshly squeezed lemon juice, or to taste
Fleur de sel
Freshly ground black pepper

Stem and halve the tomatoes. In a large bowl, combine the ingredients and toss gently to blend. Taste for seasoning.

60 calories per serving ⁂ 3 g fat ⁂ 1 g protein ⁂ 8 g carbohydrates

SPRING ONION, CUCUMBER, AND
BASIL SALAD WITH BASIL-LEMON DRESSING

Salade de Ciboule, Concombre et Basilic

Summer salads are saviors. They're quick, light, refreshing—everything we need in the heat of the summer. I have a special affinity for the trio presented here: mild yet perky spring onions, the coolness of cucumber, all bathed in a tangy basil-based dressing. 4 servings

EQUIPMENT: A mandoline or a very sharp knife.

3 spring onions (or 6 scallions), trimmed and peeled
1 European or hothouse cucumber (about 1 pound), scrubbed and trimmed (do not peel)
1 cup fresh basil leaves, left whole if small, torn if large
About 2 tablespoons Basil-Lemon Dressing (page 297)
Fleur de sel

With a mandoline or a very sharp knife, cut the onions crosswise into paper-thin slices. Separate into rings and drop into a large salad bowl. Repeat for the cucumber, cutting into thin slices and dropping into the salad bowl. Add the basil leaves. Very gently toss with just enough dressing to lightly coat the ingredients. Season with *fleur de sel*. Serve on large dinner plates.

71 calories per serving ❊ 4 g fat ❊ 2 g protein ❊ 9 g carbohydrates

"Ce ne sont pas tes oignons!" It's none of your business!

SPRING ONION, TOMATO, AVOCADO, AND BASIL SALAD WITH BASIL-LEMON DRESSING

Salade de Ciboule, Tomates-Cerises, Avocat et Basilic

The first time I made this salad our eyes lit up! The colors alone make you want to dive in; the red, white, and green are a triumvirate to applaud. Avocado is one vegetable that is not given its due: it can do more than be a major player in guacamole, as this salad proves. 4 servings

EQUIPMENT: A mandoline or a very sharp knife.

3 spring onions (or 6 scallions), trimmed and peeled
1 ripe avocado
Several tablespoons of Basil-Lemon Dressing (page 297)
30 cherry tomatoes, halved
1/4 cup fresh basil leaves, left whole if small, torn if large
Fleur de sel

With a mandoline or a very sharp knife, cut the onions crosswise into paper-thin slices. Separate into rings and drop into a large salad bowl. Peel and halve the avocado, discarding the pit. Cut each half lengthwise into thin slices and drop into the bowl. Very gently toss with enough dressing to evenly coat the onions and avocado. Add halved cherry tomatoes and toss gently once more. Sprinkle with basil and season with *fleur de sel*. Serve on large dinner plates.

↝c 163 calories per serving ✳ 12 g fat ✳ 3 g protein ✳ 15 g carbohydrates

"Faire quelque chose aux petits oignons." To do something perfectly.

BABY SPINACH, RADISH, AND MINT SALAD

Salade aux Jeunes Pousses d'Épinard, Radis et Menthe

Baby spinach is my fallback green: I love its bright color and delicate crunch. This salad is quick, pretty, delicious, and out of the ordinary, even though it's made with seemingly ordinary ingredients. 4 servings

> 1 bunch of radishes (about 30), washed and trimmed
> 4 cups (about 8 ounces) baby spinach leaves, washed and dried
> ½ cup fresh mint leaves, rinsed and cut into chiffonade
> 2 tablespoons Creamy Lemon-Chive Dressing (page 299)
> *Fleur de sel*

Cut the radishes crosswise into thin slices. Place in a large bowl with the spinach and mint. At serving time, add just enough dressing to lightly coat all the ingredients. Season with *fleur de sel*. Arrange on 4 salad plates and serve.

32 calories per serving ∗ 1 g fat ∗ 4 g protein ∗ 4 g carbohydrates

Origins: Louis XIV often ate salad and radishes at the beginning of the meal to stimulate his appetite.

TANGY COLESLAW

Chou Cru Râpé, Sauce Piquante

As a child, one of my favorite foods was coleslaw, always a version of grated cabbage salad that had a bit of an acidic tang, and one made of nothing but grated cabbage and a touch of dressing. So here it is, My Favorite Coleslaw. 4 servings

EQUIPMENT: A box grater or a food processor fitted with a shredding blade; a small jar with a lid.

¼ cabbage, cored
¼ cup light cream
2 tablespoons distilled vinegar
½ teaspoon fine sea salt

Using the largest holes of a box grater or the shredding blade of a food processor, grate the cabbage. (You should have about 4 cups.) Transfer to a large bowl. In a small jar, combine the cream, vinegar, and salt and shake to blend. Pour the dressing over the cabbage and toss until the cabbage is evenly coated. Taste for seasoning. Serve immediately.

49 calories per serving ◦ 3 g fat ◦ 1 g protein ◦ 5 g carbohydrates

"Faire chou blanc!" To draw a blank!

Folklore: Sunburn? Migraine? Place a cabbage leaf wherever it hurts and you'll be cured.

GRATED SALAD: CABBAGE, CARROTS, AND CELERY

Salade de Chou, Carottes et Céleri Râpés

This is a favorite lunchtime salad, and it's also great as part of a large summer buffet. 4 servings

EQUIPMENT: A box grater or a food processor fitted with a shredding blade; a small jar with a lid.

¼ cabbage, cored
3 carrots, trimmed and peeled
4 ribs celery, cut into very thin crosswise slices
¼ cup Creamy Lemon-Chive Dressing (page 299)
Fine sea salt

Using the largest holes of a box grater or the shredding blade of a food processor, grate the cabbage and the carrots. Combine the cabbage, carrots, and celery in a large bowl. Pour the dressing over the vegetables and toss until the vegetables are evenly coated. Taste for seasoning. Serve immediately. (The salad loses its punch if left to sit for long.)

62 calories per serving ❋ 2 g fat ❋ 6 g protein ❋ 10 g carbohydrates

Folklore: Always place a few celery seeds under your pillow to guarantee a long night's sleep and to ward off insomnia.

"Aller planter ses choux." To go plant one's cabbage, or to go live in the countryside to cultivate one's garden.

SHAVED VEGETABLE SALAD

Méli-Mélo d'Herbes et de Légumes

One glorious day in late spring a friend and I sat on the terrace of the all-organic restaurant La Chassagnette, deep in the south of France's Camargue. We had been served a version of this salad atop a slice of sourdough bread and were eating this rather messy but totally delicious *tartine,* or open-faced sandwich. I have since served it in many variations, changing the vegetables as the season fits, serving the mélange on top of a slice of smoked salmon or simply as a lovely salad. 8 servings

EQUIPMENT: A mandoline or a very sharp knife.

4 baby zucchini, rinsed and trimmed
1 carrot, scrubbed and trimmed (do not peel)
4 spring onions (or 8 scallions), trimmed and peeled
4 fresh baby artichokes, trimmed (or 4 canned artichoke hearts, drained)
2 small fennel bulbs, trimmed (any fennel fronds reserved)
Several borage flowers (optional)
½ cup fresh flat-leaf parsley leaves
½ cup fresh cilantro leaves
Several nasturtium leaves and flowers
2 tablespoons extra-virgin olive oil
Zesty Lemon Salt (page 310)

With a mandoline or a very sharp knife, cut all the vegetables into thin strips. If the vegetables are large, cut each strip into 3-inch pieces. In a large bowl, toss the vegetables, fennel fronds, herbs, and blossoms together. Add just enough extra-virgin olive oil to lightly coat the mixture. Season with the salt and serve.

83 calories per serving ⁕ 4 g fat ⁕ 3 g protein ⁕ 12 g carbohydrates

Origins: Artichokes have long been considered an aphrodisiac. As a result, during the sixteenth century, French nuns were forbidden to partake in the pleasures of this very special vegetable. Vegetable merchants used to run through the food markets shouting, "The beautiful artichoke, for the mister and the missus, to warm the heart and the soul."

SHAVED FENNEL AND PARSLEY SALAD
WITH SHEEP'S MILK CHEESE

Salade de Fenouil au Fromage de Brebis

Okay, this is the time to take out your very best extra-virgin olive oil. There is something about the springtime freshness of this salad that cries out for a top-quality oil, perhaps one from the south of France with a hint of artichoke. If there are some fennel fronds attached to the fennel bulbs, trim them off and mix them with the parsley leaves. 6 servings

EQUIPMENT: A mandoline or a very sharp knife.

3 tablespoons freshly squeezed lemon juice
4 small fennel bulbs, trimmed (any fennel fronds reserved)
½ cup fresh flat-leaf parsley leaves
About 2 tablespoons extra-virgin olive oil
Fine sea salt
A 4-ounce piece firm sheep's milk cheese, such as L'Ossau-Iraty (or Parmigiano-Reggiano), shaved
   with a vegetable peeler into very thin slices

1.   Fill a 6-cup airtight container with 1 quart cold water and add the lemon juice. Using a mandoline or a very sharp knife, cut the fennel lengthwise into very thin slices, dropping the slices into the acidulated water. Cover the container and refrigerate. This can be done up to 4 hours in advance. The fennel will crisp up, and the lemon juice will prevent it from darkening.

2.   Fill a 2-cup airtight container with 1 cup cold water and add the reserved fennel fronds and the flat-leaf parsley leaves. Cover the container and refrigerate. This can be done up to 4 hours in advance.

3.   At serving time, drain the fennel and, in a large bowl, toss with just enough olive oil to lightly coat the fennel. Arrange the slices of fennel on individual salad plates. Drain the parsley and fennel fronds and, in a small bowl, toss with just enough oil to lightly coat the parsley and fennel fronds. Arrange the parsley and fennel fronds on top of the fennel. Season with salt. Arrange the shavings of cheese on top of the parsley. Serve immediately.

✤c 136 calories per serving ❋ 10 g fat ❋ 6 g protein ❋ 6 g carbohydrates

VICTOR EMMANUEL'S SALAD

Salade Tricolore

As history tells us, a brilliant green, red, and white salad—honoring Italian king Victor Emmanuel II and celebrating the Italian tricolor—was created by a Paris restaurateur during the Second Empire. While the original salad may have consisted of mâche, beets, and celery, I have updated it to make use of the greens we most relate to Italy—arugula and radicchio—adding a touch of white with a Belgian endive. Creamy Lemon-Chive Dressing is great with this salad. 4 servings

2 cups (about 4 ounces) arugula (or watercress, mesclun, or mâche), rinsed and stemmed
2 heads of radicchio, rinsed, trimmed, and cut into thin diagonal slices
2 Belgian endives, rinsed, trimmed, and cut into thin diagonal slices
¼ cup Creamy Lemon-Chive Dressing (page 299)
Fleur de sel
Freshly ground black pepper

In a large bowl, combine the arugula, radicchio, and Belgian endive, tossing lightly to blend. Drizzle with the dressing and toss until all the leaves are evenly coated. Season with *fleur de sel* and pepper. Serve.

71 calories per serving ⊛ 3 g fat ⊛ 8 g protein ⊛ 11 g carbohydrates

Customs: Traditionally, the planting of arugula was forbidden in the convent gardens in France, for the Mediterranean green was considered to be an aphrodisiac.

Folklore: If you eat salad before consuming alcohol, you won't get drunk.

THE RED AND THE GOLD:
GRATED BEET SALAD

Salade de Betterave: Le Rouge et l'Or

One sunny Saturday morning in February, Joël Thiebault—the vegetable supplier to many of Paris's top chefs—handed me a hefty bag full of seasonal root vegetables. Included were pencil-slim leeks, all manner of potatoes (black, gold, and those tinged with red), and a bounty of fresh beets. Fresh, raw beets are actually rare in France, and even more rare are the combination of golden beets and ruby red beets. That evening, I prepared this salad, a lovely, colorful study of contrasts. 4 servings

EQUIPMENT: A box grater.

¼ cup freshly squeezed lemon juice
2 tablespoons imported French mustard
¼ cup extra-virgin olive oil
Fine sea salt
2 raw (about 8 ounces) yellow beets
2 raw (about 8 ounces) red beets

1.   In a small bowl, combine the lemon juice, mustard, and olive oil and whisk to blend. Taste for seasoning. Divide the dressing in half, placing each in a separate small bowl.

2.   Using the largest holes of a box grater, grate the yellow beets directly into the first bowl with the dressing. Grate the red beets into the second bowl. Stir each well to evenly coat the beets with the dressing. Taste each for seasoning. Serve immediately or cover and refrigerate for up to one day. To serve, place a dollop of each beet salad side by side on a plate.

162 calories per serving ❋ 14 g fat ❋ 2 g protein ❋ 9 g carbohydrates

L'ANGLE'S VEGETABLE SALAD: CARROTS, FENNEL, RADISHES, BEETS, AND ONIONS

La Salade aux Légumes d'Hiver de L'Angle du Faubourg

On one of my earliest visits to the fine Paris restaurant L'Angle du Faubourg, I sampled a version of this refreshing winter salad, one that has become a family favorite ever since. At lunch it can make a meal; for dinner it makes a fine first course or salad course. 8 servings

EQUIPMENT: A mandoline or a very sharp knife; a 5-quart pasta pot fitted with a colander; a steamer.

2 carrots, peeled
1 large bulb fennel (about 8 ounces), trimmed
Coarse sea salt
½ cup Creamy Lemon-Chive Dressing (page 299)
2 raw beets (about 8 ounces), rinsed and trimmed
1 bunch radishes, rinsed and trimmed
4 spring onions (or 8 scallions), trimmed and peeled
Fleur de sel
An 8-ounce piece of Basque sheep's milk cheese, such as L'Ossau-Iraty

1.   With a mandoline or a very sharp knife, slice the carrots and the fennel lengthwise into very thin slices.

2.   Prepare a large bowl of ice water.

3.   Fill a 5-quart pasta pot fitted with a colander with 3 quarts water. Bring to a rolling boil over high heat. Add 3 tablespoons coarse sea salt and the carrots and cook until crisp-tender, about 1 minute. Immediately remove the colander from the water, allow the water to drain from the carrots, and plunge the colander with the carrots into the ice water so they cool down as quickly as possible. (The carrots will cool in 1 minute. If you leave them longer, they will become soggy and begin to lose flavor.) Drain the carrots. Repeat, with fresh water, for the fennel. In separate bowls, toss the carrots and the fennel with just enough dressing to lightly coat the vegetables. Set aside.

4.   Steam the beets: Bring 1 quart water to a simmer in the bottom of a steamer. Place the beets on the steaming rack. Place the rack over the simmering water. Cover and steam until the beets can be pierced with a paring knife, about 20 minutes for baby beets, up to 1 hour for larger beets. (You may have to add

water from time to time to keep the steamer from running dry.) Drain and let cool just long enough so you can handle them. Most of the peel will just slip off, but stubborn patches can be peeled off with a paring knife. Cut off the root end and, with a mandoline or a very sharp knife, slice crosswise into thin slices. In a medium bowl, toss with just enough dressing to lightly coat the beets. Set aside.

5.   With a mandoline or a very sharp knife, cut the radishes into very thin slices. Place in a medium bowl and toss with just enough dressing to lightly coat the radishes. Set aside.

6.   With a mandoline or a very sharp knife, cut the spring onions into thin rings. Place in a small bowl and toss with just enough dressing to lightly coat the onions. Season lightly with *fleur de sel* to taste.

7.   Trim the rind from the cheese. With a mandoline or a very sharp knife, slice the cheese into very thin slices.

8.   On each of 8 large plates, arrange an overlapping layer of the cheese. On top of the cheese, arrange overlapping slices of carrots at one end. Repeat for the fennel, beets, and radishes. In the center, arrange a small mound of the dressed onions. Sprinkle with chives, season lightly with *fleur de sel,* and serve.

❧c 169 calories per serving ❋ 11 g fat ❋ 13 g protein ❋ 11 g carbohydrates

Note: All vegetables can be cooked up to 8 hours in advance. Store each vegetable separately in a sealed container in the refrigerator. Dress at the last minute.

"Vêtu comme un oignon." Dressed in many layers, like an onion.

Origins: The carrot was born in Europe. Charlemagne cultivated carrots in his garden, but the vegetable—always yellow at that time—was not very popular, until the Dutch cultivated an orange carrot in the seventeenth century.

MINTED JERUSALEM ARTICHOKE SALAD WITH MÂCHE

Salade de Doucette aux Topinambours et à la Menthe

Until recently, I assumed that Jerusalem artichokes had to be cooked, but they are, in fact, delightfully refreshing raw in salads, as well as pickled. 4 servings

EQUIPMENT: A mandoline or a very sharp knife.

1 tablespoon freshly squeezed lime juice
½ teaspoon fine sea salt
¼ cup extra-virgin olive oil
40 fresh mint leaves, cut into chiffonade
1 pound Jerusalem artichokes, scrubbed but not peeled
2 cups (about 4 ounces) mâche, rinsed and dried
Fleur de sel

1. In a large bowl, combine the lime juice and salt and whisk to blend. Add the oil and whisk to blend. Stir in the mint.

2. With a mandoline or a very sharp knife, cut the Jerusalem artichokes into very thin slices, dropping them immediately into the dressing. Let marinate for 10 minutes. (Do not prepare in advance or the Jerusalem artichokes will darken.)

3. At serving time, use a slotted spoon to drain the Jerusalem artichokes and arrange them in an overlapping circle at the outside edge of 4 large plates. Place the mâche in the bowl with the drained dressing and toss to evenly coat the greens with the dressing. Place a mound of dressed mâche in the center of the plate. Season lightly with *fleur de sel*.

220 calories per serving ❋ 14 g fat ❋ 3 g protein ❋ 2 g carbohydrates

SOUPS

Les Soupes et les Potages

❖

ARTICHOKE AND PARMESAN SOUP

Soupe d'Artichauts au Parmesan

Ever since I sampled this smooth, gorgeous soup at Guy Savoy's restaurant in Paris, it has been at the top of my list of favorite soups. I prepare this year-round, sometimes even for myself for lunch, because it is so filling and satisfying. I make it with fresh or frozen artichoke bottoms or even top-quality canned artichoke hearts, which have the same rich flavor of fresh artichokes with none of the labor. 12 servings

EQUIPMENT: A stock pot with a lid; a food mill with a medium blade; 12 warmed shallow soup bowls.

1 tablespoon extra-virgin olive oil
Fine sea salt
2 shallots, trimmed, peeled, and minced
2 pounds artichoke hearts (about 12), fresh, canned, or frozen
2 quarts Homemade Chicken Stock (page 294)
One 2-ounce chunk of Parmigiano-Reggiano cheese

1.   In a large, heavy-duty stock pot, combine the oil, a pinch of salt, and the shallots and stir to blend. Sweat—cook, covered, over low heat until soft but not browned—for 3 to 4 minutes. Add the artichokes and toss. Cook, covered, over very low heat, until the artichokes are soft and impregnated with oil, about 2 minutes more. Add the stock, adjusting the heat to create a gentle simmer. Cover and simmer just until the artichokes are soft and the flavors have had time to mingle, about 30 minutes. Taste for seasoning.

2.   Place a food mill fitted with a medium blade over a large bowl and purée the soup into the bowl. (Discard any fibrous bits that remain in the mill.) Return the soup to the saucepan. The soup should be a pleasant golden green and should have the consistency of a slightly runny purée. If the soup appears thin, reduce it slightly over moderate heat. (The soup can be prepared to this point several hours ahead and reheated at serving time.)

3.   With a vegetable peeler, shave the cheese into long, thick strips into a bowl. (If the chunk of cheese becomes too small to shave, grate the remaining cheese and add it to the bowl.) Set aside.

4.   Divide the hot soup among the warmed soup bowls. Place the cheese shavings on top of the soup. If done correctly, the shavings should sit delicately on top of the soup, half-melted but still intact. Serve immediately.

 107 calories per serving ✳ 4 g fat ✳ 11 g protein ✳ 6 g carbohydrates

MARINATED HEIRLOOM TOMATO SOUP

Crème Froide à la Tomate

Each summer, Johannes Sailer—chef at Les Abeilles in the Provençal village of Sablet—creates an all-tomato menu. One year he opened the meal with this stunning soup: all red, all fresh, all full of honest tomato flavor. This liquid blend of tomatoes, seasoning, top-quality olive oil, and vinegar makes you feel as though you are drinking your salad! 12 servings

EQUIPMENT: A food processor or a blender; 12 chilled shallow soup bowls.

1 ½ pounds ripe heirloom tomatoes, cored and quartered (do not peel)

½ cup tomato paste

1 tablespoon celery salt

1 teaspoon ground *piment d'Espelette* or dried Anaheim chili (or ground mild chili pepper)

2 tablespoons best-quality sherry-wine vinegar

3 tablespoons extra-virgin olive oil

20 fresh basil leaves

Combine all the ingredients with 1⅔ cups water in a food processor or a blender and purée to a smooth liquid. Taste for seasoning. The soup can be served immediately, but the flavors will benefit from ripening for 3 to 24 hours, refrigerated. At serving time, reblend the soup. Serve in chilled soup bowls.

42 calories per serving ❋ 3 g fat ❋ 1 g protein ❋ 5 g carbohydrates

---

A July Luncheon on the Sunset Terrace

Chickpea Dip with Fresh Cilantro (page 18)

Marinated Heirloom Tomato Soup

Creamy Polenta Wedges (page 148) with Red Peppers, Tomatoes, Onions, Cumin, and Espelette Pepper (page 200)

Seasonal Fruits Roasted with Honey-Lemon Sauce and Fresh Lemon Verbena (page 290)

HEIRLOOM TOMATO BROTH WITH TARRAGON

Bouillon de Tomates à l'Estragon

This delicate soup reminds me of a cool night in early fall, when the garden's tomatoes seem to be at their most flavorful. I see myself in a long white garden-party dress, surrounded by friends in finery and fine moods, and this is the first course of a multicourse feast. This is also a lifesaver recipe: it can be put together in just 5 minutes! 12 servings

EQUIPMENT: A large saucepan; 12 warmed shallow soup bowls.

2 pounds ripe heirloom tomatoes of varied colors
1½ quarts Homemade Chicken Stock (page 294)
1 teaspoon fine sea salt
⅓ cup fresh tarragon leaves, finely minced

1. Core and peel the tomatoes. Cut them into bite-sized pieces.

2. In a large saucepan, combine the stock, tomatoes, and salt. Simmer for 5 minutes. Ladle into bowls, garnish with tarragon, and serve with plenty of crusty bread.

❧c 25 calories per serving ❊ 1 g fat ❊ 1 g protein ❊ 4 g carbohydrates

CHILLED HEIRLOOM TOMATO, CORN, AND CUCUMBER SOUP WITH FRESH CILANTRO

Gaspacho de Légumes d'Été à la Coriandre

On my return from the Sunday organic market on Boulevard Raspail in Paris, this soup came together like an effortless revelation. Serve in chilled white shallow soup bowls: the vibrant contrast of colors excites the eye, and soon the contrast of textures will stimulate the palate. 8 servings

EQUIPMENT: A food processor or a blender; 8 chilled shallow soup bowls.

2 pounds ripe heirloom tomatoes, cored, peeled, seeded, and chopped
1 tablespoon freshly squeezed lemon juice
1 cup raw fresh corn kernels (1 ear)
1 small sweet white onion, finely chopped
Fine sea salt
½ cup peeled, diced cucumber
¼ cup fresh cilantro leaves for garnish

In a food processor or a blender, combine 3 cups of the tomatoes, the lemon juice, half of the corn kernels, and half of the onion and purée. Taste for seasoning. Transfer to a large bowl and cover. Refrigerate until well chilled, at least 1 hour and up to 3 hours. Stir again before serving. Taste for seasoning. Serve in chilled shallow soup bowls, garnished with the remaining tomatoes, corn, and onion, the cucumber, and the fresh cilantro leaves.

52 calories per serving ❀ trace of fat ❀ 2 g protein ❀ 12 g carbohydrates

Origins: It was not until 1793 that the tomato was entirely embraced by the French, when the vegetable growers of Marseille brought the tomato to Paris.

CHUNKY CORN SOUP WITH CILANTRO
AND SMOKED SPANISH PAPRIKA

Soupe de Maïs à la Coriandre et au Paprika Espagnol

How can two simple ingredients manage to make a soup with such color, texture, flavor? The simple marriage of fresh corn kernels, scraped from the cob and cooked—cob and all—in milk until tender, is hard to improve upon. This soup is delicious hot or cold, alone or garnished with your favorite hot peppers. I like to garnish with a few sprigs of fresh cilantro and a sprinkling of hot smoked Spanish paprika. 6 servings

EQUIPMENT: A large skillet with a lid; a food processor or a blender.

3 ears fresh corn, shucked
6 cups 1% milk
2 teaspoons fine sea salt
¼ cup fresh cilantro leaves for garnish
About 1 teaspoon hot smoked Spanish *pimentón de la Vera* or other smoked paprika for garnish

1.   With a sharp knife, slice and scrape the kernels of corn from the cob. Place the kernels and the cobs in a skillet large enough to hold the corn in a single layer. Add the milk and the salt. Cover, bring to a simmer over low heat, and cook at a bare simmer for about 45 minutes. (Watch carefully so the milk does not boil over.)

2.   Remove the corn cobs from the pot and discard. Transfer the corn kernels and cooking liquid to a food processor or a blender and purée. This may have to be done in batches. The corn kernels will break up, but the mixture will remain slightly chunky. (The soup can be prepared up to 3 days in advance, covered, and refrigerated.)

3.   Serve warm or chilled in shallow soup bowls. Garnish with cilantro and paprika and serve.

&c 164 calories per serving ⁘ 4 g fat ⁘ 10 g protein ⁘ 25 g carbohydrates

CHILLED CUCUMBER AND YOGURT SOUP WITH DILL AND FRESH MINT

Crème de Concombre à l'Aneth et à la Menthe

This popular and versatile soup is a snap to make, and its clean summer flavors make one feel light and healthy. I make it early in the morning, so we have a lovely starter for lunch on a warm summer's day. Since yogurt is a major ingredient here, search out the best you can find. If available, use sheep's milk yogurt, which has a richer, deeper flavor than that made with cow's or goat's milk. 8 servings

EQUIPMENT: A food processor, a blender, or an immersion blender; 8 chilled shallow soup bowls.

1 European or hothouse cucumber (about 1 pound)
1 teaspoon fine sea salt
2 cups nonfat yogurt
1 plump, moist clove garlic, peeled, halved, green germ removed, minced
⅓ cup finely minced fresh dill
⅓ cup finely minced fresh mint leaves

1.   Trim and peel the cucumber. Cut into chunks. In a food processor or a blender, combine the cucumber, salt, yogurt, garlic, 2 tablespoons dill, and 2 tablespoons mint. Purée. Taste for seasoning. Transfer to a bowl and cover securely with plastic wrap. Refrigerate for at least 1 hour and up to 24 hours.

2.   At serving time, reblend the soup to a smooth purée with an immersion blender, a food processor, or a blender. Pour the soup into the chilled soup bowls. Garnish with the remaining dill and mint and serve.

47 calories per serving ❋ trace of fat ❋ 4 g protein ❋ 7 g carbohydrates

Folklore: Cucumbers are a symbol of fertility and also are revered for their calming influence. And should you have a fever, sleep on a bed of cucumbers and your fever will go away.

TOMATO GAZPACHO

Gaspacho

This is one of the most instant soups I know and is always a hit when I serve it to family or friends. I like the spicy hit of raw garlic, as well as the flecks of red that come from the ripe tomato peels and red pepper. This is a thick soup and a perfect summertime first course to any meal. I am not a big "garnish" person, and while many people like to pile croutons or cubed vegetables on their fresh vegetable soups, I prefer this soup in its purest, simplest form. If you want to add a touch of spice, season the final soup at table with a bit of hot red pepper flakes or Tabasco sauce. 10 servings

EQUIPMENT: A food processor or a blender; 10 chilled shallow soup bowls.

1 European or hothouse cucumber (about 1 pound)
1½ pounds garden-fresh tomatoes, cored and quartered (do not peel)
1 red bell pepper, cored, seeded, and cut into chunks
1 small onion, peeled and cut into chunks
2 plump, moist cloves garlic, peeled, halved, green germ removed
3 tablespoons best-quality sherry-wine vinegar
2 teaspoons fine sea salt
Hot red pepper flakes or Tabasco sauce for serving (optional)

Trim the cucumber. Peel it and cut into chunks. In a food processor or a blender, purée the tomatoes. Add the remaining ingredients except the hot pepper and purée. (This may have to be done in batches. If so, stir all the puréed ingredients together in a large bowl.) Taste for seasoning. The soup can be served immediately, but the flavors will benefit from ripening for 3 to 24 hours, refrigerated. Reblend at serving time. Serve in chilled soup bowls, passing red pepper or Tabasco at the table if desired.

33 calories per serving * trace of fat * 1 g protein * 8 g carbohydrates

What's the Green Germ? The "germ" is the green sprout that runs through the center of a clove of garlic. Cut the clove in half lengthwise and you will see. Cooks differ as to what to do with the germ, which to some people can be quite indigestible. I follow a simple rule: When using raw garlic, I always remove the germ. If the garlic is being cooked, I generally do not remove the germ.

GUY SAVOY'S TOMATO COULIS
WITH ASPARAGUS AND MINT

Le Potage de Tomates aux Asperges et à la Menthe de Guy Savoy

As ever, Parisian chef Guy Savoy works his signature green color into this dish, a brilliant pairing of bright red tomatoes and bright green asparagus, all tied together with the sweet touch of fresh mint. This dish is at its refreshing best served very cold. 4 servings

EQUIPMENT: A food processor or a blender; a 5-quart pasta pot fitted with a colander; 4 chilled shallow soup bowls.

3 garden-fresh tomatoes, cored, peeled, seeded, and chopped (about 12 ounces)
1 tablespoon freshly squeezed lemon juice
1 tablespoon extra-virgin olive oil
Fine sea salt
16 spears (about 1 pound) fresh green asparagus, tips only (reserve the rest for another use)
¼ cup fresh mint leaves, finely minced

1.   In a food processor or a blender, combine the tomatoes, lemon juice, and olive oil and purée. Taste for seasoning. Transfer to a bowl and refrigerate.

2.   Prepare a large bowl of ice water.

3.   In a 5-quart pasta pot fitted with a colander, bring 3 quarts water to a rolling boil over high heat. Add 3 tablespoons salt and the asparagus. Boil, uncovered, until the asparagus tips are crisp-tender, 3 to 4 minutes. Immediately drain the asparagus and plunge into the ice water so the vegetables cool down as quickly as possible and retain their crispness and bright green color. (The vegetable will cool in 1 to 2 minutes. After that, it will soften and begin to lose crispness and flavor.) Transfer the asparagus to a colander and drain.

4.   To serve, pour the tomato sauce into chilled soup bowls. Arrange the asparagus tips on top of the coulis. Garnish with mint and serve.

69 calories per serving ◦ 4 g fat ◦ 2 g protein ◦ 9 g carbohydrates

Origins: White asparagus, popular all over Europe, comes from plants that are literally buried alive. They are cultivated by mounding soil or sand around the stalks as they grow, blocking out the light and preventing them from turning green. Asparagus grows quickly: spears can spurt 10 inches in just 24 hours.

CHILLED BEET GAZPACHO

Gaspacho de Betterave

The first time I sampled a version of this brilliant red soup was at the hands of chef Roland Durand, in his then brand-new Parisian restaurant, Passiflore. He served this chilled soup in crisp white porcelain bowls, and the contrast was breathtaking. Think of it as liquid pickled beets, with just the right amount of vinegar to wake up the palate. 4 servings

EQUIPMENT: A steamer; a food processor or a blender; 4 chilled shallow soup bowls.

2 large beets (about 1 pound), scrubbed
4 plump, moist cloves garlic, peeled, halved, green germ removed, minced
1 onion, peeled, halved, and thinly sliced
1 teaspoon imported French mustard
1 tablespoon best-quality sherry-wine vinegar
Fine sea salt
Several teaspoons finely minced fresh chives for garnish

1. Steam the beets: Bring 1 quart water to a simmer in the bottom of a steamer. Place the beets on the steaming rack. Place the rack over the simmering water, cover, and steam until the beets can be pierced with a sharp knife, about 20 minutes for baby beets and up to 1 hour for larger beets. (You may have to add water from time to time to keep the steamer from running dry.) Drain and let cool just long enough so you can handle them. Most of the peel will just slip off, but stubborn patches can be peeled off with a sharp knife. Cut off the root end and dice.

2. In a food processor or a blender, combine the beets, garlic, onion, mustard, vinegar, and 2 cups cold water. Process thoroughly to blend to a very smooth-textured purée. (This may have to be done in batches.) Taste for seasoning. Cover with plastic wrap and refrigerate for at least 2 hours and up to 24 hours to allow the flavors to blend.

3. At serving time, reblend the soup. Taste again for seasoning. Ladle into chilled soup bowls and garnish with chives.

40 calories per serving ⁂ trace of fat ⁂ 2 g protein ⁂ 9 g carbohydrates

CURRIED
BEET SOUP

Soupe de Betterave au Curry

This is the sort of vibrant-flavored, colorful soup that brightens up the day. I first sampled a version of this soup at the tiny Parisian bistro Le Timbre. I love the look of the soup when you put the beets and apples together with soft, golden onions. Neither the curry nor the ginger overwhelms the flavor of the beets but adds a nice, exotic touch. 8 servings

EQUIPMENT: A steamer; a large saucepan with a lid; a food processor or a blender; 8 warmed shallow soup bowls.

2 large beets (about 1 pound), scrubbed
1 tablespoon extra-virgin olive oil
1 medium onion, peeled, halved, and thinly sliced
Fine sea salt
2 teaspoons Curry Powder (page 308), or to taste
1 Granny Smith apple, cored and cubed (do not peel)
2 cups Homemade Chicken Stock (page 294)
1/2 teaspoon ground ginger

1.   Steam the beets: Bring 1 quart water to a simmer in the bottom of a steamer. Place the beets on the steaming rack. Place the rack over the simmering water, cover, and steam until the beets can be pierced with a sharp knife, about 20 minutes for baby beets and up to 1 hour for larger beets. (You may have to add water from time to time to keep the steamer from running dry.) Drain and let cool just long enough so you can handle them. Most of the peel will just slip off, but stubborn patches can be peeled off with a sharp knife. Cut off the root end and dice.

2.   In a large saucepan, combine the oil, onion, salt to taste, and curry powder and toss to coat the onion. Sweat—cook, covered, over low heat until soft but not browned—for 3 to 4 minutes. Add the beets, apple, and stock and simmer, covered, for 30 minutes. Season with ground ginger.

3.   Transfer the mixture to a food processor or a blender and blend to a very smooth-textured soup. (Do not place the plunger in the feed tube of the food processor or the blender or the heat will create a vacuum and the liquid will splatter.) Ladle into warmed soup bowls and serve.

✣ 60 calories per serving ✤ 3 g fat ✤ 4 g protein ✤ 6 g carbohydrates

> *"The beet is the most intense of vegetables. The radish, admittedly, is more feverish, but the fire of the radish is a cold fire, the fire of discontent, not of passion. Tomatoes are lusty enough, yet there runs through tomatoes an undercurrent of frivolity. Beets are deadly serious."*
>
> Tom Robbins, author

SPICY BUTTERNUT SQUASH SOUP

Soupe de Courge Musquée au Curry

When you serve this tangy, spicy squash soup, I'll bet that none of your guests will be able to guess what all the ingredients are. The touch of ginger here is magic, giving the soup a long, lean touch of spice that permeates through and through. An apple adds a touch of sweetness, and the parsnip helps deepen the flavors throughout. 8 servings

EQUIPMENT: A large stock pot with a lid; a food processor, a blender, or an immersion blender; 8 warmed shallow soup bowls.

2 tablespoons extra-virgin olive oil
2 medium onions, peeled, halved lengthwise, and thinly sliced
Fine sea salt
2 cups butternut squash purée (see page 62)
2 small parsnips or turnips, peeled and cubed
1 baking apple, peeled, cored, and cubed
1 quart Homemade Chicken Stock (page 294)
1 teaspoon Curry Powder (page 308)
1 teaspoon ground ginger

In a large stock pot, combine the oil, onions, and salt and sweat—cook, covered, over low heat until soft—for 3 to 4 minutes. Add the squash purée, parsnips, apple, and stock. Cook, covered, over moderate heat for 30 minutes. In a food processor or a blender or with an immersion blender, process until smooth. Add the curry powder and the ginger. Taste for seasoning. Divide among 8 warmed shallow soup bowls and serve.

119 calories per serving ⚬ 5 g fat ⚬ 7 g protein ⚬ 13 g carbohydrates

Wine Suggestion

I like a Pinot Gris with this soup: A favorite comes from the Alsatian winemaking firm of Zind-Humbrecht. The wines tend to be thick, velvety, with a touch of minerality for freshness and a touch of spice to match up to this elegant soup.

Squash or Pumpkin Purée Preheat the oven to 375 degrees F. Halve the squash crosswise and scoop out the seeds and strings. Place the halves, cut side up, on a large baking sheet. Cover the squash with foil. Roast until fork-tender. Roasting time will vary according to the size and freshness of the squash. A 3-pound squash should take about 1 hour, longer for larger squash. It should yield 2 to 3 cups of purée. When cool, scrape the pulp from the shells and purée, a little at a time, in a food processor or a blender. The water content of squash and pumpkins varies. If the purée is watery, allow it to drain in a colander to remove excess moisture.

CURRIED CHICKPEA, LENTIL, AND
SWISS CHARD STEW

Soupe de Pois Chiches, Lentilles et Blettes

As soon as cool weather arrives, I get into soup mode big-time. We eat soup almost every day at home. I love to make enough so we always have leftovers for lunch or in the freezer for days when I don't have time to cook. This dish, more of a thick stew than a soup, bursts with fresh, spicy flavors and combines some of our favorite ingredients, chickpeas and lentils. Swiss chard usually winters over in my vegetable garden in Provence, so all I need to do is don a parka and boots and harvest! If Swiss chard is not available, substitute spinach. 8 servings

EQUIPMENT: A fine-mesh sieve; a stock pot with a lid; a small skillet; 8 warmed shallow soup bowls.

1 ½ cups dried French lentils, preferably *lentilles du Puy*, rinsed and drained

2 tablespoons extra-virgin olive oil

Bouquet garni: several parsley stems, celery leaves, and sprigs of thyme, encased in a wire mesh tea infuser

1 medium onion, peeled, halved lengthwise, and thinly sliced

Fine sea salt

2 quarts Homemade Chicken Stock (page 294)

2 teaspoons Curry Powder (page 308)

½ teaspoon cayenne pepper

1 large bunch of Swiss chard, leaves only, coarsely chopped (about 12 cups)

2 cups canned chickpeas, drained and rinsed

2 teaspoons cumin seeds

1 cup Greek-style yogurt for garnish

1. Place the lentils in a fine-mesh sieve and rinse under cold running water. Set aside.

2. In a stock pot, combine the oil, bouquet garni, onion, and 1 teaspoon fine sea salt. Sweat—cook, covered, over low heat until soft but not browned—for about 3 minutes. Add the stock and bring to a simmer over moderate heat. Add the lentils, curry powder, and cayenne and stir. Simmer, covered, until the lentils are tender, about 20 minutes. (Cooking time will depend upon the freshness of the lentils—older lentils take longer to cook.) Add the chard leaves and the chickpeas and cook until the leaves are wilted, about 5 minutes more. Remove the bouquet garni. Taste for seasoning.

3.   While the stew is cooking, toast the cumin. Place the cumin seeds in a small, dry skillet over moderate heat. Shake the pan regularly until the cumin seeds are fragrant and evenly toasted, about 2 minutes. Watch carefully! They can burn quickly. Transfer the cumin to a large plate to cool. Set aside.

4.   Divide the soup among the warmed soup bowls. At the table, garnish with a spoonful of yogurt and a sprinkling of toasted cumin.

✤ᶜ 293 calories per serving ❋ 7 g fat ❋ 18 g protein ❋ 43 g carbohydrates

What I Learned: In France, we have it easy with all manner of grains, rice, and dried beans. Each package is carefully labeled, usually with the year of harvest and always a "use by" date, ensuring that the home cook will be offered the freshest possible ingredients. When shopping for any dried grains, rice, or beans, always go to a store that has good turnover and hope you get the freshest of the fresh. The rule is simple: the older the grains, rice, or beans, the longer they will take to cook and the duller the flavor. Also do yourself a favor and don't keep those ingredients on hand for years and years. Use them up as soon as you purchase them.

FRESH WHITE BEAN SOUP WITH
MORELS IN CREAM

Velouté de Haricots Blancs, Morilles à la Crème

We created this luscious dish during one of my fall classes in Provence. It was the last chance to sample the creamy, buttery white *cocos blancs*—navy beans—we buy from our local produce shop, Les Gourmandines. Dried morels are a standard in my pantry, so the dish was child's play. I love the dramatic presentation of this elegant soup: Place the morels in cream at the bottom of the soup bowl, pour the creamy white soup into a pitcher, and pour the soup over the morels at table. 12 servings.

EQUIPMENT: A stock pot with a lid; a food processor, a blender, or an immersion blender; 8 warmed
   shallow soup bowls.

2 pounds fresh small white beans in the pod, shelled, or 1 pound dried white beans
3 tablespoons extra-virgin olive oil
2 bay leaves, preferably fresh
3 plump, moist cloves garlic, minced
Large bunch of fresh thyme
4 quarts Homemade Chicken Stock (page 294)
1 teaspoon fine sea salt, or to taste
1 recipe Wild Morel Mushrooms in Cream (page 189), kept warm in a small saucepan

1.   For fresh beans: In a stock pot, combine the olive oil, bay leaves, and garlic and stir to coat the garlic with the oil. Place over moderate heat and cook until the garlic is fragrant and soft, about 2 minutes. Do not let it brown. Add the thyme, reserving some leaves for garnish, and beans, stir to coat with oil, and cook for 1 minute more. Add the stock and stir. Cover, bring to a simmer over moderate heat, and simmer for 15 minutes. Season with salt. Continue cooking at a gentle simmer until the beans are tender, about 15 minutes more. Stir from time to time to make sure the beans are not sticking to the bottom of the pan. (Cooking time will vary according to the freshness of the beans.) Taste for seasoning. Remove and discard the bay leaves and thyme. Purée in a food processor, in a blender, or with an immersion blender.

For dried beans: Rinse the beans, picking them over to remove any pebbles. Place the beans in a large bowl, add boiling water to cover, and set aside for 1 hour. Drain the beans, discarding the water. In a stock pot, combine the olive oil, bay leaves, and garlic and stir to coat the garlic with the oil. Cook over moderate heat, until the garlic is fragrant and soft, about 2 minutes. Do not let it brown. Add the thyme, reserving some leaves for garnish, and the beans, stir to coat with oil, and cook for 1 minute more. Add the stock and stir. Cover, bring to a simmer over moderate heat, and simmer for 30 minutes to 1 hour. Season with salt. Continue cooking at a gentle simmer until the beans are tender, about 30 minutes more. Stir from time to time to make sure they are not sticking to the bottom of the pan. (Cooking time will vary according to the freshness of the beans.) Taste for seasoning. Remove and discard the bay leaves and thyme. Purée in a food processor, in a blender, or with an immersion blender.

2.   At serving time, transfer the warm soup to a large pitcher. Place several spoonfuls of warm morels in the bottom of each warmed soup bowl. At the table, pour the warm soup over the morels in the bowl. Garnish with fresh thyme leaves.

✳ᶜ 304 calories per serving ❋ 16 g fat ❋ 12 g protein ❋ 29 g carbohydrates

ROASTED ORANGE PEPPER SOUP

Crème de Poivrons Oranges

This gorgeous soup wins raves every time I prepare it. It's a favorite with my students, and I think we all agree that orange and yellow peppers are easily available yet somehow underutilized. 12 servings

EQUIPMENT: A stock pot with a lid; a rimmed, foil-lined baking sheet; a food processor, a blender, or an immersion blender; 8 warmed shallow soup bowls.

2 tablespoons extra-virgin olive oil
1 medium onion, peeled and thinly sliced
Fine sea salt
6 (about 2 pounds) orange or yellow bell peppers, roasted, peeled, and sliced (see page 69)
2 quarts Homemade Chicken Stock (page 294)
2 medium potatoes, peeled and diced
Freshly ground white pepper
About 3 tablespoons pistachio, walnut, or extra-virgin olive oil for garnish

1.   In a stock pot, combine the oil, onion, and salt to taste and sweat—cook, covered, over low heat until soft—for 3 to 4 minutes. Add the sliced peppers and cook for 4 to 5 minutes more. Add the stock and the potatoes and cover. Cook until the potatoes are soft, about 20 minutes.

2.   In a food processor or a blender or with an immersion blender, purée in batches. (Do not place the plunger in the feed tube of the food processor or the blender or the heat will create a vacuum and the liquid will splatter.) Taste for seasoning. Serve in warmed soup bowls. Drizzle with best-quality olive oil or a nut oil of your choice.

135 calories per serving ⁕ 3 g fat ⁕ 4 g protein ⁕ 24 g carbohydrates

For Perfect Roasted Peppers

• Select thick-fleshed, thick-skinned peppers. They have more flavor and will better withstand the heat.

• Preheat a broiler. Place the peppers on the foil-lined baking sheet at least 3 inches from the heat of the broiler, so they do not come in direct contact with the intense heat and they roast and steam at the same time, making for more moist and tender peppers. Peppers can also be roasted on a grill, over a gas flame, or in a very hot (500 degree F.) oven.

• Do not pierce the peppers. You want to save that beautifully oily liquid within.

• Watch the peppers carefully as they cook. Turn them often, using tongs that won't puncture the flesh. The skin should blister but not burn. (If the skin turns black and charred long before it begins to pull away from the pepper, the heat is too intense.) The entire roasting process should take about 15 minutes.

• Once the skin shrinks and peels away from the peppers on all sides, remove the peppers from the heat, place them in a large bowl, and cover the bowl with plastic wrap. Let them cool thoroughly, about 10 minutes. Remove them from the bowl, being careful not to lose any of the juices. Remove the charred skin from the peppers, carefully remove the seeds, and slice the peppers into lengthwise strips. Do not rinse the peppers once they are peeled or you will lose the flavorful juices.

AUTUMN CELERIAC, CELERY, AND CHESTNUT SOUP WITH PARMESAN AND ROSEMARY

Soupe d'Automne au Céleri-Rave, Céleri et Marrons

This soup combines some of my favorite autumnal ingredients—the tang of celeriac, the delicacy of celery, and the richness of chestnuts. Laced with a touch of cheese and the fresh hint of rosemary, this soup will wake up every palate at the table. 12 servings

EQUIPMENT: A stock pot with a lid; a food processor, a blender, or an immersion blender; 12 warmed shallow soup bowls.

20 vacuum-packed roasted chestnuts (from a 14-ounce jar)
1½ pounds celeriac, quartered, peeled, and cubed
3 cups diced celery
2 teaspoons fine sea salt
1½ quarts Homemade Chicken Stock (page 294)
One 2-ounce chunk of Parmigiano-Reggiano cheese
About 1 tablespoon finely minced fresh rosemary for garnish

1. Coarsely chop the chestnuts, reserving 4 chopped chestnuts for garnish. Set aside.

2. In a stock pot, combine the chestnuts, celeriac, celery, salt, and stock. Bring to a boil over high heat. Reduce to a simmer and cover, cooking just until all the ingredients are soft, about 20 minutes.

3. In a food processor, in a blender, or with an immersion blender, blend the soup to a smooth purée. Return to the casserole to keep it warm. (The soup can be made one day in advance, covered, and refrigerated. At serving time, reheat and reblend.)

4. With a vegetable peeler, shave the cheese into long, thick strips into a bowl. (If the chunk of cheese becomes too small to shave, grate the remaining cheese and add it to the bowl.) Set aside.

5. To serve, divide the hot soup among the warmed soup bowls. Garnish with chopped chestnuts. Place the cheese shavings on top of the soup. If done correctly, the shavings should sit delicately on top of the soup, half melted but still intact. Garnish with rosemary and serve.

83 calories per serving ※ 2 g fat ※ 4 g protein ※ 12 g carbohydrates

JERUSALEM ARTICHOKE SOUP WITH HAZELNUT OIL

Crème de Topinambours, Huile de Noisette

This is a quick, beautiful, and delicious winter soup that warms the soul. Parisian chef Pierre Gagnaire introduced me to this method of cooking Jerusalem artichokes—or *topinambours*—in milk, to create a pristine white creation. The hazelnut oil nicely echoes the earthy, nutty flavor of this winter vegetable. 8 servings

EQUIPMENT: A large saucepan; a food processor or a blender; 8 warmed shallow soup bowls.

1 quart 1% milk
Fine sea salt
1 pound Jerusalem artichokes, scrubbed
About 2 tablespoons best-quality hazelnut oil

1. Pour the milk into a large saucepan. Add 1 teaspoon fine sea salt. Peel the Jerusalem artichokes, chop coarsely, and drop immediately into the milk. (This will stop the vegetable from turning brown as it is exposed to the air.) When all the Jerusalem artichokes are prepared, place over moderate heat and cook gently until soft, about 25 minutes. Watch carefully so the milk does not boil over.

2. Transfer the mixture in small batches to a food processor or a blender. Purée. (Do not place the plunger in the feed tube of the food processor or the blender or the heat will create a vacuum and the liquid will splatter.) Purée continuously, until the mixture is perfectly smooth and silky.

3. Return the soup to the saucepan and reheat gently. Taste for seasoning. Pour into the warmed soup bowls and drizzle with hazelnut oil.

124 calories per serving * 5 g fat * 5 g protein * 16 g carbohydrates

WINTER ROOT VEGETABLE PISTOU

Pistou aux Légumes d'Hiver

I think of this colorful vegetable soup as my winter *soupe au pistou,* for it's a great mix of seasonal vegetables seasoned at serving time with a robust watercress pesto and enriched with freshly grated Parmigiano-Reggiano cheese. I like adding tomatoes to the mix, for they impart a welcome touch of color as well as a sense of summer freshness. 12 servings

> EQUIPMENT: A mandoline or a very sharp knife; a stock pot with a lid; 12 warmed shallow soup bowls.
>
> 2 parsnips, trimmed and peeled
> 5 carrots, trimmed and peeled
> 4 turnips, trimmed and peeled
> 1½ quarts Homemade Chicken Stock (page 294)
> 2 teaspoons fine sea salt
> 1 cup tomato juice or canned tomato purée
> Bouquet garni: several parsley sprigs, thyme sprigs, and bay leaves, encased in a wire mesh tea infuser
> A wire mesh tea infuser filled with rinds of Parmigiano-Reggiano (see note)
> ¾ cup freshly grated Parmigiano-Reggiano cheese for garnish
> ¾ cup Watercress Pesto (page 303) for garnish

1.   With a mandoline or a very sharp knife, slice all the vegetables into thin rounds. If the turnips are large, quarter each slice so all the vegetables remain about the same size.

2.   Place the chicken stock in the stock pot. Add all the vegetables, the salt, tomato juice, bouquet garni, and cheese rinds. Cook at a gentle simmer, partially covered, until the vegetables are soft, 15 to 20 minutes. Taste for seasoning. Remove the bouquet garni and cheese rinds.

3.   At serving time, ladle the soup into the warmed soup bowls. Pass a bowl of freshly grated Parmigiano-Reggiano cheese and another of watercress pesto at the table and allow guests to season their soup individually.

✤c 97 calories per serving ❖ 4 g fat ❖ 6 g protein ❖ 12 g carbohydrates

What I Learned: Years ago I realized that thick rinds of Parmigiano-Reggiano cheese are one great flavor booster for any soup. I never throw them out, but rather save them in a small zippered bag in the refrigerator. Placing them, as well as herbs, in a wire mesh tea infuser means that you don't have to worry about fishing them out of the soup before you serve it!

FISH AND SHELLFISH

Les Poissons, Coquillages et Fruits de Mer

❖

SIX-MINUTE FRESH COD STEAMED
ON A BED OF ROSEMARY

Cabillaud Cuit à la Vapeur de Romarin

Steamed fish is quick, easy, and healthy. Years ago, I became fond of this method of steaming fish on a bed of herbs, after my Provençal fishmonger Eliane Berenger suggested I try it. You could use a variety of herbs here, but I find the sturdiness of the rosemary branch, as well as the herb's dense and aromatic richness, to be ideal. The older, woodier stems can be used for steaming; save the younger, more tender herbs for garnish. The cod should be ultra-fresh, glistening, and snow white, without a hint of dryness. 4 servings

EQUIPMENT: A tweezers; a large, deep skillet with a lid; 4 warmed dinner plates.

1 pound fresh cod fillet, skin intact
Several sprigs of fresh rosemary
Fine sea salt
Freshly ground white pepper
Finely minced fresh rosemary for garnish
Almond or pistachio oil for garnish
Fleur de sel

1.   Run your fingers over the top of the cod fillets to detect any tiny bones that remain in the fish. With tweezers, remove the bones. Cut the cod into 4 even 4-ounce portions. Season with fine sea salt and pepper.

2.   Place the rosemary and about ¹/₂ cup water in a large skillet. The water should be about ¹/₂ inch deep. Bring to a boil over high heat. Place the fish on top of the branches of rosemary: The fish should not touch the water. Cover and simmer gently until the fish is cooked through, about 6 minutes. Remove from the heat and allow the fish to rest for 2 to 3 minutes. Carefully transfer the fish to warmed dinner plates. Garnish with minced rosemary, a drizzle of almond or pistachio oil, and a light sprinkling of *fleur de sel*.

113 calories per serving ❊ 3 g fat ❊ 20 g protein ❊ 0 carbohydrates

Garden Advice from on High

In the year 800, Charlemagne declared in a legislative act the ninety different vegetables that should be grown in a vegetable garden, including peas, arugula, and pumpkin squash. On the list are many herbs and vegetables grown primarily for medicinal use. Among them are rosemary, mustard greens, sage, and many varieties of mint, used for creating ointments, salves, and poultices.

CELERIAC SALAD WITH FRESH CRABMEAT

Rémoulade de Céleri-rave au Crabe

When fresh crabmeat is in season in the winter months, I can't get enough of this sweet, tender treat. I first sampled a version of this dish at the wonderful fish bistro L'Ecailler du Bistrot on Rue Paul-Bert in Paris's eleventh arrondissement. The fish and shellfish are always at the peak of freshness there, and the menu always tempts me to try something new and different. I sampled this one day in December. Here fresh and tangy celeriac—also known as *celery root*—is cut into a fine julienne, tossed with a light and creamy dressing, and topped with tasty fresh crabmeat. It's a white-on-white dish that appeals, brightening up gray winter days. 6 servings

EQUIPMENT: A mandoline fitted with a julienne blade; a fine-mesh sieve.

1 cup Creamy Lemon-Chive Dressing (page 299)
10 ounces celeriac, peeled and trimmed
6 ounces fresh crabmeat

1. Place the dressing in a large, shallow bowl. With a mandoline fitted with a julienne blade, cut the celeriac into a fine julienne, grating it right into the bowl with the dressing. Toss to evenly coat the celeriac.

2. At serving time, place a large fine-mesh sieve over a large bowl. Transfer the celeriac to the sieve and allow any excess dressing to drain off.

3. Place the crabmeat in a small bowl and toss with just enough of the drained dressing to evenly coat the crabmeat.

4. Arrange a mound of the dressed celeriac on each of 6 salad plates. Arrange a small mound of the dressed crabmeat on top of the celeriac. Serve immediately.

⁂ 127 calories per serving ⁕ 8 g fat ⁕ 8 g protein ⁕ 7 g carbohydrates

Wine Suggestion

The first time I sampled this dish, we sipped a fine Sauvignon Blanc, the famed Sancerre from the Loire Valley. The forward, grassy flavors of the wine stand up to the tang of the celeriac and complement the sea-fresh flavors of crabmeat. A good bet is the Sancerre from Domaine Lucien Crochet.

AVOCADO AND CRAB "RAVIOLI"

"Raviole" d'Avocat au Crabe

The very first time I dined at Paris's Astrance, chef Pascal Barbot presented me with this stunningly simple first course. Instead of a classic pasta base, the luscious avocado plays the role of the ravioli, with the sweet crabmeat salad sandwiched in between. Top-rate ingredients are a must here, but the rest is child's play. 4 servings

EQUIPMENT: 4 chilled dinner plates.

1 pound fresh crabmeat, cooked
Zest and juice of 2 limes, preferably organic
Zest of 2 oranges, preferably organic
½ cup finely minced fresh chives
Fine sea salt
Coarsely ground white pepper
2 ripe avocados, halved lengthwise, pitted, and peeled
1 tablespoon almond oil or extra-virgin olive oil
Fleur de sel

1.   In a large bowl, combine the crabmeat, lime juice, orange zest, and chives. Season to taste with salt and freshly ground white pepper. Set aside.

2.   With a very sharp knife, slice each avocado half lengthwise into 4 slices. Place 2 slices on each of 4 chilled dinner plates. Mound a quarter of the crabmeat on top of the avocado slices on each of the chilled plates. Cover each mound of crab with 2 slices of avocado. Drizzle the slices of avocado with the almond oil. Season generously with *fleur de sel,* white pepper, and the lime zest. Serve immediately.

306 calories per serving ❀ 20 g fat ❀ 26 g protein ❀ 8 g carbohydrates

Wine Suggestion
We sampled this salad with a mineral-rich Riesling, the Domain Ostertag Clos Mathis 2002.

MUSSELS WITH CHORIZO AND CILANTRO

Moules au Chorizo et Coriandre

The afternoon I first sampled this dish, at La Chassagnette, a Camargue restaurant just outside of Arles, the waiter announced the dish as he placed it before us. What he said was *moules au chorizo,* but my dining companion heard *moules Shapiro.* In our house, this lively, bright, flavorful dish has gone by that name ever since! I love the sharp hit of fresh cilantro at the end. 4 servings

EQUIPMENT: A large fine-mesh sieve; dampened cheesecloth.

2 pounds fresh mussels
2 tablespoons extra-virgin olive oil
2 onions, peeled, halved, and finely sliced
½ teaspoon fine sea salt
½ cup dry white wine
3 ounces thinly sliced chorizo sausage, cut into julienne strips
Freshly ground black pepper
1 cup cilantro leaves, coarsely chopped

1.   Thoroughly scrub the mussels and rinse with several changes of water. If an open mussel closes when you press on it, it is good; if it stays open, discard it. Debeard the mussels. (Do not debeard the mussels more than a few minutes in advance or they will die and spoil. Note that in some markets mussels are preprepared, in that the small black beard that hangs from the mussel has been clipped off but not entirely removed. These mussels do not need further attention.) Set aside.

2.   In a large saucepan, combine the oil, onions, and salt and stir to blend. Sweat—cook, covered, over low heat until soft but not browned—for about 3 minutes. Add the wine. Bring to a boil and boil, uncovered, for 5 minutes. Add the mussels, cover, and cook just until the mussels open, about 5 minutes. Do not overcook. Discard any mussels that do not open. Transfer the mussels to a large bowl. Add the chorizo. Place a sieve over a bowl and line the sieve with several thicknesses of dampened cheesecloth. Carefully strain the liquid into the sieve. Transfer the strained liquid into the bowl with the mussels and chorizo. Shower with black pepper and cilantro. Serve, with plenty of crusty bread. Supply each guest with a moistened hand towel.

307 calories per serving ⁕ 18 g fat ⁕ 20 g protein ⁕ 10 g carbohydrates

MUSSELS WITH SWISS CHARD AND SAFFRON CREAM

Moules aux Blettes en Crème Safranée

We sat on the terrace of Les Abeilles in the nearby village of Sablet one warm Saturday afternoon in July as the cicadas chirped along and we sheltered ourselves from the sun beneath the dense sycamore trees. Chef Johannes Sailer offered this gorgeous first course, a classic blend of mussels and saffron, enhanced by the earthy flavor of Swiss chard. Since my garden is overrun with chard in the summer months, this was a welcome addition to my repertoire. Interestingly enough, the saffron becomes almost spicy in the company of the Swiss chard. And there's nothing more beautiful than a saffron-colored sauce. 8 appetizer servings

EQUIPMENT: A steamer; 2 small saucepans; a 5-quart pasta pot fitted with a colander; 8 warmed small bowls.

2 pounds fresh mussels
Freshly ground black pepper
2 tablespoons freshly squeezed lemon juice
10 large Swiss chard leaves and ribs (about 1 1/2 pounds total)
1 1/2 cups light cream
1/4 teaspoon saffron threads

1.   Thoroughly scrub the mussels and rinse with several changes of water. If an open mussel closes when you press on it, it is good; if it stays open, discard it. Debeard the mussels. (Do not debeard the mussels more than a few minutes in advance or they will die and spoil. Note that in some markets mussels are preprepared, in that the small black beard that hangs from the mussel has been clipped off but not entirely removed. These mussels do not need further attention.) Set aside.

2.   Bring 1 quart of water to a simmer in the bottom of a steamer. Place the mussels on the steaming rack. Season generously with freshly ground black pepper. Place the rack over the simmering water, cover, and steam just until the mussels open, 2 to 3 minutes. Do not overcook. Discard any mussels that do not open. Separate the mussels from their shells, reserving 8 pairs of the prettiest shells for decoration. Place the mussels in a small bowl. Set aside.

3.   Add the lemon juice to a large bowl of water. Trim and remove any large, fibrous strings from each rib of Swiss chard. Cut the ribs crosswise (against the grain of the rib, much as you would cut celery) into thin, even slices. Drop the slices into the bowl of acidulated water. Once all the ribs are sliced, drain and

place in a small saucepan. Add 1 cup of the cream and a pinch of saffron threads. Cover and bring to a simmer. Cook just until the ribs are tender, about 5 minutes.

4. Cut the Swiss chard leaves into fine chiffonade. In a 5-quart pasta pot fitted with a colander, bring 3 quarts of water to a rolling boil over high heat. Plunge the leaves into the boiling water and blanch, uncovered, just until softened, 2 to 3 minutes. Drain and rinse under the coldest possible water. Squeeze the leaves to rid them of liquid. Place in a small saucepan. Add the remaining 1/2 cup of cream and a pinch of saffron threads. Cover and bring to a simmer. Cook just until the leaves are warmed through, 1 to 2 minutes.

5. To serve, add the mussels to the cream and rib mixture. Reheat over low heat just until warmed through. Place a spoonful of the Swiss chard leaf mixture on the bottom of each of the warmed bowls. Carefully spoon the rib, mussel, and cream mixture on top. Decorate each bowl with a pair of reserved mussel shells. Serve immediately.

⁂c 155 calories per serving ⁂ 9 g fat ⁂ 5 g protein ⁂ 5 g carbohydrates

What I Learned: This dish is also delicious cold: I like to serve it in tiny glass bowls.

> ## Wine Suggestion
>
> The first time I sampled this dish, we drank one of my favorite Provençal white wines, the fine, mineral-rich Sablet blanc from winemaker Yves Gras's Santa Duc. A blend of Viognier, Grenache Blanc, and Bourboulenc, it is crisp and fresh and fine for a warm summer day's sipping.

A Springtime Bistro Meal

Cucumber, Spring Onion, and Goat Cheese Salad Le Cinq-Mars (page 26)
Artichoke and Parmesan Soup (page 48)
Mussels with Swiss Chard and Saffron Cream
Individual Chocolate Custards with Espelette Pepper (page 272)

WARM OYSTERS WITH SPINACH
AND SPICY CREAM SAUCE

Huîtres Chaudes aux Épinards, Sauce Epicée

I eat oysters whenever and wherever I can. I love their bright, briny flavor, the rituals that go with them (salty butter on dense, fragrant rye bread, a touch of lemon or a touch of coarsely ground black pepper). But there are days when I also like to serve them warm, and this is one of my current favorite preparations: the oysters are topped with a touch of spicy cream, then a hefty dose of wilted spinach. For eating raw, I like the tiniest oysters I can find, for I feel that they have a more intense flavor. But when serving them warm, go for the monsters. A dish that is gorgeous, healthy, delicious! 12 appetizer servings

EQUIPMENT: An oyster knife and glove; a fine-mesh sieve; a heat-proof serving dish.

12 large fresh oysters
About 1½ cups coarse salt (11 ounces)
½ cup crème fraîche or sour cream
Grated zest of 1 lemon, preferably organic
½ teaspoon ground *piment d'Espelette* or dried Anaheim chili (or ground mild chili pepper)
1 recipe Just Spinach! (page 203)

1.   Open the oysters and filter the oyster liquor through a fine-mesh sieve into a small bowl. Reserve the oyster liquor.

2.   Cover the bottom of a heat-proof serving dish (I use a shallow copper omelet pan) with a thin layer of coarse sea salt. Place the opened oysters on the bed of salt to keep them stable. Refrigerate. Within about 15 minutes, the oysters will give off a second, even more flavorful oyster liquor. Pour off the second oyster liquor, again through a fine-mesh sieve set over the small bowl.

3.   Preheat the broiler.

4.   In a small bowl, whisk together the cream, lemon zest, reserved oyster liquor, and *piment d'Espelette*. Spoon the cream sauce over the oysters. Carefully arrange a dollop of spinach on top of the cream. Place the dish under the broiler just until warmed through, about 10 seconds. Serve immediately.

55 calories per serving ∘ 4 g fat ∘ 4 g protein ∘ 4 g carbohydrates

A crisp young Muscadet is an ideal wine here: it's an underrated wine that is mineral-rich, bone-dry, and smoky. It's a wine that makes you salivate and, of course, eat! The qualities of the wine—made from the rarely seen Melon de Bourgogne grape—nicely mirror this dish, with a bit of creaminess, touches of spice, and the sea. Try the offering from the vineyard of Domaine Brégeon.

Oysters and Rye Bread

Years ago I set out to find the origins of the combination of rye bread and oysters. In France, oysters are traditionally accompanied by rye bread slathered with butter. I asked chefs and oyster growers, restaurateurs and oyster shuckers, but no one could even begin to suggest the origin of the combination. Finally it occurred to me that I was looking in the wrong direction. So I asked Parisian bread baker Lionel Poilâne and got a quick response: "It was the Romans. Their word for rye bread was 'oyster bread.'" From now on, when searching for origins, I'll check with the Romans first!

SALMON WRAPPED IN SPINACH LEAVES
WITH CAPER, LEMON, AND OLIVE SAUCE

Saumon en Chemise d'Épinards, Sauce aux Olives

Salmon is on our menu on an almost daily basis, and in this version I wrap the fresh fish in wilted spinach leaves, steam the packets, and serve it with a pungent and colorful sauce of capers, lemons, and extra-virgin olive oil. It's quick, it's elegant, it's lively. 4 servings

EQUIPMENT: A 5-quart pasta pot fitted with a colander; a small saucepan; tweezers; a steamer; 4 warmed dinner plates.

The Fish

3 tablespoons coarse sea salt

8 large spinach leaves, rinsed and stemmed

1 pound skinless fresh salmon fillet

Fine sea salt

The Sauce

1 cup best-quality drained green olives (preferably a mix of Picholine and Lucques), pitted

¼ cup capers in vinegar, drained

2 tablespoons freshly squeezed lemon juice

¼ cup extra-virgin olive oil

1.   In a 5-quart pasta pot fitted with a colander, bring 3 quarts water to a rolling boil over high heat. Add the coarse salt and drop the spinach leaves into the pot. Blanch just until wilted, about 30 seconds. Remove the spinach with a slotted spoon and rinse the leaves in cold water to stop the cooking and help them maintain their brilliant green color. Lay them open and flat on a layer of paper towels to dry. Set aside.

2.   Run your fingers over the top of the salmon fillet to detect any tiny bones that remain in the salmon. With tweezers, remove the bones. Cut the salmon into 4 even 4-ounce portions. Season each piece of salmon with fine sea salt. Wrap each piece of salmon in a spinach leaf, folding the leaf evenly and neatly around the fish. If necessary, secure with a toothpick. Set aside.

3.   Prepare the sauce: In a small saucepan, combine all the ingredients and bring just to a simmer over moderate heat. Remove from the heat and cover.

4.   Bring 1 quart water to a simmer in the bottom of a steamer. Place the salmon packets on the steaming rack. Place the rack over simmering water, cover, and steam until the salmon is lightly cooked, 3 to 4 minutes. (Steam for a few more minutes if you prefer fully cooked salmon.) Remove the salmon packets from the steaming rack, drain, and transfer 1 packet to each of 4 warmed dinner plates. Spoon the sauce over the packets and serve immediately.

✤c 297 calories per serving ❋ 21 g fat ❋ 23 g protein ❋ 3 g carbohydrates

Wine Suggestion

Although wild salmon once grew abundantly in the Loire River, it no longer does. That doesn't stop me from making the "what grows together goes together" link and, more often than not, a turn to a favorite Loire Valley white in my cellar. Try the 100 percent Chenin Blanc Montlouis, from winemaker Jacky Blot. The wines from his Domaine de la Taille aux Loups have both great acid and fruit, with an intriguing finish of raw honey.

QUICK-CURED SARDINES WITH
SHALLOTS ON RYE BREAD

Sardines Marinées aux Échalotes sur Toast de Seigle

Sardines are quick, inexpensive, healthy fare in France, and we indulge often. One evening in December I dreamed up this very quick dish, one that can be served as an appetizer or a first course. I like these quick-cured sardines served on a piece of toasted bread, making for a good contrast of textures and flavors. 8 servings

EQUIPMENT: A scissors.

¼ cup minced shallot
3 tablespoons extra-virgin olive oil
2 teaspoons coarse sea salt
8 very fresh small sardines
Freshly ground black pepper
8 slices rye bread, toasted

1. In a small bowl, combine the shallot, oil, and salt and toss to blend. Set aside.

2. Clean the sardines: Rinse them under cold running water, gently rubbing the scales off. Gently twist the head off, pulling the guts with it. Discard the head and guts. With your fingertips, gently press down the belly side, pressing the sardine open like a book. With your fingertips, gently pull the central bone from head to tail, being careful not to tear the flesh. With the scissors, gently detach the bone from the flesh. Discard the bone. Leave the sardines whole, with both fillets intact. Open the sardines flat.

3. Place each sardine, skin side down, in a flat, shallow dish. Once all of the sardines are cleaned and placed in the dish, scatter with the shallot mixture. The sardines can be served immediately or left to marinate, covered and refrigerated, for up to 8 hours. To serve, place a sardine on a slice of rye toast.

179 calories per serving ⁕ 9 g fat ⁕ 9 g protein ⁕ 16 g carbohydrates

Wine Suggestion

I love sampling these sardines with sips of Domaine de la Monardière white Vacqueyras, a rare and exciting blend of Grenache Blanc, Roussanne, and Viognier. I love it when the fruits and acids marry so nicely with the sea-fresh flavors of the sardines. Try for a white with a touch of minerality.

SARDINES IN PARCHMENT WITH TOMATOES AND ONIONS

Sardines en Papillote aux Tomates et Oignons

Gorgeous, sparkling fresh tiny sardines can be found almost all year round, coming either from the chilled Atlantic or the warmer Mediterranean. These protein-rich, light, and filling little fish seem to love Mediterranean-style accompaniments, such as tomatoes, onions, bay leaves, and thyme. Here the sardines are cooked in a single parchment paper packet, making for a quick, colorful, festive treat. 4 servings as a first course

EQUIPMENT: A scissors; a 12-inch square of parchment paper or aluminum foil; a baking sheet;
   4 warmed dinner plates.

12 very fresh small sardines
2 small, oval fresh tomatoes, cored and cut lengthwise into thin slices
2 spring onions or 4 scallions, peeled and cut lengthwise into thin slices
Several branches fresh thyme
Several bay leaves, preferably fresh
2 teaspoons coarse sea salt
1 tablespoon extra-virgin olive oil

1.   Preheat the oven to 425 degrees F.

2.   Prepare the sardines: Rinse them under cold running water, gently rubbing the scales off. Gently twist the head off, pulling the guts with it. Discard the head and guts. With your fingertips, gently press down the belly side, pressing the sardine open like a book. With your fingertips, gently pull the central bone from head to tail, being careful not to tear the flesh. With scissors, gently detach the bone from the flesh. Discard the bone. Leave the sardine whole, with both fillets intact. Fold the fillets together, closing each sardine.

3.   Place the parchment paper or aluminum foil on a baking sheet. Arrange the sliced tomatoes, sliced onions, thyme, and bay leaves in the center of the paper or foil. Arrange the sardines on top. Sprinkle with coarse salt. Drizzle with oil. If using parchment paper, carefully fold the paper over the fish, closing it like a book. To seal the package, double-fold the top and secure with several staples. Double-fold the two sides and secure each side with several staples. If using foil, simply bring the foil up into a ball, securing the vegetables and fish, and close the foil firmly.

4.   Place the baking sheet in the center of the oven and bake for 15 minutes.

5.   Remove the baking sheet from the oven and let the package rest for at least 5 minutes. At serving time, carefully open the package with scissors, being cautious of the steam that will rise from the package.

6.   Use a slotted spoon to transfer the fish and vegetables to warm serving plates. Serve immediately.

   ❧c 206 calories per serving ❋ 12 g fat ❋ 19 g protein ❋ 8 g carbohydrates

Wine Suggestion

I love this with a white from the Loire: A good choice is the 100 percent Chenin Blanc, a Saumur Domaine des Roches Neuves l'Insolite, from winemaker Thierry Germain. Chenin Blanc is one of the world's most misunderstood, as well as ignored, grapes. It is full of rich, complex minerality but light and versatile enough to pair with this vibrant, assertive combination of sardines and tomatoes.

Folklore: You can use an onion to forecast the winter weather. Peel an onion and note the number of papery leaves that surround it. The more leaves, the colder the upcoming winter!

SEA SCALLOPS ON A BED OF LEEKS

Coquilles Saint-Jacques, Fondue de Poireaux

Scallops and leeks are a popular French combination, and when the first-of-season scallops appear on menus come October, this specialty becomes ubiquitous. It is, in fact, a brilliant marriage, a combination that wins on color contrast alone. 4 servings

> EQUIPMENT: A 5-quart pasta pot fitted with a colander; a large skillet with a lid; a large nonstick skillet; 4 warmed small plates.
>
> Coarse sea salt
> 8 leeks, white portion only, trimmed, rinsed, halved lengthwise, and cut into thin half-moon slices
> 8 large sea scallops (1½ to 2 inches)
> ¼ cup crème fraiche or top-quality heavy cream
> Fine sea salt
> Freshly ground white pepper
> 1 tablespoon Classic Vinaigrette (page 296)
> 2 tablespoons finely minced fresh chives
> 2 tablespoons finely minced fresh flat-leaf parsley leaves
> 2 tablespoons finely minced fresh chervil leaves or tarragon leaves
> *Fleur de sel*

1.   Prepare a large bowl of ice water.

2.   Fill a 5-quart pasta pot fitted with a colander with 3 quarts water and bring to a rolling boil over high heat. Add 3 tablespoons coarse salt and the leeks. Blanch until crisp-tender, about 1 minute. Immediately remove the colander from the water, allow the water to drain from the leeks, and plunge the colander with the leeks into the ice water so they cool down as quickly as possible. (The leeks will cool in 1 minute. If you leave them longer, they will become soggy and begin to lose flavor.) Drain the leeks and wrap them in a thick towel to dry. (The leeks can be cooked up to 1 hour in advance. Keep them wrapped in the towel at room temperature.)

3.   Gently and lightly rinse the scallops and pat dry with paper towels. Remove the little muscle on the side of the scallop and discard. Cut each scallop in half horizontally. Set aside.

4.   At serving time, place the blanched leeks in the large lidded skillet and reheat, adding enough crème fraîche to evenly coat the leeks. Cover and keep warm over low heat.

5.   In the large nonstick skillet over high heat, sear the scallops and cook just until they brown around the edges, 30 seconds to 1 minute on each side. Season each side after it has cooked. (Cooking time will vary according to the size of the scallops. For scallops that are cooked all the way through, sear for 1 minute or more on each side.)

6.   On each warmed plate, arrange a bed of warm leeks. Top with the seared scallops. Drizzle lightly with the vinaigrette. Sprinkle with herbs. Season with *fleur de sel*. Serve.

❋c 221 calories per serving ❋ 6 g fat ❋ 8 g protein ❋ 36 g carbohydrates

Wine Suggestion

Look for a buttery white wine that has a touch of creaminess. Try the 100 percent Chardonnay Chablis Domaine Bessin, cuvée Montmains. It's a wine with a highly developed nose, a touch of fattiness, and great expression.

LA CAGOUILLE'S POACHED SKATE
WITH SAUCE GRIBICHE

L'Aile de Raie de La Cagouille, Sauce Gribiche

I could return to the simple but spectacular Parisian fish restaurant La Cagouille once a week just to sample their ample main-course preparation of skate—*raie*—served with an enriching sauce gribiche. Here the gribiche—rather than the usual glorified mayonnaise—appears as a main player, with cubes of carrots, potatoes, turnips, capers, chives, chopped hard-cooked eggs, and a dose of sherry-wine vinegar. 6 servings

EQUIPMENT: A steamer; a double boiler; a large, shallow skillet; a large, wide spatula; 6 warmed dinner plates.

Sauce Gribiche
4 large eggs, at room temperature
3 small carrots, peeled and cut into 1/2-inch slices
3 potatoes, peeled and cut into 1/2-inch cubes
3 turnips, peeled and cut into 1/2-inch cubes
1 tablespoon sherry-wine vinegar
2 teaspoons imported French mustard
2 tablespoons capers in vinegar, drained
1/4 cup extra-virgin olive oil
30 cornichons, cut crosswise into thin slices
1/2 teaspoon fine sea salt
1/2 cup finely minced fresh chives

Poaching Liquid
2 medium onions, peeled, quartered, and stuck with 4 cloves
Several sprigs flat-leaf parsley
6 whole peppercorns
4 fresh or dried bay leaves

2 pounds skate wing, with skin
1/4 cup finely minced fresh parsley for garnish

1.   Place the eggs in a saucepan. Cover generously with water. Cook, uncovered, over medium-high heat until the first large bubbles rise steadily from the bottom of the pan. Reduce the heat so the water continues to simmer gently but never boils. Simmer for 8 minutes. The cooked eggs should have a firmly set yolk and white. Pour off the hot water. Stop the cooking by running cold water over the eggs for 1 minute. When the eggs are cool, peel them. Separate the whites and the yolks. With a fork, mash the yolks into a fine purée. Finely chop the whites. Set aside.

2.   Bring 1 quart water to a simmer in the bottom of a steamer. Place the carrots, potatoes, and turnips on the steaming rack. Place the rack over the simmering water, cover, and steam until the vegetables are soft and cooked through, about 10 minutes.

3.   While the vegetables are steaming, in a large bowl, combine the vinegar, mustard, capers, olive oil, cornichons, and salt and blend with a fork. Add the chives and toss once more.

4.   As soon as the vegetables are cooked through, remove from the steaming rack, drain, and toss immediately into the sauce. Stir to coat the vegetables. Set aside.

5.   In a large, shallow skillet large enough to hold the skate wing, combine the poaching liquid ingredients with 1 quart cold water. Add the skate wing and bring just to a boil over high heat. Reduce the heat to medium and gently simmer, uncovered, until the skate is cooked through, turns white at the edges, and the skin begins to wrinkle, about 20 minutes.

6.   With a large, wide spatula, carefully lift the skate wing from the skillet. Using a sharp knife, gently scrape off all of the skin and any of the gristle underneath it, being careful not to disturb the pattern of the skate wing. Trim away and discard the thin layer of brown meat.

7.   To serve, cut the skate wing vertically into 6 pieces. Carefully arrange on 6 warmed dinner plates. Pour equal amounts of the sauce over the fish. Garnish with equal amounts of the egg yolk, egg white, and parsley. Serve immediately.

✳c 381 calories per serving ✳ 13 g fat ✳ 17 g protein ✳ 48 g carbohydrates

Wine Suggestion

A wine on the La Cagouille wine list that I love—for its flavor as well as its price—is a Macon-Villages, the 100 percent Chardonnay Comte Lafon Macon Milly-Lamartine 2000, a stony, mineral-rich delight that one could imagine sampling each day at lunch with a different fish offering.

Origins: In France during the fourteenth century, the turnip was considered the meat substitute of the poor.

SEARED BABY SQUID WITH PARSLEY AND GARLIC

Soupions à l'Ail et au Persil

Dishes don't get much simpler than this. The popular French duo of parsley and garlic get top billing here, adding zest and texture to the delicate nature of these sweet, tiny squid. 4 servings as a first course

EQUIPMENT: **A large skillet.**

8 ounces small squid
4 plump, moist cloves garlic, peeled, halved, green germ removed, minced
1 cup fresh flat-leaf parsley leaves, finely minced
2 tablespoons extra-virgin olive oil
Fleur de sel

1. Gut, clean, and rinse the squid, reserving the tentacles and leaving the bodies whole. (Or have your fishmonger do this for you.)

2. In a medium bowl, combine the garlic and parsley and toss to blend. Set aside.

3. In a large skillet over high heat, heat the oil until hot but not smoking. Add the squid and tentacles and sear, tossing for even cooking, for 1 minute. With a slotted spoon, transfer the squid and tentacles to the bowl of garlic and parsley and toss to evenly coat the squid. Season with *fleur de sel* and serve.

121 calories per serving ⁕ 8 g fat ⁕ 10 g protein ⁕ 4 g carbohydrates

Wine Suggestions

Our Parisian wine merchant, Juan Sanchez, has introduced me to dozens of wines that have become daily favorites in our house. We love his Jurançon Sec, Clos d'Uroulat Cuvée Marie, a blend of 90 percent Gros Manseng and 10 percent Courbu, from the southwest of France. It's got life, zest, and punch and can stand up to this garlic-rich dish. Another fine bet is the Jurançon Sec from Domaine Cauhape, Chant des Vignes. It has lots of body and a nice, clean finish.

History: In 1568 French surgeon Ambroise Paré advised the working class to eat cloves of garlic and shallots with bread, butter, and good wine—if they could afford it—to prevent an outbreak of the plague.

BABY SQUID SALAD WITH GARLIC, OLIVES, TOMATOES, AND PARSLEY

Salade de Petits Calmars à la Provençale

This dish comes straight from the Mediterranean, where delicate baby squid can be found during many months of the year. These tender cephalopods cook in just forty-five seconds, then while still warm are bathed in a pungent mix of raw garlic, pimiento-stuffed olives, cherry tomatoes, and plenty of parsley. 4 servings

EQUIPMENT: A 5-quart pasta pot fitted with a colander.

8 ounces small squid

6 plump, moist cloves garlic, peeled, halved, green germ removed, minced

2 tablespoons extra-virgin olive oil

2 tablespoons freshly squeezed lemon juice

20 cherry tomatoes, stemmed and halved

20 pimiento-stuffed olives, halved crosswise

½ cup coarsely chopped flat-leaf parsley

3 tablespoons coarse sea salt

Fleur de sel

1.   Gut, clean, and rinse the squid. Reserve the tentacles and cut the bodies into ¼-inch rings. (Or have your fishmonger do this for you.)

2.   In a medium bowl, combine the garlic, oil, lemon juice, tomatoes, olives, and parsley and toss to blend. Set aside.

3.   In a 5-quart pasta pot fitted with a colander, bring 3 quarts water to a boil over high heat. Add the coarse salt. Add the squid rings and tentacles and cook for 45 seconds, from the time the squid enter the water. Drain immediately. Add the squid to the bowl with the garlic mixture. Toss gently to blend. Taste and season with *fleur de sel*. The salad can be prepared several hours in advance. At serving time, taste for seasoning. Serve at room temperature, with crusty bread to absorb the sauce.

166 calories per serving ※ 11 g fat ※ 10 g protein ※ 9 g carbohydrates

Folklore: Garlic will make you both brave and courageous, especially if you have it for breakfast!

TUNA STRIPS WITH ESPELETTE PEPPER

Lanières de Thon au Piment d'Espelette

In the summer months when gorgeous, fresh Mediterranean tuna is in season, this dish appears on the table almost every week. The idea of cutting the tuna into long strips came to me while looking for a way to get away from the cliché of cooking a single, big steak of tuna. The dish is fast, packed with plenty of spicy flavor from the *piment d'Espelette,* and provides plenty of good, lean protein. We call it Tuna Bing, Bang, Boom, since it cooks in a flash. I love to serve this with Butter-Warmed Corn Kernels with Fresh Cilantro Leaves (page 174). 4 servings

EQUIPMENT: A large skillet; 4 warmed large dinner plates.

1 pound ultra-fresh tuna fillet
2 tablespoons extra-virgin olive oil
2 teaspoons ground *piment d'Espelette* or dried Anaheim chili (or ground mild chili pepper)
Fleur de sel

1. Cut the tuna into strips about ¾ inch thick and 4 inches long. In a large bowl, combine the strips of tuna fillet, the olive oil, and the pepper powder. Toss to blend. Marinate at room temperature for 10 minutes.

2. Heat a large, dry skillet over high heat. When hot, remove the strips of tuna from the marinade, without draining, and place in the skillet. Working quickly, sear the fish for about 15 seconds on each side for rare tuna, longer for tuna that is well cooked. Immediately transfer the tuna strips to warmed plates. Season with *fleur de sel* and serve.

226 calories per serving ◦ 13 g fat ◦ 27 g protein ◦ 1 g carbohydrates

✳ Variation: In place of Espelette pepper powder, use either sweet or hot Spanish paprika, to taste.

Wine Suggestions

When you think Basque country, think Irouléguy, the tiniest vineyard in Europe. Vines cover the steeply terraced hillsides of the colorful region. The reds are rustic, made from the Cabernet Franc, Tannat, and Cabernet Sauvignon grapes. The easy-drinking whites, made from Gros Manseng and Courbu grapes, have plenty of acidity and a nice balance of fruit. My favorite winemaker there is Etienne Brana.

TUNA CONFIT WITH TOMATOES, CAPERS, AND WHITE WINE

Confit de Thon aux Tomates, Câpres et Vin Blanc

Fashion in food often surprises people. Tuna is one of those fashion statements. Twenty years ago, raw or rare-cooked tuna was unheard of, save for a few remote sushi restaurants. Then, tuna was cooked like the "chicken of the sea" we grew up with, almost like a pot roast. There are merits to this method, for a thick fillet of tuna can indeed stand up to long, slow cooking. In this recipe, not only is the tuna cooked very slowly and gently, but the pan is set in a water bath, so the tuna comes out evenly cooked but still quite rare and flaky. The onions, tomatoes, and capers are perfect accompaniments, allowing the tuna to retain its moisture. The size of the pan here is important: the tuna should fit snugly. 12 servings

EQUIPMENT: A roasting pan; a heavy-duty casserole, 8 inches in diameter, with a lid.

2 pounds tuna fillet in a single piece, cut 2 inches thick
½ cup dry white wine
½ cup extra-virgin olive oil
1 pound tomatoes, cored and chopped
2 onions, peeled, halved crosswise, and thinly sliced
1 teaspoon hot red pepper flakes, or to taste
¼ cup capers in vinegar, drained
Fine sea salt
Freshly ground black pepper

1.   Preheat the oven to 225 degrees F.

2.   Fill a roasting pan with 2 inches of water. Over high heat, bring the water to a boil.

3.   Place the tuna in the casserole. It should fit snugly, in a single layer. Pour the wine and olive oil over the tuna. The liquid should come almost to the top of the fish. Scatter the tomatoes, onions, hot pepper, and capers over the tuna. Season with salt and pepper. Cover.

4.   Place the roasting pan in the oven. Place the covered casserole in the roasting pan. Cook for 1 hour. The tuna should be cooked through, but barely, and be tender and flaky. Serve warm or at room temperature, slicing the tuna into thick slices. Pour the cooking juices over the tuna.

✢ᶜ 287 calories per serving ✲ 12 g fat ✲ 28 g protein ✲ 10 g carbohydrates

Wine Suggestion

The Mediterranean notes of tomatoes, onions, hot peppers, and capers suggest a rich red, but not one that's too fancy. Try an unusual wine from the Domaine de la Janasse in Châteauneuf-du-Pape. Their Vin de Pays de la Principauté d'Orange Terre de Buissière (that's a mouthful!) is an uncommon blend of Merlot, Cabernet Sauvignon, Syrah, and Grenache. Each grape adds its own touch of character here, and the complexity helps it stand up to the tuna just fine.

LE KAIKU'S TUNA, CHIVE, AND SHALLOT TARTARE

Tartare de Thon à la Ciboulette Le Kaiku

One warm, bright evening in July I sat on the colorful terrace of the historic Saint-Jean-de-Luz restaurant Le Kaiku and savored this Basque-inspired tuna tartare, studded with chives and the gentle crunch of finely minced shallot. As my plate was cleared I asked the waitress, "Do you sometimes give diners the recipe for this?" She laughed, responding, "Even I don't know the secret." I think I've come pretty close here: the key is mixing the tartare at the very last moment, so the seasoning does not compete with the lusciousness of the fish. You can drizzle the finished product with a touch of good-quality sherry-wine vinegar. And of course a touch of the famed *piment d'Espelette*! 4 servings

EQUIPMENT: 4 chilled salad plates.

1 pound ultra-fresh tuna fillet, cut into tiny rectangles and well chilled
4 shallots, trimmed, peeled, and finely minced
1 cup finely minced fresh chives
3 tablespoons extra-virgin olive oil, or as needed
½ teaspoon ground *piment d'Espelette* or dried Anaheim chili (or ground mild chili pepper)
Fleur de sel
Sherry-wine vinegar for garnish

Place the tuna in a large bowl. Add the shallots and chives and toss gently. Add just enough olive oil to evenly coat the tartare, tossing gently. Season with Espelette pepper and *fleur de sel* and toss once more. Arrange in a mound on chilled plates. Drizzle with vinegar and serve immediately.

275 calories per serving ❋ 16 g fat ❋ 28 g protein ❋ 5 g carbohydrates

Wine Suggestion

That evening we drank one of my favorite whites from the southwest of France, a white Jurançon Sec. This little-known wine is made from two rather obscure grape varietals, Gros Manseng and Petit Courbu. It's a citrusy wine that is both exotic and full-bodied and exciting enough to stand up to the forward flavors of this tartare. A fine choice is the wine from Domaine Bru-Baché.

SUSAN'S MONKFISH WITH SAVOY CABBAGE AND SPANISH HAM

Les Queues de Lotte au Chou Vert et au Bellota de Susan

My good friend Susan Hermann Loomis shared this delightful winter dish with me. It's perfect for a cold night: somehow cabbage and pork warm the soul. Use the finest Spanish ham you can find and the crispiest head of savoy cabbage. 4 servings

EQUIPMENT: A small skillet; a 10-quart pasta pot fitted with a colander; 2 large skillets, 1 with a lid; 4 warmed dinner plates.

1 savoy cabbage (about 2 pounds)
4 small monkfish tails (each about 8 ounces)
$\frac{1}{3}$ cup shelled almonds
3 tablespoons coarse sea salt
2 tablespoons extra-virgin olive oil
1 tablespoon unsalted butter
2 ounces Spanish ham, cut into thin matchsticks
1 plump, moist clove garlic, peeled, halved, green germ removed, cut into thin slivers
Fine sea salt
Freshly ground white pepper
$\frac{1}{2}$ cup all-purpose flour
$\frac{1}{2}$ teaspoon ground ginger
$\frac{1}{4}$ teaspoon ground *piment d'Espelette* or dried Anaheim chili (or ground mild chili pepper)
1 tablespoon grapeseed oil
Fleur de sel

1. Trim and quarter the cabbage. Cut the quarters into thin $\frac{1}{4}$-inch strips. Set aside.

2. Remove the outer and inner skins from the monkfish tails. Remove the central bone. Set aside.

3. Toast the almonds: Place the almonds in a small, dry skillet over moderate heat. Shake the pan regularly until the nuts are fragrant and evenly toasted, about 2 minutes. Watch carefully! They can burn quickly. Transfer the nuts to a large plate to cool. Chop them coarsely. Set aside.

4.   Prepare a large bowl of ice water.

5.   In a 10-quart pasta pot fitted with a colander, bring 8 quarts water to a rolling boil over high heat. Add the coarse sea salt and the cabbage. Cook, uncovered, just until the cabbage turns a very bright, almost translucent green, about 5 minutes. Transfer the cabbage to the ice water, and when the cabbage is completely cooled, let it drain until it is almost, but not quite, dry.

6.   In a large skillet, heat the olive oil and the butter over moderate heat until melted. Add the ham, garlic, and cabbage. Toss until all the ingredients are combined. Season lightly with fine sea salt and pepper and cook until the cabbage is wilted but still bright green, about 8 minutes. Taste for seasoning. Remove from the heat and cover to keep warm.

7.   While the cabbage is cooking, sift together the flour, ginger, *piment d'Espelette,* and 1/4 teaspoon fine sea salt onto a plate or piece of parchment paper. Dredge the monkfish in the coating.

8.   In a large skillet over high heat, heat the grapeseed oil. When the oil is hot but not smoking, add the monkfish and cook, covered, turning regularly until the fish is an even golden brown and cooked through, 7 to 8 minutes.

9.   To serve, evenly divide the cabbage and ham among 4 warmed dinner plates, dropping the cabbage onto the plates from a certain distance above the plate so it falls nicely. Place 2 pieces of monkfish on top of the cabbage and sprinkle each plate with an equal amount of toasted almonds. Garnish with *fleur de sel* and serve immediately.

&c 473 calories per serving ⁕ 21 g fat ⁕ 44 g protein ⁕ 29 g carbohydrates

Wine Suggestion

Cabbage always makes me think of Alsace, so it follows that a crisp chilled Riesling would be right at home here.

POULTRY AND MEATS

Les Volailles et les Viandes

❖

GRILLED CHICKEN WITH SHALLOT VINAIGRETTE

Poulet en Crapaudine à la Vinaigrette d'Échalote

Sweet shallots work their magic in this dish, where they are sliced into rings and marinated in walnut oil and lemon juice. Once the chicken is grilled, the mixture smothers the chicken as it rests, warming the shallots to a delicate tenderness. This method works fine for grilled or roasted chicken as well as grilled or roasted squab, quail, or guinea hen. 8 servings

EQUIPMENT: Poultry shears or a heavy-duty scissors; a roasting pan.

1 best-quality farm chicken (about 5 pounds)
Coarse sea salt
Freshly ground black pepper
12 shallots, trimmed, peeled, and cut into thin rings
1/2 cup walnut, hazelnut, or extra-virgin olive oil (see Note)
2 tablespoons freshly squeezed lemon juice
1/2 teaspoon fine sea salt

1. Preheat the broiler for about 15 minutes. Or prepare a wood or charcoal fire. The fire is ready when the coals glow red and are covered with ash.

2. Prepare the chicken: Place the chicken, breast side down, on a flat surface. With a pair of poultry shears, split the bird lengthwise along the backbone. Open it flat and press down with the heel of your hand to flatten completely. With a sharp knife, make slits in the skin near the tail and tuck the wing tips in to secure them. The bird should be as flat as possible to ensure even cooking.

3. Season the chicken lightly with the coarse sea salt and pepper. With the skin side toward the heat, place the chicken on a roasting pan set beneath the broiler or directly on the grill about 5 inches from the heat so that the poultry cooks evenly without burning. Cook until the skin is evenly browned, basting occasionally, about 15 minutes. Using tongs so you do not pierce the meat, turn and cook the other side, basting occasionally, about 15 minutes more. To test for doneness, pierce the thigh with a skewer. The chicken is done when the juices run clear.

4. While the chicken is cooking, combine the shallots, oil, lemon juice, and fine sea salt in a large, shallow platter large enough to hold the chicken. Set aside.

5.   Remove the chicken from the heat and season lightly with coarse salt and pepper. Place on the platter and spoon the shallot mixture over the chicken, turning the poultry to coat it evenly with the mixture. Cover securely with aluminum foil and let the chicken rest for 15 minutes.

6.   To serve, quarter the chicken and slice the breast meat, arranging it on a serving platter.

Note: If you broil the chicken, you may prepare a sauce with the drippings: Place the broiler pan over moderate heat, scraping up any bits that cling to the bottom. Cook for several minutes, continuing to scrape and stir until the liquid is almost caramelized but not burned. Spoon off any excess fat and deglaze with several tablespoons cold water (hot water would cloud the sauce). Bring to a boil. Reduce the heat and simmer until thickened, about 5 minutes. Strain the sauce through a fine-mesh sieve and transfer to a sauceboat. Serve immediately with the chicken.

✳c 460 calories per serving (less if the skin is not consumed) ✳ 32 g fat ✳ 33 g protein ✳ 7 g carbohydrates

Wine Suggestion

Pair this dish with a young Côtes-du-Rhône, either white or red. A favorite in my cellar comes from the Châteauneuf-du-Pape vineyards Clos du Caillou. Their white Côtes-du-Rhône, Les Garrigues blanc, could pass for a Châteauneuf, with its complex flavors and crisp minerality. The red, Bouquet des Garrigues, has a beautiful nose, with a touch of pepper and spice.

Source Note: Top-quality oils from Leblanc in Burgundy can be ordered on-line at honestfoods.com and Gourmetcountry.com.

CHICKEN BREASTS WITH MINT, CAPERS, AND WHITE WINE

Blancs de Poulet à la Menthe

The soothing nature of white breast meat, the sunny flavor of fresh mint, and the tangy firmness of capers join to make this a winning dish. It's quick, it's festive, it's efficient, for nights when you want something special but don't have a lot of time. Serve this with Baby Spinach, Radish, and Mint Salad (page 34). 4 servings

EQUIPMENT: A meat mallet or a heavy-duty skillet; a large skillet.

4 skinless, boneless chicken breast fillets (each about 4 ounces)
¼ cup fresh mint leaves
2 tablespoons extra-virgin olive oil
Fine sea salt
1 cup dry white wine
2 tablespoons capers in vinegar, drained

1. Cut each chicken breast in half. Cover with plastic wrap and, with a meat mallet or a heavy-duty skillet, flatten the meat to about ¼-inch thickness. In a shallow bowl, combine the chicken, mint, and 1 tablespoon of the olive oil. Cover and marinate for at least 15 minutes.

2. In a large skillet over moderate heat, heat the remaining tablespoon of oil until hot but not smoking. Add the chicken and cook for about 2 minutes. Season with salt and turn, cooking the other side for about 2 minutes more. Season the second side and transfer to a warm serving platter. Cover with foil to keep warm. Slowly add the wine to the skillet, scraping up any bits of chicken that cling to the pan. Add the capers and boil, uncovered, for 2 to 3 minutes or until the sauce is reduced and syrupy. Drizzle the sauce over the chicken.

✦c 237 calories per serving ⁂ 10 g fat ⁂ 26 g protein ⁂ 1 g carbohydrates

Wine Suggestion

Drink the white wine used in cooking: Try a white from the Savoie, the elegant Chignin-Bergeron, or any wine based on the elegant Roussanne grape, with notes of hazelnuts and the pale color of straw. Try the Chignin-Bergeron from winemakers André and Michel Quénard.

SEARED DUCK BREAST WITH
ESPELETTE PEPPER JELLY

Magrets de Canard à la Gelée de Piment d'Espelette

Quick, easy, and a dish that delights everyone, this moist, meaty duck breast is the perfect recipe for entertaining. Since the duck breast benefits from resting once it is cooked—the juices are reabsorbed into the meat, making it even more moist and tender—the dish can be cooked in advance. I have made it as much as two hours in advance, and it was delicious. I like this with a sauce, here one made with tangy, spicy Espelette Pepper Jelly. This dish is equally good with a homemade cherry jam and will pair well with a cherrylike red wine, such as a rich red Rhône. 6 servings

EQUIPMENT: A large skillet; 6 warmed dinner plates; a small saucepan.

2 fatted duck breasts (*magrets de canard*), each about 12 ounces
Coarse sea salt
½ cup Espelette Pepper Jelly (page 307)

1. Using a sharp knife, make 12 diagonal incisions in the skin of each duck breast. Make 12 more diagonal incisions to create a crisscross pattern. The cuts should be deep but not go all the way through to the flesh. The scoring will help the fat melt while cooking and will stop the duck breast from shrinking up as it cooks. Sprinkle both sides of the breasts with salt.

2. Heat a large, dry skillet over medium-high heat. When the pan is hot but not smoking, place the duck breasts, skin side down, in the pan. Reduce the heat to medium and cook until the skin is a uniform deep golden brown, 8 minutes. Watch carefully and do not let the skin burn and blacken. The duck will be rare. Turn the duck breasts and cook them skin side up for 3 minutes more. Turn once again and cook skin side down for 3 minutes more. There will be a good deal of fat in the pan and, in fact, the meat will almost fry in its own fat. There will be some splattering. If cooking over a gas burner, be careful to avoid flames.

3. Remove the duck breasts from the pan and transfer to a warm platter. Season both sides with salt. Arrange the duck breasts, side by side, skin side up (to keep the skin crispy) on the platter. Cover securely with foil and let the duck rest for at least 10 minutes and up to 1 hour, to allow the juices to retreat into the meat. (The duck will retain most of its heat as it rests. If desired, keep the duck warm in a low oven.)

4. To serve, slice the duck: Holding a knife at a 45-degree angle, cut the duck across the grain into ½-inch-thick slices and arrange on warmed dinner plates.

5.   Heat the Espelette Pepper Jelly in a small saucepan over low heat. Add the juices that have pooled in the platter as the duck rests. Stir, cooking just until warmed through. Arrange 3 or 4 pieces of sliced duck on each warmed dinner plate. Spoon the pepper sauce over the duck and serve.

❀ 253 calories per serving (assuming the skin is not consumed) ❀ 6 g fat ❀ 18 g protein ❀ 34 g carbohydrates

Note: Fatted duck breasts—Moulard duck breasts—half or whole, can be ordered on-line from D'Artagnan at dartagnan.com.

Wine Suggestion

If you can get your hands on a fine Rhône with cherrylike overtones, go for it! I've loved this with the Sabon family's Domaine de la Janasse. Their Côtes-du-Rhône Les Garrigues is a powerful 100 percent Grenache wine made from vines sixty to eighty years old. It's a textbook example of wine from the Châteauneuf-du-Pape region, one of both power and finesse.

Piment d'Espelette

History tells us that the first seeds of the *piment d'Espelette* were brought from Mexico to the Basque region in the southwest of France by a member of Christopher Columbus's crew. In the beginning, the pepper was used as a medicine, but by 1650 the long, shiny red pepper was used as a condiment to help preserve the local hams and charcuterie. Since 1967, the ten villages that share the proper climate to cultivate the pepper have held an annual pepper festival the last week of October in the town of Espelette.

SAUTÉED QUAIL WITH
MUSTARD AND FENNEL

Cailles Poêlées à la Moutarde

If you love the clean, pure, and dense flavor of poultry as much as I do, then you will love this quick, efficient recipe for sautéed quail. This is an easy last-minute dish, and in the summertime it means no lighting the oven and heating up the kitchen! 4 servings

EQUIPMENT: Poultry shears; 2 large skillets; a pastry brush.

4 large fresh quail (each about 6 ounces), butterflied
Fine sea salt
4 tablespoons extra-virgin olive oil
2 tablespoons imported French mustard
2 teaspoons fennel seeds

Season the birds with salt. Heat 2 tablespoons of oil in each of 2 large skillets over moderate heat until hot but not smoking. Add the quail to the pans and sauté skin side down until golden brown, about 5 minutes. Turn and sauté until tender and still juicy, another 5 minutes. Transfer the birds to a platter. Season with salt. Place them breast side up on the platter. With a pastry brush, brush the mustard all over the breast side of the quail. Sprinkle with the fennel seeds. Cover loosely with foil and let rest for 5 to 10 minutes. Serve, offering finger bowls or a moistened hand towel for each diner.

369 calories per serving ⁂ 29 g fat ⁂ 25 g protein ⁂ 2 g carbohydrates

Wine Suggestion

We last sampled this with a bright, young red Vacqueyras from Domaine des Amouriers, cuvée Les Genestes, a blend of Grenache, Syrah, and Mourvèdre, aged totally in stainless steel and a fine, clean partner for the tender, meaty bird.

To Butterfly Quail Place the quail, breast side down, on a flat surface. With a pair of poultry shears, split the bird lengthwise along the backbone. Open it flat and press down with the heel of your hand to flatten it completely. Turn the quail skin side up and press down once more to flatten. With a sharp knife, make tiny slits in the skin near the top of each drumstick. Tuck the opposite drumstick through the slit to cross the bird's legs. The bird should be as flat as possible to ensure even cooking.

"La moutarde me monte au nez!" I'm beginning to see red!

BRAISED RABBIT WITH BLACK OLIVES, RED WINE, AND PINE NUTS

Lapin au Vin Rouge et aux Olives Noires

Leftover bits of wine or over-the-hill bottles that would serve better for cooking than drinking will find a useful purpose with this rustic dish, a fine blend of rabbit, salty olives, rich red wine, and a nice crunch of toasted pine nuts. Serve with Creamy Polenta Wedges (page 148). 8 servings

EQUIPMENT: A food processor or a blender; a large, heavy-duty, flame-proof casserole with a lid; a small skillet; 8 warmed dinner plates.

One 28-ounce can peeled Italian plum tomatoes in their juice
3 tablespoons extra-virgin olive oil
1 fresh rabbit or chicken (about 3 pounds), cut into serving pieces
Fine sea salt
Freshly ground white pepper
10 plump, moist cloves garlic, peeled, halved, green germ removed
1 cup dry red wine
1 teaspoon fresh or dried thyme leaves
4 bay leaves, preferably fresh
1 cup pitted best-quality French brine-cured black olives
½ cup pine nuts

1.   In a food processor or a blender, purée the tomatoes. Set aside.

2.   In a large, heavy-duty, flame-proof casserole, heat the oil over moderately high heat until hot but not smoking. Add the rabbit, turn the heat to low (to keep the rabbit meat from drying out), cover, and cook gently, shaking the pan from time to time, until the rabbit is tender and brilliantly golden but still moist, about 5 minutes. This may have to be done in batches. (Cooking time will vary according to the size of the pieces.) As each piece of rabbit is browned, transfer it to a platter and season lightly with salt and pepper.

3.   In the fat that remains in the casserole, sear the garlic for 1 to 2 minutes. Add the red wine and bring to a boil. Add the tomato purée, thyme, and bay leaves. Return the rabbit to the casserole, cover, and simmer over low heat until the rabbit is cooked through, 25 to 30 minutes. Add the olives. Simmer, uncovered, to allow the sauce to reduce, about 5 minutes.

4.   Meanwhile, toast the pine nuts: In a small, dry skillet over moderate heat, toast the nuts, shaking the pan regularly, until they are fragrant and evenly toasted, about 2 minutes. Watch carefully! They can burn quickly. Transfer the nuts to a large plate to cool.

5.   To serve, arrange portions of rabbit on warmed dinner plates, spooning the sauce over it all. Sprinkle with the toasted pine nuts.

⁂c 392 calories per serving ⊛ 22 g fat ⊛ 38 g protein ⊛ 8 g carbohydrates

Wine Suggestion

One of my favorite wines in the world comes from winemaker Michèle Aubéry-Clément. Her Domaine Gramenon red Côtes-du-Rhône, cuvée La Sagesse, is a dream of a wine. Made from 100 percent Grenache, it is fresh and fruity and pairs beautifully with this rustic winter dish.

Words on Wine: "Save young wines for spring and summer when they taste of fruit, and old wines for fall and winter, when you taste the roots."

Fabrice Langlois, sommelier at Château du Beaucastel in Châteauneuf-du-Pape

"Ils nous sont tombés sur le râble!" They sure laid into us! (The râble is the small of the back.)

RABBIT WITH ARTICHOKES AND PISTOU

Lapin aux Artichauts et au Pistou

Parisian restaurateur Dominique Versini—better known as Olympe—kindly shared this recipe with me. It has that zesty Mediterranean flavor of her Corsican heritage. Make it when fresh artichokes are in season in early spring. 8 servings

EQUIPMENT: A food processor or a blender; a large, heavy-duty skillet with a lid.

One 28-ounce can peeled Italian plum tomatoes in their juice
1 lemon, preferably organic
4 large artichokes
3 tablespoons extra-virgin olive oil
1 fresh rabbit or chicken (about 3 pounds), cut into serving pieces
Fine sea salt
Freshly ground white pepper
1 cup dry white wine
8 plump, moist garlic cloves, peeled but left whole
4 fresh or dried bay leaves
¼ cup Light Basil Purée (page 301)

1.   In a food processor or a blender, purée the tomatoes. Set aside.

2.   Prepare the artichokes: Prepare a large bowl of cold water, adding the juice of 1 lemon, plus the halved lemon, to the water. Rinse the artichokes under cold running water. Using a stainless-steel knife to minimize discoloration, trim the stem of an artichoke to about 1½ inches from the base. Carefully trim and discard the stem's fibrous exterior. Bend back the tough outer green leaves, one at a time, and snap them off at the base. Continue snapping off leaves until only the central cone of yellow leaves with pale green tips remains. Lightly trim the top cone of leaves to just below the green tips. Trim any dark green areas from the base. Halve the artichoke lengthwise. With a small spoon, scrape out and discard the hairy choke. Cut each trimmed artichoke bottom into 8 even wedges. Return each wedge to the acidulated water. Repeat for the remaining 3 artichokes. Set aside.

3.   In a large, heavy-duty skillet, heat the oil over moderately high heat until hot but not smoking. Add the rabbit, turn the heat to low (to keep the rabbit meat from drying out), cover, and cook gently, shaking the pan from time to time, until the rabbit is tender and brilliantly golden but still moist, about 5 minutes.

This may have to be done in batches. (Cooking time will vary according to the size of the pieces.) As each piece of rabbit is browned, transfer it to a platter and season lightly with salt and pepper.

4.   Slowly add the wine to the casserole, scraping up any brown bits that stick to the bottom of the pan. Add the rabbit, tomatoes, drained artichokes, garlic, and bay leaves. Cover and simmer over low heat until the rabbit is cooked through, 25 to 30 minutes. At serving time, stir in the Light Basil Purée. Serve atop polenta, pasta, or rice.

&c 346 calories per serving ⁕ 13 g fat ⁕ 38 g protein ⁕ 16 g carbohydrates

Wine Suggestion

I love this with a chilled white Chardonnay. A favorite in my cellar comes from the village of Saint-Aubin in Burgundy, where Hubert Lamy makes a pure and beautiful white Saint-Aubin, one that is floral and has a touch of minerality and seems to be at home with the combination of the poultry with tomatoes, artichokes, and basil.

Origins: The artichoke was introduced to France in the sixteenth century by Catherine de Médicis, and the vegetable is now cultivated in Provence as well as Brittany.

Words on Wine: "Wine is the most expressive and memorable way in which human beings can taste geography, can taste places on earth, can taste the world."

Andrew Jefford, British wine writer

BRAISED BEEF WITH CARROTS

Boeuf Braisé aux Carottes

It was New Year's Eve day, and my husband, Walter, and I were having lunch at our favorite neighborhood café on Rue du Bac in Paris. Out of the blue, he announced that he was going to make the famed French specialty, *boeuf-carottes,* for the next day's dinner. I was stunned, for he had barely cooked for years, save for preparing another homey dish, *blanquette de veau.* The next day he did indeed prepare this glorious dish, and it quickly became a winter classic. The glory of this dish is in its simplicity and the tidy list of ingredients: just beef, carrots, wine, stock, tomato paste, and herbs. Use a lean cut of meat and you'll find this light, digestible dish is made for the way we eat today. I have altered the classic recipe, doubling the amount of carrots. Maybe we'll rename this version *Carottes Braisées au Bœuf*! 12 servings

EQUIPMENT: A large, heavy-duty, skillet with a lid; 12 warmed dinner plates.

3 tablespoons unsalted butter
3 pounds beef in a single piece from the top or bottom round, heel of round, shoulder arm, or
    shoulder blade
Fine sea salt
Freshly ground black pepper
3 pounds carrots, trimmed, peeled, and very thinly sliced
Two 6-ounce cans tomato paste
3 cups dry red wine, such as a Côtes-du-Rhône
3 cups Homemade Chicken Stock (page 294)
Bouquet garni: several bay leaves, sprigs of thyme, and sprigs of parsley, encased in a wire mesh tea
    infuser

1.   In a large, heavy-duty skillet with a lid, heat the butter over moderate heat until hot. Add the meat and thoroughly brown on all sides, regulating the heat to avoid scorching the meat. Be patient: good browning is essential for the meat to retain flavor and moistness and will take about 6 minutes. When browned on all sides, season generously with salt and pepper. Add the carrots, tomato paste, wine, stock, and bouquet garni. Bring just to a simmer over moderate heat. Reduce the heat to low and cook, covered, maintaining a very gentle simmer, until the meat is very tender, 3 to 4 hours. Turn from time to time to evenly coat the meat with the liquid.

2.　　To serve, remove the bouquet garni. Cut the meat into thin slices and arrange on warmed dinner plates. Spoon the carrots alongside. Spoon the sauce over all. Serve with steamed rice.

❖c 328 calories per serving ✻ 14 g fat ✻ 26 g protein ✻ 16 g carbohydrates

Wine Suggestion

A good red, such as a Gigondas or a Vacqueyras. Current favorites include Yves Gras's Gigondas from Domaine Santa Duc and Domaine des Amouriers' Vacqueyras Les Genestes, a lively, non-oaked blend of Grenache, Syrah, and Mourvèdre.

Words on Wine: "Wines taste like the names of the villages: Gigondas is soft and round. Vacqueyras is dark, black, deep, and square."

Fabrice Langlois, sommelier, Château du Beaucastel, Châteauneuf-du-Pape

"Les carottes sont cuites!" The game is up!

Folklore: Eating carrots will make you friendlier.

ROAST LEG OF LAMB WITH HONEY AND MINT CRUST

Gigot d'Agneau en Chemise de Menthe et de Miel

The pairing of lamb and mint has become a sad cliché, calling up visions of sugar-sweet mint jelly and over-cooked lamb. Think again! Rare-roasted lamb with a zesty fresh mint crust is a fine tonic. A soothing mint and yogurt sauce is poured over the meat, making for a lovely modern dish if there ever was one. 12 servings

EQUIPMENT: A roasting pan; a food processor or a blender; 12 warmed dinner plates.

1 leg of lamb with bone (about 5 pounds), with trimmings and bones from upper leg, carefully
    trimmed of fat and tied (ask your butcher to do this)
Fine sea salt
Freshly ground black pepper

Mint and Honey Topping
4 cups (2 bunches) fresh mint, leaves only
3 tablespoons strong-flavored honey, such as heather honey
1 cup fine dried bread crumbs

Mint and Yogurt Sauce
4 cups (2 bunches) fresh mint, leaves only
1 cup nonfat yogurt, preferably sheep's milk

1.   Preheat the oven to 425 degrees F.

2.   In the bottom of a roasting pan, scatter the lamb trimmings and bones. Place the lamb on top or on a roasting rack. Season generously all over with salt and pepper. Place in the oven and roast, allowing 10 to 12 minutes per pound for medium-rare, 15 minutes for medium. Turn the lamb several times during cooking and baste occasionally.

3.   Meanwhile, prepare the topping: Blanch and refresh the mint leaves. Squeeze them dry. Place in the bowl of a food processor or a blender and chop finely. Add the honey and blend to a paste. Add the bread crumbs and blend. Set aside.

4. Prepare the yogurt sauce: Blanch and refresh the mint leaves. Squeeze them dry. Place in a food processor or a blender and chop finely. Add the yogurt and blend. Transfer to a small bowl. Set aside.

5. Remove the lamb from the oven and, once again, season generously. On a large carving board, place a salad plate upside down on a dinner plate. Transfer the lamb, exposed bone in the air, at an angle to the upside-down plate. Cover with foil. Let rest for at least 25 minutes.

6. Preheat the broiler.

7. To finish the lamb: With your hands, evenly spread a thin layer of the topping all over the lamb. Place the lamb about 3 inches from the broiler, turning and broiling until the crust is golden brown, about 6 minutes. Watch carefully and do not let it burn. Remove from the oven. Carve the lamb and arrange on 12 warmed dinner plates. Serve with the Mint and Yogurt Sauce.

₰ᶜ 433 calories per serving ❖ 26 g fat ❖ 31 g protein ❖ 18 g carbohydrates

Wine Suggestion

The last time I prepared this dish, we served it with the complex, rich Côtes-de-Provence Château de Roquefort, cuvée Rubrum Obscurum, a healthy blend of 70 percent Grenache, 15 percent Carignan, and 15 percent Mourvèdre, a rustic combination that makes you sit up and take notice!

On Storing Fresh Herbs

Leafy herbs such as parsley and mint, as well as chives, should be stored like bouquets of flowers: Place them in a tall glass, cut ends down, in about 1 inch of cold water. Cover the top loosely with a perforated plastic bag to allow some air to circulate. (Airtight containers will trap moisture and encourage spoilage.) Change the water daily.

Woody herbs such as sage, thyme, and rosemary should be placed in a perforated bag or loosely wrapped in plastic and stored in the vegetable drawer of the refrigerator.

LAMB COUSCOUS WITH CHICKPEAS AND ZUCCHINI

Couscous d'Agneau aux Courgettes et Pois Chiches

This satisfying one-dish meal makes a great weeknight dinner, when you want something substantial but don't have the time to fuss. The essential here is to sear the meat really well, so the outside is almost caramelized and the center remains beautifully rare. I love the nice hit of spice here and can never get enough chickpeas or zucchini. I make this dish regularly, from spring into fall, when firm, slender zucchini are plentiful. Serve with a bowl of Fresh Cilantro Sauce as a zippy, lively condiment. 12 servings

EQUIPMENT: A medium saucepan; 2 large skillets; 12 warmed dinner plates.

1 teaspoon ground cumin

³/₄ teaspoon ground ginger

¹/₂ teaspoon ground cayenne pepper

³/₄ teaspoon ground cinnamon

Fine sea salt

2 pounds meat from a 3-pound leg of lamb, cut into 1¹/₂-inch cubes

1 cup instant couscous

4 tablespoons extra-virgin olive oil

2 teaspoons *harissa,* or to taste

2 cups Homemade Chicken Stock (page 294)

Freshly ground black pepper

3 cups cooked chickpeas

One 15-ounce can peeled Italian plum tomatoes in their juice

1¹/₂ pounds slender zucchini, washed, trimmed, and sliced into ¹/₄-inch rounds

¹/₂ cup mint leaves, cut into chiffonade

Fresh Cilantro Sauce (page 302) as a condiment

1.   In a large bowl, combine the cumin, ginger, cayenne, cinnamon, and ¹/₂ teaspoon fine sea salt. Toss to blend. Add the cubed lamb and toss to evenly coat the meat. Set aside.

2.   Place the couscous in a heat-proof bowl, such as a large Pyrex measuring cup. Add 1 tablespoon of the olive oil, 1 teaspoon of the *harissa,* and ¹/₂ teaspoon salt and stir to blend. In a medium saucepan, bring the chicken stock to a boil over high heat. Pour the boiling stock over the couscous, stir with a fork, and cover the bowl with foil. Set aside.

3.   In a large skillet, heat 2 tablespoons of the remaining oil over high heat until hot but not smoking. Add the lamb and brown well on all sides. This is the most crucial part of the dish: the lamb should be seared well but remain rare in the center. Do this in small batches and do not crowd the pan. As each batch is cooked, transfer the meat to a platter and season lightly with salt and black pepper. Return the meat and any cooking juices that have pooled on the platter to the skillet, along with the chickpeas, remaining teaspoon of *harissa,* and the canned tomatoes and their liquid. Bring to a simmer over moderate heat and simmer for 2 minutes. The mixture should be brothlike. Taste for seasoning.

4.   In another large skillet, heat the remaining tablespoon of oil over moderate heat until hot but not smoking. Sear the zucchini, cooking just until it begins to brown at the edges. Season lightly with salt. Arrange spoonfuls of the couscous on the warmed dinner plates. Spoon the lamb mixture alongside. Spoon the zucchini over the lamb. Garnish with mint. Pass a bowl of Fresh Cilantro Sauce.

✤ 293 calories per serving ❈ 10 g fat ❈ 22 g protein ❈ 30 g carbohydrates

Wine Suggestion

This demands a good, bright young red with lots of muscle. Try the *vin de table* Petit Vin d'Avril from the Domaine Clos des Papes, in Châteauneuf-du-Pape. This good-quality wine is a nonvintage blend of Merlot, Cabernet Sauvignon, Grenache, and Mourvèdre. Wine critic Robert Parker calls this "an ideal bistro red meant for uncritical consumption." I'll second that!

GARLIC-RICH SEVEN-HOUR
LEG OF LAMB

Gigot de Sept Heures à l'Ail

Simplicity at its finest: three ingredients team up to create a soothing, complex-tasting dish. The forceful, fulsome fragrance of garlic fills the kitchen, while the distinct aroma of freshly roasted lamb wafts through the air. This is French comfort food at its finest. The *seven* in the title is a bit of a misnomer, since the original recipe from France's Southwest was made with mutton rather than tender young lamb. The concept is simple: brown the meat in olive oil, add chicken stock and an avalanche of garlic, cover, and braise in a warm oven until the meat is literally falling off the bone. The French say it should be tender enough to eat *à la cuillère,* or with a spoon. A five-pound leg of lamb will usually cook in four to five hours. This is delicious with Broccoli Purée with a Hint of Mint (page 167) and Potato Gratin from the Savoy (page 222). 12 servings

EQUIPMENT: A large, heavy-duty skillet with a lid; 12 warmed dinner plates.

1 leg of lamb with bone (about 5 pounds), with trimmings and bones from upper leg, carefully
    trimmed of fat and tied (ask your butcher to do this)
½ teaspoon Espelette Pepper Salt (page 311)
3 plump, moist heads of garlic, cloves separated and peeled but left whole
3 cups Homemade Chicken Stock (page 294), or more if needed

1.   Preheat the oven to 350 degrees F.

2.   In a large, heavy-duty skillet that will hold the lamb snugly, heat the oil over moderate heat until hot but not smoking. Add the lamb and sear well on all sides, about 10 minutes total. Remove from the skillet, place on a large platter, and season lightly with the salt. Return the lamb to the pan and add the garlic and the stock. Bring to a simmer over moderate heat. Cover, place in the oven, and cook until the meat is tender and falling off the bone, 4 to 5 hours. Check the meat every 30 minutes or so, turning it from time to time, making sure the liquid is not evaporating too much. Add more stock if necessary.

3.   To serve, transfer the lamb to a large carving board. Carve the meat or pull it apart with your fingers. Transfer a serving to each of 12 warmed dinner plates. With a slotted spoon, transfer several cloves of garlic to each plate. With a large spoon, spoon a bit of sauce over each plate. Serve.

378 calories per serving ⚬ 26 g fat ⚬ 30 g protein ⚬ 4 g carbohydrates

Dinner for a Chilly January Night

Bistrot Paul Bert's Watercress Salad with Creamy Bacon and Poached Egg (page 22)

Celeriac Salad with Fresh Crabmeat (page 78)

Garlic-Rich Seven-Hour Leg of Lamb

Cauliflower Purée (page 172)

Broccoli Purée with a Hint of Mint (page 167)

Rosemary-Apple-Cranberry Galette (page 268) with Buttermilk Sorbet (page 271)

PORK SAUSAGE WITH POTATOES AND RED WINE VINAIGRETTE

Cervelas Pistaché, Vinaigrette au Vin Rouge

I created this dish for our special wine week, when we have a plentiful supply of half-empty bottles of red wine, left over from various tastings. This is an ideal one-dish meal for cold weather: it perfumes the kitchen as the smoky pork sausages, potatoes, and red wine vinaigrette work their magic. 6 servings

EQUIPMENT: 2 large saucepans, 1 with a lid.

1 plump, coarse-textured smoked pork sausage, such as kielbasa (about 2 pounds)
8 small yellow-fleshed potatoes (such as Yukon Gold), scrubbed and peeled
Several fresh or dried bay leaves
Several sprigs of celery leaves

Red Wine Vinaigrette
1 cup fruity, red wine
1/3 cup extra-virgin olive oil
1/4 cup best-quality red-wine vinegar
1 tablespoon cooked beet juice (optional)
Fine sea salt
Freshly ground black pepper

Fresh flat-leaf parsley leaves for garnish

1.   In a large saucepan, combine the sausage, potatoes, bay leaves, and celery leaves and cover with cold water. Bring to a gentle simmer and simmer, covered, until the sausage and potatoes are cooked through, about 20 minutes.

2.   While the potatoes and sausage are cooking, prepare the red wine vinaigrette: Pour the wine into a large saucepan and reduce to 1/4 cup over high heat. Add the oil, vinegar, and beet juice (if using) and whisk to blend. Taste for seasoning.

3.   Drain and cut the potatoes and the sausage into thin, even rounds. Arrange alternating rounds of the potatoes and the sausage on a platter and drizzle with the warm vinaigrette. Garnish with parsley leaves and serve.

✧c 370 calories per serving ※ 27 g fat ※ 11 g protein ※ 13 g carbohydrates

Wine Suggestion

A Beaujolais, of course. A favorite is the Fleurie from Domaine Chignard, a velvety wine that's like liquid black cherries and blueberries.

Words on Wine: "Wine has a mysterious side to its character. Its ability to lift out dark profundities of flavor from the earth is an example of this. No one knows why wines sometimes taste of the soil in which they grow—but they do."

Andrew Jefford, British wine writer

History: Until the end of the eighteenth century, the French still considered the potato food for the poor. But after the terrible famine of 1769–1770, the interest in finding agricultural solutions became more serious. A competition was held to find the most suitable vegetable to help feed people and eliminate famine. French agronomist and nutritionist Parmentier won first prize by proposing the potato.

To convert the French court to becoming potato lovers, Parmentier offered King Louis XVI a feast-day gift of a basket of the finest potatoes, which the king had cooked for the court.

To convince the public, Parmentier grew potatoes on the plains of Sablons just outside of Paris. He guarded the garden by day but not by night. Potatoes were stolen, and, as the story goes, potatoes earned respect from the common man.

Vineyard Wisdom: In the vineyard, there are also proverbs to guide the French winemaker. Our former winemaker Ludovic Cornillon used to say:

Taille tôt, ou taille tard,
Rien ne vaut une taille de mars.

Prune early, or prune late,
but nothing's as good as pruning in March.

PASTA, RICE, BEANS, AND GRAINS

Les Pâtes, Riz, Légumes Secs et Céréales

◈

WARM GOAT CHEESE AND ARTICHOKE CANNELLONI THE LANCASTER

Cannelloni de Chèvre Tiède et Artichauts Hôtel Lancaster

When I sampled the original version of this dish at the Hotel Lancaster in Paris, where chef Michel Troisgros is consultant, I thought briefly of running to the front desk, reserving a room, taking a nap, and coming back for dinner. Instead I decided to re-create the dish at home, for dinner the next evening. My version is a bit more rustic, but I'm enthusiastic about this dish. I hope you'll be, too. 4 servings

EQUIPMENT: A food processor or a blender; a grapefruit spoon or a melon baller; a mandoline or a very sharp knife; a 10-quart pasta pot fitted with a colander; a rectangular baking dish.

6 ounces fresh goat's milk cheese
2 large eggs, lightly beaten
Grated zest of 2 lemons, preferably organic
Fine sea salt
A 12-inch-square sheet of fresh pasta (about 6 ounces)
1/4 cup freshly squeezed lemon juice
2 fresh baby artichokes
3 tablespoons coarse sea salt
1/4 cup freshly grated Parmigiano-Reggiano cheese for garnish
Minced fresh fennel fronds for garnish
Minced fresh parsley leaves for garnish
Minced fresh chives for garnish

1. Preheat the oven to 350 degrees F.

2. In a food processor or a blender, combine the goat cheese, eggs, and lemon zest. Process to blend. Season to taste with fine sea salt. Set aside. (The filling can be prepared up to 4 hours in advance, covered, and refrigerated.)

3. Cut the sheet of pasta into sixteen 3-inch squares. Set aside.

4. In a large, shallow salad bowl, whisk together the lemon juice and 1/4 teaspoon fine sea salt. Set aside.

5.   Prepare the artichokes: As you would break off the tough ends of an asparagus spear, break off the stem of the artichoke to about 1 inch from the base. Carefully trim and discard the stem's fibrous exterior, leaving the edible and highly prized inner, almost-white stem. Cut off the top fourth of the artichoke. Bend back the tough outer green leaves, one at a time, letting them snap off naturally at the base. Continue snapping off leaves until only the central cone of yellow leaves with pale green tips remains. Lightly trim the top cone of leaves to just below the green tips. Trim any dark green areas from the base. Halve the artichoke lengthwise. With a grapefruit spoon or melon baller, scrape out and discard the hairy choke, if present. With a mandoline or a very sharp knife, slice the halved artichoke lengthwise into paper-thin slices. Toss the slices with the lemon and salt mixture. Repeat for the other artichoke. (This can be done up to 2 hours in advance. Set aside, covered, at room temperature.)

6.   Prepare a large bowl of ice water. Set aside.

7.   In a 10-quart pasta pot fitted with a colander, bring 8 quarts water to a rolling boil over high heat. Add the coarse salt and the pasta, stirring to prevent the pasta from sticking. Precook just until the pasta is soft and pliable, about 2 minutes. Drain thoroughly and drop each sheet of pasta into the ice water to stop it from cooking and keep it from sticking. Drain.

8.   Place a square of pasta on a clean work surface. Spread about 2 teaspoons of cheese and egg filling evenly along one edge of the square. Carefully roll the pasta and place in a baking dish, seam side down. Continue rolling the remaining sheets of pasta until all the filling is used. Place the rolled cannelloni side by side in a single layer in the baking dish. Sprinkle the grated cheese over the top of each cannelloni.

9.   Cover the baking dish securely with foil, place in the center of the oven, and bake until bubbling, about 20 minutes. Transfer 4 pieces of cannelloni to a warmed salad plate. Arrange 4 slices of artichoke on top of each piece of cannelloni. Scatter the herbs over the pasta. Serve immediately.

⁕ᶜ 242 calories per serving ⁕ 8 g fat ⁕ 14 g protein ⁕ 31 g carbohydrates

> ## Wine Suggestion
>
> That day we sampled a 100 percent Chenin Blanc, a Montlouis from Domaine Chandon, and it was a perfect match for Troisgros's modern fare. Dry, yet tasting like a fresh bonbon, it handled every dish on the menu with flair. Another worthy dry Montlouis comes from Clos du Breuil, from winemaker François Chidaine. The wine is mineral-rich with a lively acidity.

Artichokes might be considered the lobster of the vegetable family: they make for labor-intensive eating. When you get to the heart of the matter—the creamy heart—you've hit pay dirt, much like finally getting to the lobster's tail.

PENNE WITH FAVA BEANS, BASIL PURÉE, AND PARMESAN

Penne aux Fèves

Green on green, the wholesome, hearty pasta dish is a delight and combines many of my favorite ingredients—fava beans, pasta, basil, and Parmigiano-Reggiano cheese. When time is of the essence, use frozen fava beans, which saves a lot of labor. This is a filling, dense dish, so I serve it in very small portions. 8 servings

EQUIPMENT: A 10-quart pasta pot fitted with a colander; 8 warmed shallow soup bowls.

½ cup Light Basil Purée (page 301)
7 tablespoons coarse sea salt
2 pounds fava beans in their pods, shelled (3 cups fava beans)
1 pound imported Italian penne
½ cup freshly grated Parmigiano-Reggiano cheese

1.   Place the basil purée in a large salad bowl.

2.   In a 10-quart pasta pot fitted with a colander, bring 8 quarts water to a rolling boil over high heat. Add 3 tablespoons of the salt and the shelled fava beans. Cook until tender, about 3 minutes. To check for doneness, remove a bean and rinse it under cold running water. Slice the inner skin of each bean with a fingernail and pop out the bean. If it pops out easily, the beans are ready. Remove the pasta pot from the heat. Remove the colander, drain over a sink, and rinse with cold running water for 1 to 2 minutes. Skin the remaining beans, dropping them into the bowl of basil purée.

3.   In the same 10-quart pasta pot fitted with a colander, bring 8 quarts water to a rolling boil over high heat. Add the remaining 4 tablespoons salt and the pasta, stirring to prevent the pasta from sticking. Cook until tender but firm to the bite, about 11 minutes. Remove the pasta pot from the heat. Remove the colander and drain over a sink, shaking to remove excess water. Immediately transfer the drained pasta to the basil purée and fava beans in the bowl. Toss to evenly coat the pasta. Add the cheese and toss once more. Transfer to individual warmed shallow soup bowls and serve.

✣c 465 calories per serving ⁕ 9 g fat ⁕ 22 g protein ⁕ 76 g carbohydrates

SPAGHETTI WITH GREEN OLIVES, GARLIC, AND FRESH MINT

Spaghetti aux Olives Vertes et à la Menthe

When fresh mint is at hand, use that, or try a good dose of top-quality dried mint, with its even, haunting flavors. The touch of raw garlic wakes up the palate, while the green olives add a fine hint of acidity. This beautifully chunky sauce—which makes just 1 cup—can double as a dip for raw vegetables. 4 servings

EQUIPMENT: A food processor or a blender; a 10-quart pasta pot fitted with a colander; 4 warmed shallow soup bowls.

1 cup pitted green olives
2 plump, moist cloves garlic, peeled, halved, green germ removed
1 cup fresh mint leaves or ½ cup dried
⅓ cup extra-virgin olive oil
⅔ cup freshly grated Parmigiano-Reggiano cheese
Freshly ground black pepper
¼ cup coarse sea salt
1 pound imported Italian spaghetti

1.   In a food processor or a blender, combine the olives, garlic, mint, oil, and half of the cheese. Pulse to create a roughly chopped, not smooth, sauce. Season with pepper. Transfer to a shallow bowl large enough to hold the sauce and the pasta and toss gently. Set aside.

2.   In a 10-quart pasta pot fitted with a colander, bring 8 quarts water to a rolling boil over high heat. Add the salt and the pasta, stirring to prevent the pasta from sticking. Cook until tender but firm to the bite, about 6 minutes. Remove the pasta pot from the heat. Remove the colander and drain over a sink, shaking to remove excess water. Immediately transfer the pasta to the sauce in the bowl. Toss to evenly coat the pasta. Toss with the remaining cheese. Season generously with pepper. Transfer to warmed bowls and serve.

472 calories per serving ⁂ 19 g fat ⁂ 15 g protein ⁂ 61 g carbohydrates

Wine Suggestion

Garlic and mint always make me turn to a white wine: Try Comte Lafon's Mâcon-Milly-Lamartine, cuvée Clos du Four. It's clean, neat, and has a touch of oak and a nice minerality.

PEA AND MINT RISOTTO

Risotto aux Petits Pois et à la Menthe

Color means a lot to me on a plate: it boosts one's mood, enhances the table, just makes one feel good and happy. I love the crisp white and green contrast of this dish, as well as the surprise flavor of the mint, whose color appears in camouflage, hidden among the green of the peas. When I served this dish to my husband, Walter, for the first time, he announced, "I love peas, just love peas." Funny, we'd been married twenty-seven years at the time, and I never knew of his passion for peas. I guess I don't serve them often enough. 4 servings

EQUIPMENT: A 5-quart pasta pot fitted with a colander; 2 large saucepans, 1 with a lid; 4 warmed shallow soup bowls.

The Peas and Mint
3 tablespoons coarse sea salt
3 pounds fresh peas, in the pod, shelled (3½ cups peas), or frozen peas
1 cup fresh mint leaves, cut into chiffonade

The Rice
About 5 cups Homemade Chicken Stock (page 294)
1 tablespoon extra-virgin olive oil
1 plump, moist clove garlic, peeled, halved, green germ removed
1 shallot, trimmed, peeled, and minced
Fine sea salt
1½ cups Italian Arborio rice
½ cup freshly grated Parmigiano-Reggiano cheese

1.   In a 5-quart pasta pot fitted with a colander, bring 3 quarts water to a rolling boil over high heat. Add the salt and the peas and cook for just 1 minute, so they remain crisp and retain their bright green color. Immediately remove them from the heat, drain, and rinse under cold running water to stop the cooking and help preserve the bright green color. Drain well and set aside.

2.   In a large saucepan, heat the stock and keep it simmering, at barely a whisper, while you prepare the risotto.

3.   In another large saucepan, combine the oil, the halved garlic clove, the shallot, and fine sea salt

and sweat—cook, covered, over low heat until soft but not browned—for 3 to 4 minutes. Remove and discard the garlic. Add the rice and stir until the rice is well coated with the fat, 1 to 2 minutes. (This step is important for good risotto: the heat and fat will help separate the grains of rice, ensuring a creamy consistency in the end.)

4.   When the rice becomes glistening and semitranslucent, add a ladleful of the stock. Cook, stirring constantly until the rice has absorbed most of the stock, 1 to 2 minutes. Add another ladleful of the simmering stock and stir regularly until all the stock is absorbed. Adjust the heat as necessary to maintain a gentle simmer. The rice should cook slowly and should always be covered with a veil of stock. Continue adding ladlefuls of stock, stirring frequently and tasting regularly, until the rice is almost tender but firm to the bite, about 17 minutes total. The risotto should have a creamy, porridgelike consistency.

5.   Remove the saucepan from the heat and stir in the cheese, the reserved peas, and half of the mint. Taste for seasoning. Transfer the risotto to warmed, shallow soup bowls. Garnish with the remaining mint chiffonade. Serve immediately.

✻c 475 calories per serving ✤ 8 g fat ✤ 18 g protein ✤ 79 g carbohydrates

What I Learned: This is a "pantry and freezer" dish if there ever was one, meaning you can come home from work and find what you need at hand. Now I always keep a package of frozen peas in the freezer, there is always frozen homemade chicken stock there, and with Arborio rice in the pantry, Parmigiano-Reggiano cheese in the refrigerator, and mint in the garden, dinner is half made!

Wine Suggestion

Although we may consume peas year-round, I think of their spring freshness and like to pair them with a light, springy wine, such as a Sauvignon Blanc. Try a Sancerre from the Loire Valley, such as that from Domaine Sautereau, aged in stainless steel, one that can double as a perfect aperitif. Just a sip will make you begin to salivate—and that extra touch of fruit here stands up to the pea and mint combination.

History: King Louis XIV was crazy about peas. As soon as peas were introduced from Italy in 1660, peas became a favorite of the French court. The snobbish trend of eating vast quantities of peas lasted for more than thirty years. In a letter dated May 16, 1696, the king's second wife, Madame de Maintenon, wrote, "Oh that the chapter of peas lasts forever. Impatient to eat them, the pleasure once eaten, and then the joy of eating some more. . . ."

PUMPKIN AND SAGE RISOTTO

Risotto au Potiron et à la Sauge

A roaring fire, a sip of crisp white wine, and this warming fall and winter dish put me in a happy mood at the end of a chilly day. This dish wins on looks alone, the alabaster of the rice, the bright reddish orange of the pumpkin, with aromatic and colorful touches of fresh sage. When I make risotto I sit on a stool near the stove as I stir the risotto, a glass of chilled white wine at my side. 4 servings

EQUIPMENT: A medium saucepan with a lid; 2 large saucepans, 1 with a lid; 4 warmed shallow soup bowls.

The Pumpkin
1 tablespoon extra-virgin olive oil
1 shallot, trimmed, peeled, and minced
Fine sea salt
2 cups ½-inch cubes of peeled pumpkin or butternut squash
8 leaves fresh sage, cut into fine chiffonade
2 cups Homemade Chicken Stock (page 294)

The Rice
About 5 cups Homemade Chicken Stock (page 294)
1 tablespoon goose fat or unsalted butter
1 plump, moist clove garlic, peeled, halved, green germ removed
1 shallot, trimmed, peeled, and minced
Fine sea salt
1½ cups Italian Arborio rice
½ cup freshly grated Parmigiano-Reggiano cheese

A chunk of Parmigiano-Reggiano cheese for grating as garnish
Coarsely ground white pepper for garnish
Pistachio oil for garnish (optional)

1.   In a medium saucepan, combine the oil, shallot, and salt and sweat—cook, covered, over low heat until soft but not browned—for 3 to 4 minutes. Add the cubed pumpkin, half the sage, and the 2 cups stock. Cover and simmer until the pumpkin is cooked but still slightly firm, about 10 minutes.

2.   In a large saucepan, heat the 5 cups stock and keep it simmering, at barely a whisper, while you prepare the risotto.

3.   In another large saucepan, melt the goose fat or butter over low heat. Add the garlic, shallot, and salt and sweat—cook, covered, over low heat without coloring until soft and translucent—3 to 4 minutes. Remove and discard the garlic. Add the rice and stir until the rice is well coated with the fat. (This step is important for good risotto: the heat and fat will help separate the grains of rice, ensuring a creamy consistency in the end.)

4.   When the rice becomes glistening and semitranslucent, add a ladleful of the stock. Cook, stirring constantly until the rice has absorbed most of the stock, 1 to 2 minutes. Add another ladleful of the simmering stock and stir regularly until all the stock is absorbed. Adjust the heat as necessary to maintain a gentle simmer. The rice should cook slowly and should always be covered with a veil of stock. Continue adding ladlefuls of stock, stirring frequently and tasting regularly, until the rice is almost tender but firm to the bite, about 17 minutes total. The risotto should have a creamy, porridgelike consistency.

5.   Remove the saucepan from the heat and stir in the cheese and the cooked, drained pumpkin. Taste for seasoning. Transfer the risotto to warmed soup bowls. Garnish with shavings of fresh Parmesan and the remaining chiffonade of sage leaves. Season with coarsely ground white pepper. If using, drizzle with pistachio oil. Serve immediately.

    ✻c 430 calories per serving ⁕ 10 g fat ⁕ 14 g protein ⁕ 73 g carbohydrates

What I Learned: To safely cut a pumpkin, cut off about ½ inch of the bottom half so it can stand firmly and evenly on the cutting board. Then carefully cut the pumpkin in half, removing and discarding the seeds and fibrous interior. When peeling pumpkins and squash, I use a strong vegetable peeler to remove the tough outer skin.

Wine Suggestion

I like a crisp, bright white here and for a real treat will open a bottle of Zind-Humbrecht's Riesling, Herrenweg de Turckheim. The wine is mineral rich, all aged in steel so there is no wood to mask the wine's innate character. It is also dense, thick, deep, almost creamy, a fine match for this elegant risotto.

GOLDEN CAULIFLOWER AND RICE PILAF

Riz Pilaf au Chou-Fleur et aux Épices

This golden, fragrant rice dish can be eaten as a quick main dish at lunchtime or as a side dish at dinner. And, I confess, leftovers make for quite an invigorating treat at breakfast time. I prepare this with a golden rice from the Camargue in the south of France, but any top-quality long-grain rice would be fine here. 8 servings

EQUIPMENT: A medium saucepan with a lid.

2 tablespoons extra-virgin olive oil
1½ cups rice
2 cups Homemade Chicken Stock (page 294)
12 cardamom seeds
1 teaspoon cumin seeds
¼ teaspoon ground *piment d'Espelette* or dried Anaheim chili (or ground mild chili pepper)
½ teaspoon Curry Powder (page 308)
1 stick cinnamon
1 teaspoon fine sea salt
8 ounces cauliflower florets (about 2 cups)
Fresh cilantro leaves for garnish

In a medium saucepan, heat the oil over moderate heat until hot but not smoking. Add the rice and cook for 1 minute, stirring to coat with oil. Add the stock and bring to a boil. Add the cardamom, cumin, *piment d'Espelette*, curry powder, cinnamon, salt, and cauliflower. Cover. Reduce the heat to simmer and cook until the rice is tender, about 20 minutes. Remove from the heat; remove and discard the cinnamon. Serve with a garnish of fresh cilantro.

199 calories per serving ◦ 4 g fat ◦ 4 g protein ◦ 36 g carbohydrates

Wine Suggestion

While this dish is most often served as a side dish, it can serve as a main dish. Riesling—which renowned wine writer Jancis Robinson calls "the world's greatest white wine grape"—is all too often ignored and/or undervalued. Try anything from Zind-Humbrecht or Domaine Ostertag.

ROASTED CHICKPEAS, MUSHROOMS, ARTICHOKES, AND TOMATOES

Pois Chiches, Champignons, Tomates et Artichauts au Four

This is one of our favorite weeknight winter suppers, a quick and warming dish to sample with a light red, sitting in front of the fire. Think of a few slices of toasted whole wheat bread and a crispy green salad, and you're in heaven. 4 servings

EQUIPMENT: A small skillet; a spice grinder; a 1-quart gratin dish.

2 teaspoons cumin seeds
2 cups canned chickpeas, drained and rinsed
2 cups canned artichoke hearts, drained
8 ounces fresh mushrooms, cleaned, trimmed, and thinly sliced
1 cup Rustic Oven-Roasted Tomato Sauce (page 306)
Fine sea salt

1. Preheat the oven to 425 degrees F.

2. Toast the cumin: Place the cumin in a small skillet over moderate heat. Shake the pan regularly until the cumin seeds are fragrant and evenly toasted, about 2 minutes. Watch carefully! They can burn quickly. Transfer the cumin to a large plate and set aside to cool. Grind to a fine powder in a spice grinder.

3. In a large bowl, combine the chickpeas, artichokes, mushrooms, tomato sauce, and cumin. Season to taste. Transfer to a 1-quart gratin dish, smoothing out the mixture with the back of a spoon. Place in the center of the oven and bake until bubbly, about 30 minutes.

235 calories per serving ❋ 3 g fat ❋ 12 g protein ❋ 47 g carbohydrates

❋ Variation: Instead of chickpeas, use best-quality fresh, precooked dried or canned white beans to make a version of a vegetarian cassoulet.

Wine Suggestion

Mushrooms make me think of Pinot Noir. Try the elegant, gorgeous, fine light red Marsannay from Domaine Bruno Clair, cuvée Les Longeroies.

CREAMY POLENTA WEDGES

Polenta Poêlée

I could serve caviar, lobster, foie gras, but almost no dish gets raves and requests for seconds like a good slice of polenta. I love the simplicity of this dish and the soothing satisfaction one derives from the creamy flavor, smooth texture, and golden hue of a well-made polenta. Favorite accompaniments include a dollop of Chunky Fresh Tomato Sauce (page 305) with Butter-Warmed Corn Kernels with Fresh Cilantro Leaves (page 174) and Red Peppers, Tomatoes, Onions, Cumin, and Espelette Pepper (page 200). 8 servings

EQUIPMENT: A large saucepan; a 10-inch round glass or porcelain baking dish; a large skillet.

3 cups 1% milk

1 teaspoon fine sea salt

½ teaspoon freshly grated nutmeg

1 cup instant polenta

1 cup freshly grated Parmigiano-Reggiano cheese

1 tablespoon extra-virgin olive oil

1. In a large saucepan, bring the milk, salt, and nutmeg to a boil over high heat. (Watch carefully, for milk will boil over quickly.) Add the polenta in a steady stream and, stirring constantly with a wooden spoon, cook until thickened and the polenta leaves the side of the pan as it is stirred, about 2 minutes.

2. Remove from the heat. Stir in the cheese, stirring to blend thoroughly. Pour into the baking dish. Even out the top with a spatula. Cool until firm, about 5 minutes.

3. Cut the polenta into 8 even wedges. In a large skillet, heat the oil over moderate heat until hot but not smoking. Add the polenta wedges and warm on both sides, about 1 minute per side. To serve, place a wedge of polenta on a plate, with the accompaniment of choice.

162 calories per serving ⬧ 6 g fat ⬧ 9 g protein ⬧ 18 g carbohydrates

Wine Suggestions

A favorite in summer and winter, this dish demands wine without pretension. Our own Clos Chanteduc red Côtes-du-Rhône (Grenache, Syrah, and Mourvèdre) is a fine choice, or the white Domaine de la Janasse Vin de Pays de la Principauté d'Orange (100 percent Viognier).

COUSCOUS, GRAINS, AND CHICKPEAS

Couscous, Pois Chiches et Flocons Variés

This quick and delicious grain mixture is a standby in our household. It seems to go with everything, at just about every meal. (I've been known to enjoy a small bowl for breakfast.) Serve it alongside grilled meats, poultry, or fish or as part of a vegetable buffet. 4 servings

½ cup medium-grain instant couscous
½ teaspoon fine sea salt
1¼ cups boiling Homemade Chicken Stock (page 294)
1 tablespoon extra-virgin olive oil
½ cup spelt flakes
1 tablespoon barley flakes
1 tablespoon oat flakes
½ cup canned chickpeas, drained and rinsed
½ cup finely minced fresh parsley leaves

In a heat-proof glass or metal container, combine the couscous and salt. Add the boiling stock and the oil. Stir to blend. Cover and set aside for 8 minutes. Stir with a fork to blend again. Stir in the grain flakes, chickpeas, and parsley. Taste for seasoning. Serve warm or at room temperature.

189 calories per serving ⁕ 4 g fat ⁕ 7 g protein ⁕ 31 g carbohydrates

COUSCOUS SALAD WITH SPINACH, PARSLEY, AND SPRING ONIONS

Taboulé aux Épinards

During the summer months, we frequently entertain large groups of friends, always dining outdoors. I like to have a broad range of foods, up to a dozen different vegetables and salads, along with a roast chicken cooked in the bread oven. This quick and easy salad is a favorite: the colors are lively, the flavors forward, and it's just as good as a leftover the following day. 12 servings

EQUIPMENT: A food processor or a blender.

1 cup medium-grain instant couscous

1 teaspoon fine sea salt

1⅓ cups hottest possible tap water

1 tablespoon freshly squeezed lemon juice

1 bunch fresh parsley, leaves only (2 cups loosely packed)

1 tablespoon extra-virgin olive oil

3 spring onions or 6 scallions, trimmed and cut into very thin rings

5 ounces fresh spinach, rinsed, dried, stems removed, and cut into chiffonade (4 cups loosely packed)

3 tablespoons Creamy Lemon-Chive Dressing (page 299)

1. In a large, shallow bowl, combine the couscous and the salt. Toss with a fork to blend. Add the water and fluff until the grains are evenly separated. Set aside and occasionally fluff and toss the grains until all the liquid has been absorbed, about 3 minutes.

2. In a food processor or a blender, combine the lemon juice, parsley leaves, and olive oil and process until the parsley is finely chopped. Toss the parsley mixture and the spring onions with the couscous. (This can be prepared up to 8 hours in advance and refrigerated.)

3. At serving time, toss the spinach chiffonade with just enough dressing to evenly coat the greens. Add the dressed spinach to the couscous mixture and toss gently to blend evenly. Serve.

77 calories per serving ◦ 1 g fat ◦ 3 g protein ◦ 14 g carbohydrates

Jardin de Curé

In France, they are known as *jardins de curé* or *jardins de simple* in reference to the unpretentious gardens the priest traditionally cultivated in the churchyard. The concept dates from Charlemagne's time, when he carefully listed the plants and trees he hoped to see grow in his empire. From medieval times, the priest's garden represented both edible and medicinal plants, as well as flowers for the altar. Then the gardens were set out in square beds, laid out to represent a cross. Always the garden included borage, fennel, marjoram, parsley, and carnations, usually with a border of boxwood, yew, or santolina. Whatever is grown in a traditional *jardin de curé*, it should give the impression of profusion, mystery, and surprise and evoke the pleasure of a simple life!

CUMIN-SCENTED CHICKPEAS WITH ROASTED EGGPLANT AND RUSTIC TOMATO SAUCE

Pois Chiches et Aubergine au Cumin en Sauce Tomate

This versatile vegetable combo fits in just about anywhere, anytime. Serve it as a side dish with grilled poultry or meat or as part of a lavish summer vegetable buffet. I love the contrast of colors—the paleness of the chickpeas, the jet-black skin of the eggplant, the ruby tomatoes—as well as the varied textures, from soft to crunchy, smooth to chunky. 6 servings

EQUIPMENT: A nonstick baking sheet; a small skillet; a spice grinder.

1 small, elongated, Asian-type eggplant (about 4 ounces), rinsed
2 cups canned chickpeas, drained and rinsed
1 cup Rustic Oven-Roasted Tomato Sauce (page 306)
2 teaspoons cumin seeds

1.   Preheat the oven to 475 degrees F.

2.   Trim and discard the ends of the eggplant. Cut the eggplant lengthwise into 4 even slices, each about ½ inch thick. Place the eggplant, cut side down, on a nonstick baking sheet. Place on a rack in the center of the oven and roast, turning from time to time, until the eggplant is soft in the center, about 10 minutes total.

3.   Remove from the oven and let cool. Once cooled, cut crosswise into 1-inch strips. Set aside.

4.   Toast the cumin: Place the cumin in a small, dry skillet over moderate heat. Shake the pan regularly until the cumin seeds are fragrant and evenly toasted, about 2 minutes. Watch carefully! They can burn quickly. Transfer the cumin to a large plate and set aside to cool. Grind to a fine powder in a spice grinder.

5.   In a large bowl, combine the eggplant, chickpeas, and tomato sauce. Toss to blend. Add the cumin. Serve at room temperature or slightly chilled. Store in an airtight container in the refrigerator for up to 2 days.

186 calories per serving ※ 2 g fat ※ 8 g protein ※ 36 g carbohydrates

GREAT GRAINS:
QUINOA, SPELT, RICE, MILLET, AND SESAME

Méli-Mélo de Graines et Céréales

I call this mixture Great Grains, for it's such a gratifying, healthy blend of grains and seeds. Beautiful, too! I make this dish all year round, serving it warm in the winter months with roast poultry or fish and at room temperature in the summertime as a satisfying grain salad, dressed with Creamy Lemon-Chive Dressing (page 299).
6 servings

EQUIPMENT: A small skillet; a fine-mesh sieve; a 1-quart saucepan.

⅓ cup quinoa
⅓ cup precooked *épeautre* (farro, spelt, or substitute wheat berries)
¼ cup precooked brown rice
⅓ cup millet
2 tablespoons sesame seeds
2½ cups Homemade Chicken Stock (page 294)
2 bay leaves, preferably fresh
½ teaspoon fine sea salt

1. In a small, dry skillet, toast the quinoa over medium heat, stirring regularly, until it crackles and becomes aromatic, 3 to 5 minutes. Transfer to a fine-mesh sieve and rinse thoroughly.

2. In a 1-quart saucepan, combine the grains and seeds, the stock, the bay leaves, and the salt. Bring to a boil over high heat. Immediately reduce the heat to low, cover, and cook until the liquid is absorbed and the grains are puffed and tender, about 20 minutes. Let stand, covered, for at least 5 minutes before serving. Remove and discard the bay leaves. Taste for seasoning. Serve warm or at room temperature.

161 calories per serving * 3 g fat * 9 g protein * 24 g carbohydrates

VEGETABLES

Les Légumes

❖

BABY ARTICHOKES WITH AVOCADO, PINE NUTS, AND PARMESAN

Petits Artichauts aux Pignons et au Parmesan

The melting warmth of Parmesan cheese, the rich nuttiness of toasted pine nuts, the soothing texture of a perfectly ripe avocado, and the haunting, earthy flavor of artichokes team up to make a spirit-lifting dish that seems at home at all tables, all year round. Consider it a salad, a first course, a side dish—whatever your desires dictate. 4 servings

EQUIPMENT: A grapefruit spoon or a melon baller; a small skillet; a steamer; a large skillet.

1 lemon, preferably organic
4 large or 8 baby artichokes
1/4 cup pine nuts
12 shavings of Parmigiano-Reggiano cheese (about 1 ounce)
Fleur de sel
1/4 cup basil leaves, cut into chiffonade
1 ripe avocado
1 tablespoon pine nut oil or extra-virgin olive oil

1.   Prepare the artichokes: Prepare a large bowl of cold water, adding the juice of 1 lemon, plus the halved lemon, to the water. Rinse the artichokes under cold running water. Using a stainless-steel knife to minimize discoloration, trim the stem of an artichoke to about 1 1/2 inches from the base. Carefully trim and discard the stem's fibrous exterior. Bend back the tough outer green leaves, one at a time, and snap them off at the base. Continue snapping off leaves until only the central cone of yellow leaves with pale green tips remains. Lightly trim the top cone of leaves to just below the green tips. Trim any dark green areas from the base. Halve the artichoke lengthwise. With a grapefruit spoon or melon baller, scrape out and discard any hairy choke. Cut each trimmed artichoke half lengthwise into 8 even slices for large artichokes, 4 slices for baby artichokes. Return each slice to the acidulated water. Repeat for the remaining artichokes. (This can be done up to 2 hours in advance. Set aside, uncovered, at room temperature.)

2.   Place the pine nuts in a small, dry skillet over moderate heat. Toast, regularly shaking the pan until the nuts are fragrant and evenly browned, about 2 minutes. Watch carefully! They can burn quickly. Transfer the nuts to a large plate to cool. Set aside.

3.   Place 3 shavings of cheese onto each of 4 salad plates. Set aside.

4.   Bring 1 quart water to a simmer in the bottom of a vegetable steamer. Place the artichokes on the steamer rack. Place the rack over the simmering water, cover, and steam until the artichokes are tender, 2 to 3 minutes. Remove the steaming rack and let drain.

5.   Heat a large, dry skillet over high heat. When hot, add the drained sliced artichokes and sauté until browned on both sides, 3 to 4 minutes. Transfer the warm artichokes to the prepared salad plates, placing them on top of the shaved cheese. Season with *fleur de sel*. Sprinkle with the pine nuts and the basil chiffonade. Peel, halve, and pit the avocado. Cut the 2 avocado halves lengthwise into very thin slices. Arrange the slices around the artichokes. Drizzle each plate with pine nut oil and serve.

✢c 281 calories per serving ☀ 19 g fat ☀ 12 g protein ☀ 25 g carbohydrates

The artichoke "bottom" is really the firm-fleshed base of a large artichoke. The "heart" actually comes from tiny whole artichokes, which have almost no choke. When choosing frozen or canned artichokes, choose the "hearts," for they will be much more tender and elegant.

GRILLED ARTICHOKES AND LEMONS WITH SPICY GARLIC MAYONNAISE

Artichauts Grillés à l'Aïoli

Elegant, beautiful, delicious, this springtime treat makes a great first course or side dish. Use your imagination for a dipping sauce: a spicy homemade aïoli, or garlic mayonnaise, would be right at home here, or a mayonnaise seasoned with fresh lemon zest. 4 servings

EQUIPMENT: A steamer.

4 large artichokes
4 lemons, halved crosswise
2 teaspoons pistachio oil (or walnut, hazelnut, or extra-virgin olive oil)
Fleur de sel
Spicy Garlic Mayonnaise (page 304)

1.   Trim the stem from each artichoke and peel the stem. Bring 3 cups water to a simmer in the bottom of a steamer. Place the artichokes and peeled stems on the steaming rack. Place the rack over the simmering water, cover, and steam until the artichokes are cooked through, about 30 minutes. (The artichoke is cooked when the outer leaves can easily be pulled from the artichokes and the stem end is tender when pierced with a knife.) Cut the artichokes lengthwise in half and scoop out the hairy choke. Halve the stems lengthwise.

2.   Heat a grill and spread the coals out when they are red and dusted with ash.

3.   Lightly oil the grill rack and place it about 3 inches above the coals, allowing it to preheat for a few minutes. Place the artichoke halves, stems, and the lemon halves on the grill rack cut side down. Grill just until the artichokes and lemons are nicely browned and lightly streaked with grill marks, 2 to 3 minutes. With tongs, transfer each artichoke half—grilled side up—and half of a stem to a small salad plate. Drizzle immediately with oil and *fleur de sel*. Place a lemon half, cut side up, alongside. Squeeze the smoky lemon juice over the artichoke. Place a large bowl in the center of the table to hold discarded artichoke leaves. Serve with garlic mayonnaise. Supply a finger bowl or moistened hand towel for each guest.

✾c 52 calories per serving ⁕ 1 g fat ⁕ 3 g protein ⁕ 13 g carbohydrates

ASPARAGUS WITH GRUYÈRE AND SMOKED HAM

Asperges Vertes au Jambon Fumé

This is the sort of vegetable dish one can make a meal of. Or at least a main dish that's accompanied by a tossed green salad. The fresh green spears of asparagus are quickly cooked in a touch of oil, salt, rosemary, and bay leaves, then drained, rolled in cheese, and wrapped in ham. A final sauté transforms them into creamy, smoky, crisp delights. 4 servings

EQUIPMENT: A large skillet with a lid.

2 tablespoons extra-virgin olive oil
16 small spears (about 1 pound) fresh green asparagus, rinsed and tough ends trimmed
1 teaspoon coarse sea salt
½ cup freshly grated Swiss Gruyère cheese
16 thin slices best-quality smoked ham (about 10 ounces)

1.   In a skillet large enough to hold the asparagus in a single layer, combine the oil, asparagus, and salt. Sprinkle with several tablespoons of cold water. Cover. Cook over high heat just until the oil and water mixture begins to sizzle. Reduce the heat to medium and braise the asparagus, turning from time to time, just until the vegetable begins to brown in spots, 8 to 10 minutes.

2.   Place the cheese on a large plate. Roll the asparagus in the cheese. Wrap each asparagus spear in a slice of ham and secure with a toothpick.

3.   Return the asparagus to the skillet and cook until the ham is crispy and brown, turning the asparagus with tongs, about 2 minutes. Serve immediately.

252 calories per serving · 14 g fat · 26 g protein · 5 g carbohydrates

Asparagus and Wine

Cooks have long disparaged the idea of wine and asparagus, with the understanding that the acidity of wine alters the flavor of asparagus. I'd rather search for a positive marriage than a cruel divorce. Here are some asparagus-friendly wines, suggested by Les Caves Taillevent in Paris: a Chardonnay such as a Bourgogne Aligoté, a Chardonnay such as a Petit Chablis, a Sauvignon Blanc such as a Menetou-Salon.

ASPARAGUS BRAISED WITH FRESH ROSEMARY AND BAY LEAVES

Asperges Braisées au Romarin

If you want to bring out the best in asparagus, try braising it. All of its mineral-rich, woodsy flavors come forth, rewarding you with rich, haunting pleasures. I actually created this dish in Paris one Sunday in the spring. I had just returned from the weekend market, braised the fresh asparagus in a large cast-iron casserole, and showered it with plenty of fresh, home-grown rosemary and basil leaves. They don't need any more embellishment—trust me!
4 servings

EQUIPMENT: A large skillet with a lid.

16 plump spears (about 2 pounds) fresh white or green asparagus
1 tablespoon extra-virgin olive oil
1 teaspoon coarse sea salt
Several sprigs fresh rosemary
Several bay leaves, preferably fresh

Rinse the asparagus and trim the tough ends. In a skillet large enough to hold the asparagus in a single layer, combine the oil, asparagus, salt, rosemary, and bay leaves. Sprinkle with several tablespoons of cold water. Cover. Cook over high heat just until the oil and water mixture begins to sizzle. Reduce the heat to medium and braise the asparagus, turning from time to time, just until the vegetable begins to brown in spots, 8 to 10 minutes (depending on the thickness of the asparagus). Serve immediately.

68 calories per serving ⁂ 4 g fat ⁂ 3 g protein ⁂ 8 g carbohydrates

Wine Suggestion

A Chardonnay, such as Mâcon-Milly-Lamartine Clos du Four from Domaine Les Héritiers des Comtes Lafon.

Folklore: If you have a toothache, rub the teeth and gums with asparagus and you'll be cured.

ROASTED ASPARAGUS WITH ARUGULA AND SHALLOT VINAIGRETTE

Asperges au Four, Vinaigrette à l'Échalote

Roasting is another excellent way of drawing dense, rich flavors from fresh green asparagus. Here a shallot vinaigrette soothes and softens flavors and keeps the vegetable moist as it roasts. Once roasted, the asparagus is placed atop a piquant arugula salad dressed with the same vinaigrette. Shavings of Parmigiano-Reggiano cheese enrich and embellish it all. 4 servings

EQUIPMENT: A rimmed baking sheet.

16 thin spears fresh green asparagus (about 1 pound)
2 tablespoons Shallot Vinaigrette (page 300)
Coarse sea salt
6 cups lightly packed arugula (about 5 ounces)
¼ cup finely chopped fresh chives
12 shavings of Parmigiano-Reggiano cheese (about 1 ounce)
Fleur de sel

1. Preheat the oven to 450 degrees F.

2. Rinse the asparagus and trim the tough ends. Arrange the asparagus on a baking sheet large enough to hold the asparagus in a single layer. Drizzle with the vinaigrette. Sprinkle with coarse salt. Roll the asparagus around to coat the spears with the vinaigrette and salt. Sprinkle with about 2 tablespoons water.

3. Place the baking sheet in the oven and roast until the asparagus are cooked through, though still slightly firm and browned at the tips, about 12 minutes.

4. Meanwhile, combine the arugula and chives in a large bowl. Add just enough vinaigrette to lightly coat the greens and toss. Transfer to individual dinner plates. When the asparagus are cooked, place them on top of the arugula salad. Scatter the shavings of cheese on top of the asparagus, season with *fleur de sel*, and serve.

103 calories per serving ⁕ 7 g fat ⁕ 7 g protein ⁕ 7 g carbohydrates

"Asparagus inspires gentle thoughts."

Charles Lamb, English essayist (1775–1834)

Origins: Louis XIV loved asparagus so much that he persuaded his gardener to grow it twelve months of the year, in greenhouses.

GREEN BEANS WITH SUMMER SAVORY

Haricots Verts à la Sarriette

Young, tender green beans and summer savory are a Provençal marriage made in heaven. The vibrant mint-like flavor of the herb serves as a perfect foil for the herbal sweetness of fresh green beans. Serve this as a side dish or as a first course. It should be served warm, to best enhance the pungency of the herb. 6 servings

EQUIPMENT: A 10-quart pasta pot fitted with a colander; a large skillet.

¼ cup coarse sea salt
1 pound green beans, rinsed and trimmed at both ends
1 tablespoon finely chopped fresh summer savory leaves
2 tablespoons unsalted butter

1.   Prepare a large bowl of ice water.

2.   Fill a 10-quart pasta pot fitted with a colander with 8 quarts water and bring to a rolling boil over high heat. Add the salt and the beans and cook until crisp-tender, about 5 minutes. (Cooking time will vary according to the size and tenderness of the beans.) Immediately remove the colander from the water, allow the water to drain from the beans, and plunge the colander with the beans into the ice water so they cool down as quickly as possible. (The beans will cool in 1 to 2 minutes. If you leave them longer, they will become soggy and begin to lose flavor.) Drain the beans and wrap them in a thick towel to dry. (The beans can be cooked up to 4 hours in advance. Keep them wrapped in the towel and refrigerate, if desired.)

3.   At serving time, place the beans in a large skillet over moderate heat. Add the summer savory and butter. Warm the mixture, tossing to coat the beans, for 1 to 2 minutes. Serve warm.

55 calories per serving ※ 4 g fat ※ 1 g protein ※ 5 g carbohydrates

Summer Savory, or *sarriette,* is a perennial herb that is intensely aromatic, reminiscent of both thyme and mint. The herb is used often and sparingly in salads, cheese dishes, and herb blends. In Provence, it is also called the bean herb, for it is often found paired with green beans. Its leaves are a bit larger and more rounded than its hardy perennial cousin, winter savory.

Ice Saints and More

Although there may be dramatic climatic changes from year to year, the French vegetable gardener remains faithful to a series of proverbs that follow the rhythm of the seasons, according to the feast days of the Catholic saints.

For the feast of Sainte Agathe (February 5) gardeners are advised to *"Fais tes poireaux, sème ton oignon, sans réflexion, même dans la glace."* Or "Plant your leeks and sow your onions, without taking the time to think, even if the ground is frozen."

The feast day of Saint Didier falls on May 23, when gardeners in the eastern regions of France, such as the Vosges, are advised, *"Qui sème les haricots à la Saint Didier les arrachera à poignées."* Or "He who plants the seeds for green beans on May 23 will harvest them by the handful."

If gardeners live in the southern, or warmer regions of France, they are advised to sow green beans on May 3: *"Sème tes haricots à la Sainte-Croix, tu en récolteras plus que pour toi."* Or "Sow green beans on May 3, and you will harvest for more than yourself."

In Provence, there are three critical dates in May when temperatures can drop dramatically, and there can be frosts, ruining any fragile vegetables or budding and flowering fruits. The days are May 11 (the feast day of Saint Mamert), May 12 (Saint Pancrace), and May 13 (Saint Servais), and these saints are generally known as "the ice saints." Tradition also suggests that when planting your vegetable garden you always wait for the feast days of the ice saints to pass so tender vegetables do not risk a sudden freeze.

BROCCOLI PURÉE WITH A HINT OF MINT

Purée de Brocoli à la Menthe

I love it when recipes begin as a simple conversation. One wintry Saturday morning the Parisian restaurateur Louis-Jacques Vanucci of Le Soleil picked me up to take me to the market to meet the vegetable king, Joël Thiebault. We were talking food, of course, and Louis-Jacques mentioned that he had just made a purée of broccoli and added just a hint of mint and that little touch of brightness turned an ordinary purée into one with deep complex flavors, the mint exhaling its menthol richness. I went home and prepared this dish that evening. It's been a staple ever since. 12 servings

EQUIPMENT: A steamer; a food processor or a blender.

2 pounds broccoli florets and stems, trimmed and rinsed
1 cup fresh mint leaves and stems, rinsed
Fine sea salt

Bring 1 quart water to a simmer in the bottom of a steamer. Place the broccoli on the steaming rack. Place the rack over the simmering water, cover, and steam until the broccoli is soft and cooked through, about 10 minutes. With a slotted spoon, transfer the broccoli to a food processor or a blender. Add the mint and salt and purée to a smooth-textured purée.

❀ᶜ 30 calories per serving ❀ trace of fat ❀ 3 g protein ❀ 6 g carbohydrates

SAUTÉED BRUSSELS SPROUTS WITH GARLIC AND OLIVE OIL

Choux de Bruxelles Sautés à l'Ail

When tender, tiny green Brussels sprouts appear in the farmers' markets, we know it's a sure sign of autumn. We want warm food then, with forceful, forward flavors, and this dish fills the bill. Rather than cooking the baby cabbages as whole vegetables, I like to peel away and separate the leaves, making for a more elegant and unusual presentation. 4 servings

EQUIPMENT: **A large skillet.**

1 pound Brussels sprouts, trimmed
2 tablespoons extra-virgin olive oil
4 plump, moist cloves garlic, peeled, halved, green germ removed, slivered
½ teaspoon fine sea salt
Freshly ground black pepper

1.   Peel away and separate the leaves of the Brussels sprouts. Discard the cores.

2.   In a large skillet, combine the oil, garlic, and salt. Cook over moderate heat, just until the garlic is golden, 2 to 3 minutes. Add the Brussels sprout leaves and cook just until crisp, 2 to 3 minutes more. Season to taste. Serve immediately.

113 calories per serving ⋄ 7 g fat ⋄ 4 g protein ⋄ 1 g carbohydrates

"It is not really an exaggeration to say that peace and happiness begin, geographically, where garlic is used in cooking."

Marcel Boulestin, British chef (1878–1943)

STEAMED BRUSSELS SPROUTS WITH BACON AND CREAM

Choux de Bruxelles à la Crème et au Bacon

Give me cabbage with bacon any day. This combination of Brussels sprouts, bacon, and cream makes a perfect winter specialty, a top-of-the-stove dish that takes just minutes to prepare but rewards you with plenty of rich, savory kitchen aromas as well as flavors. 4 servings

EQUIPMENT: A steamer; a large skillet.

1 pound Brussels sprouts, trimmed
2½ ounces smoked bacon, rind removed, cut into ¼-inch cubes (¾ cup)
¼ cup *crème fraîche* or heavy cream
Fine sea salt
Freshly ground black pepper

1.   With a sharp knife, cut an X in the base of each Brussels sprout, to prevent the vegetable from falling apart while cooking.

2.   Bring 1 quart water to a simmer in the bottom of a steamer. Place the Brussels sprouts on the steaming rack. Place the rack over the simmering water, cover, and steam until the sprouts give just the slightest resistance when pierced with a sharp knife, about 7 minutes.

3.   While the sprouts are steaming, cook the bacon. In a large, skillet pan with no added fat, brown the bacon over moderate heat until crisp and golden, about 5 minutes. With a slotted spoon, transfer the bacon to several layers of paper towel to absorb the fat. Blot the top of the bacon with several layers of paper towel to absorb any additional fat. Set aside.

4.   When the Brussels sprouts are cooked, add the sprouts, bacon, and *crème fraîche* to the skillet and heat through, about 2 minutes. Season to taste. Serve immediately.

﹡c 180 calories per serving ⁘ 12 g fat ⁘ 10 g protein ⁘ 11 g carbohydrates

STEAMED, CREAMY CABBAGE

Chou à la Crème

❧ This light and creamy bed of cabbage serves as a backdrop for all sorts of dishes. I like to steam salmon or codfish and set it atop a bed of this crisp winter specialty. 4 servings

EQUIPMENT: A box grater or a food processor fitted with a shredding blade; a steamer.

1 pound cabbage
4 tablespoons light cream
1 tablespoon freshly squeezed lemon juice
¾ teaspoon fine sea salt
Freshly ground black pepper

1.   Using the largest holes of a box grater or a food processor fitted with a shredding blade, grate the cabbage. You should have 4 cups. Set aside.

2.   Combine the cream, lemon juice, salt, and pepper in a large bowl. Toss to blend. Set aside.

3.   Bring 1 quart water to a simmer in the bottom of a steamer. Place the cabbage on the steaming rack. Place the rack over the simmering water, cover, and steam until the cabbage is tender, about 7 minutes. Do not overcook.

4.   With a slotted spoon, carefully transfer the cabbage to the bowl with the cream dressing. Toss to coat evenly with the dressing. Taste for seasoning. Serve warm.

❧ 61 calories per serving ◦ 3 g fat ◦ 2 g protein ◦ 7 g carbohydrates

CAULIFLOWER PURÉE

Purée de Chou-fleur

Delicate, pure white, and fragrant, this wintertime purée brightens the table on those long, cold days. I like to serve this quick and easy purée with Seared Duck Breast with Espelette Pepper Jelly (page 111) as well as the Broccoli Purée with a Hint of Mint (page 167). 8 servings

EQUIPMENT: A large saucepan; a food processor or a blender.

1 whole cauliflower (about 2 pounds), trimmed and broken into florets
½ cup 1% milk
½ cup light cream
½ teaspoon fine sea salt, or more to taste
1 teaspoon unsalted butter
½ teaspoon freshly grated nutmeg

In a large saucepan, combine the cauliflower, milk, cream, and salt and simmer, uncovered, over medium heat until tender, about 15 minutes. Stir from time to time to prevent the cauliflower from sticking to the pan. Drain, reserving any liquid, and transfer to a food processor or a blender. Process to blend. Add the butter and nutmeg and process to a fine purée. Add just enough of the reserved liquid to give it a smooth, light consistency. Season to taste. Serve warm.

69 calories per serving * 4 g fat * 3 g protein * 7 g carbohydrates

What I Learned: Because this dish contains milk and cream, it can easily scorch. Watch the cauliflower carefully as it cooks, to prevent the dish from coloring.

BUTTER-WARMED CORN KERNELS WITH FRESH CILANTRO LEAVES

Maïs à la Coriandre

Butter, fresh corn, and coriander leaves seem to be a trio made in heaven. Corn calls out for just a touch of salted butter, and the haunting flavor of fresh coriander leaf seems to echo the marriage of butter and corn. Here the kernels are cut from the cob and warmed for just a minute, so the vegetable retains its crunch, color, flavor, and aroma. Season with a touch of homemade lemony *fleur de sel* and you have a colorful, flavorful vegetable dish. This is a recipe that even my French dentist will approve of, since he is constantly admonishing me, "No corn on the cob!" 6 servings

EQUIPMENT: A large skillet.

3 ears fresh corn, shucked
1 tablespoon salted butter
¼ cup fresh cilantro leaves, coarsely chopped
Zesty Lemon Salt (page 310)

With a sharp knife, scrape the kernels of corn from the cob. Melt the butter in a large skillet over moderate heat and cook the corn just until warmed through, tossing the corn in the skillet for about 1 minute. Transfer to a bowl, shower with the coriander leaves, and season with lemon salt.

56 calories per serving ⁕ 2 g fat ⁕ 2 g protein ⁕ 9 g carbohydrates

What I Learned: There are many people who do not relish the flavor of fresh cilantro leaf as I do. Easy substitutes include parsley and/or chives, to retain that colorful touch of green.

"Compter pour du beurre." To count for nothing.

EGGPLANT, TOMATO, BASIL, AND CHEESE TIMBALES

Timbales d'Aubergines, Tomates et Basilic

This is the sort of dish I could eat for breakfast, lunch, and dinner. And have. The thinly sliced, broiled egg-plant takes on an almost sweet, candylike flavor, and how can one go wrong with the combination of egg-plant, tomato, basil, and cheese? I've also made this dish substituting zucchini for the eggplant, with great success. 4 servings

> EQUIPMENT: A baking sheet; parchment paper or a silicone mat; a pastry brush; four ½-cup ramekins; 4 warmed salad plates.
>
> 1 small, firm eggplant (about 8 ounces), stem end trimmed
> 1 tablespoon extra-virgin olive oil
> Fine sea salt
> 12 Oven-Roasted Cherry Tomatoes (page 208)
> 24 large fresh basil leaves
> 8 ounces fresh goat's milk cheese
> 2 teaspoons Basil Oil (page 312) for garnish

1.   Preheat the broiler. Place an oven rack about 3 inches below the heat. Line a baking sheet with parchment paper or a silicone mat. Set aside.

2.   Cut the eggplant lengthwise into 12 very thin slices. Brush both sides of the eggplant slices lightly with oil and sprinkle lightly with salt. Place the slices side by side on the baking sheet.

3.   Place the baking sheet on the oven rack and broil until the eggplant is browned around the edges, about 2 minutes per side. Remove from the oven. (Do not turn off the broiler.)

4.   Line each of four ½-cup ramekins with 3 slices of grilled eggplant, allowing the eggplant to drape over the edge. Place 3 tomatoes on top of the eggplant in the ramekins. Cover the tomatoes with 2 leaves of fresh basil. Place about 2 ounces of cheese on top of the basil, then add 2 more leaves of fresh basil, pressing down on the cheese to make a compact timbale. Fold the overhanging eggplant onto the preparation, pressing down once more. (The timbales can be prepared up to this point up to 4 hours in advance and kept at room temperature.)

5.   Remove and discard the parchment paper or remove the silicone mat. Place the ramekins on the baking sheet, place on the oven rack, and broil just until warmed through, about 2 minute. Remove from

the oven. Turn the ramekins out, unmolding them onto 4 warmed salad plates. Garnish with 2 leaves of fresh basil. Drizzle with Basil Oil and serve.

❀ᶜ 120 calories per serving ❀ 9 g fat ❀ 4 g protein ❀ 6 g carbohydrates

Origins: In the seventeenth century, colorful purple eggplant tweaked the curiosity of King Louis XIV, who asked his gardener to cultivate the *béringere,* its Spanish name. But his gardener wrote, "We cultivate it purely out of curiosity," and in a seed catalog dating from 1760 it was sold as an ornamental plant. Due to its form, it was nicknamed "the laying hen" or "the vegetable egg" and was used to decorate desserts and fruit baskets. By 1800, it was being cultivated all over the south of France as an edible plant, and soon one could find it everywhere. In 1809, a French book called *The Good Gardener* mentions the eggplant's culinary use as a dessert, declaring, "It's a ragoût fantasy!" By 1825, eggplant had arrived in Parisian markets and begun to appear in cookbooks.

EGGPLANT DAUBE

Daube d'Aubergines

My husband, Walter, is always telling me to make it easy for myself. I take his advice most days and think of this recipe as filling the bill. Easy as pie and so delicious. When the garden is overflowing with eggplant and tomatoes, I make a double batch and feast on it for lunch as well as dinner. It's a dish that can be eaten warm or at room temperature and seems to improve with age. 6 servings

EQUIPMENT: A large skillet with a lid.

2 tablespoons extra-virgin olive oil
1 large onion, peeled, halved, and thinly sliced
Fine sea salt
5 small, elongated, Asian-type eggplants (about 2 pounds), cubed (do not peel)
4 large tomatoes (about 2 pounds), cored, peeled, seeded, and chopped
2 plump, moist cloves garlic, peeled, halved, green germ removed
Bouquet garni: several parsley stems, celery leaves, and sprigs of thyme, encased in a wire mesh tea infuser
Grated zest of 1 orange, preferably organic
2 cups dry white wine

In a large skillet, combine the oil, onion, and salt. Sweat—cook, covered, over low heat until soft but not browned—for about 3 minutes. Add the eggplants, tomatoes, garlic, bouquet garni, orange zest, and wine. Stir to combine. Cook, covered, over the lowest possible heat until the mixture is soft, 1 to 1 1/2 hours. Taste for seasoning. Remove the bouquet garni. Serve warm or at room temperature.

✻c 172 calories per serving ✻ 5 g fat ✻ 3 g protein ✻ 20 g carbohydrates

The Right Pan for the Task

After years of watching students cook in my classes, I have decided the one mistake cooks make time after time is selecting a pan that's too small for the task. I like ingredients to have plenty of room in a pan. When ingredients are crushed together and there is no "air" left in the pan, I find ingredients cook too slowly.

For many dishes—such as this Eggplant Daube—I favor cast-iron or enameled cast-iron cookware. It's sturdy, pretty, and I like the results I get when I am looking for a nice, evenly cooked dish. I have an old black cast-iron pot that was in the house when we acquired it. The pot must be forty years old and will probably outlive me.

What's a Daube?

In Provence, the most popular *daube* is made of beef marinated in red wine and vegetables. A *daube* is cooked in a *daubière*, traditionally an oval clay pot with a handle and a lid. The *daubière* was set beside the fire, on top of the stove or in the oven, and designed for long, slow cooking. Today *daubes* are made in all sorts of vessels and can be made with many ingredients—vegetables, meats, or fish. What they all have in common is long, slow cooking.

EGGPLANT AND TOMATOES FROM
THE VELLERON MARKET

Aubergines et Tomates, Marché de Velleron

Around 5:30 most summer evenings dozens of shrewd shoppers line up along a gated chain-link fence in a parking lot in the village of Velleron, not far from the antiques capital of L'Isle-sur-la-Sorgue. People elbow one another, keep a sharp watch on their timepieces, eyes darting from one vegetable merchant to the other as the merchants set up shop behind the fence. At six o'clock sharp a whistle blows, the gates open, and shoppers rush to buy some of the freshest and prettiest produce in all of Provence. On one visit, a merchant handed me a little promotional brochure on tomatoes, with this recipe included. I am always looking for new ways to cook eggplant, especially ways that do *not* involve lighting the oven and heating the kitchen in the dead of summer. I think of this as an eggplant sandwich: The eggplant is slit about halfway through, lengthwise, then slices of fresh tomato are tucked inside. The eggplant is then cooked, covered, on top of the stove, making for a fragrant, moist, unforgettably delicious and ridiculously simple dish. As a variation, one could add bits of grated cheese, olives, capers, or all three. 4 servings

EQUIPMENT: A large casserole with a lid.

4 small garden-fresh tomatoes (1 pound)
4 small, elongated, Asian-type eggplants (1 pound)
Fine sea salt
1 teaspoon dried oregano
2 tablespoons extra-virgin olive oil

Rinse and core the tomatoes, but do not peel. Slice lengthwise into 4 even slices. Make a lengthwise cut—from stem end to bottom—through each eggplant, cutting about halfway through. Season the inside with salt. Carefully place several slices of tomato inside each eggplant. Lay the eggplant side by side in a casserole that will hold them tightly. Sprinkle with the oregano and drizzle with the oil. Cover and cook over the lowest possible heat, watching carefully to avoid scorching the eggplant, cooking until the eggplant is soft when pierced with the tip of a knife, 25 to 30 minutes. Serve warm or at room temperature.

 117 calories per serving ∗ 7 g fat ∗ 2 g protein ∗ 14 g carbohydrates

STEAMED EGGPLANT WITH BUTTERMILK-THYME DRESSING

Aubergines Vapeur au Thym

Steamed food is a bit of a miracle to me. These little strips of eggplant cook in a flash, retaining all their character and goodness, ready to absorb a generous sprinkling of sharp, minced raw garlic and the soothing Buttermilk-Thyme Dressing. 4 servings

EQUIPMENT: A steamer.

2 to 3 small, elongated, Asian-type eggplants (about 1 pound)
4 plump, moist cloves garlic, peeled, halved, green germ removed, minced
Fine sea salt
2 tablespoons Buttermilk-Thyme Dressing (page 298)

1. Cut the eggplants lengthwise—from stem end to bottom—into very thin slices. Do not peel.

2. Bring 1 quart water to a simmer in the bottom of a steamer. Place the eggplant slices—slightly overlapping—on the steaming rack. Place the rack over the simmering water, cover, and steam until the eggplant is soft and cooked through, about 15 minutes. With a slotted spoon, transfer the slices to a large platter. Sprinkle with the garlic, season with salt, and drizzle with the dressing. Toss gently to coat the eggplant. Serve immediately. This dish should be eaten warm!

&c 32 calories per serving ⊛ trace of fat ⊛ 1 g protein ⊛ 7 g carbohydrates

Words on Wine: "Gigondas wine tastes like a postcard from the village, all black cherries, licorice, rosemary, and thyme."

Fabrice Langlois, sommelier at Château du Beaucastel in Châteauneuf-du-Pape

JOHANNES'S PICNIC EGGPLANT

Les Aubergines du Pique-nique de Johannes

During my June and August fitness classes in Provence, our Wednesday hike is a glorious uphill trek on the ragged mountains of Gigondas, known as Les Dentelles de Montmirail. Once we get to the top, we hike farther uphill to a lookout point, where we have a gorgeous 360-degree view of the surrounding vineyards and villages. Our reward is a lavish picnic, catered by chef Johannes Sailer of the restaurant Les Abeilles in the neighboring village of Sablet. During one class, this simple and sublime eggplant dish was part of that buffet. 4 servings

EQUIPMENT: **A large skillet; a 1-quart gratin dish.**

2 small, firm eggplants (about 1 pound), stem end trimmed (do not peel)
⅓ cup extra-virgin olive oil
Fine sea salt
2 cups Chunky Fresh Tomato Sauce (page 305)

1.   Preheat the oven to 425 degrees F.

2.   Cut each eggplant lengthwise into 4 even slices. Set aside.

3.   In a large skillet, heat 2 tablespoons of the oil over moderate heat until hot but not smoking. Add 4 slices of eggplant and cook until golden brown on one side, about 45 seconds. Turn and brown the other side, about 45 seconds more. Transfer the cooked eggplant slices to the gratin dish. Season lightly with salt. Repeat for the remaining slices, arranging each slice on top of the others in the gratin dish.

4.   Pour the tomato sauce over the eggplant. Place the gratin dish in the center of the oven and bake until bubbly, about 25 minutes. Serve warm or at room temperature.

*C 234 calories per serving * 18 g fat * 3 g protein * 18 g carbohydrates

Wine Suggestion

During the picnic we were honored with the presence of winemaker Yves Gras, of the Domaine Santa Duc vineyard in Gigondas. The day we sampled this eggplant gratin, Yves offered tastes of his red Côtes-du-Rhône, cuvée Les Quatre Terres, or the four soils. The wine is made from grapes of four distinct soils—sandy, rocky, limestone-rich, and claylike—in vineyards of four neighboring villages: Seguret, Vacouevras, Roaix, and Rasteau.

ROASTED FRESH GARLIC

Têtes d'Ail au Four

When fresh, tender purple-tinged garlic is in the market in late spring, this dish finds its way to my table rather frequently. The idea for this recipe comes from Raoul Reichrath, a fine chef and friend who runs Le Grand Pré in Roaix, a favorite haunt in Provence. 8 servings

EQUIPMENT: A large skillet; a large baking dish.

8 whole heads of fresh garlic
2 tablespoons extra-virgin olive oil
1 tablespoon sugar

1.   Preheat the oven to 425 degrees F.

2.   With a sharp knife, horizontally trim off the top third of each head of garlic. (Reserve the top portion for stock or use while roasting poultry or meat.)

3.   Heat the oil in a large skillet over moderate heat. When the oil is hot but not smoking, place the heads of garlic, cut side down, in the skillet and cook until the garlic turns a golden brown, 3 to 4 minutes. Check carefully that the garlic does not burn.

4.   With tongs, place the heads of garlic, cut side up, side by side in a baking dish. Sprinkle with the sugar. Roast, uncovered, until the garlic cloves are meltingly soft, about 45 minutes. Check from time to time and reduce the heat or cover with foil if the garlic seems to be drying out. Serve one head of garlic per guest. This is delicious with any roast meat or poultry.

66 calories per serving ☼ 4 g fat ☼ 1 g protein ☼ 8 g carbohydrates

What I Learned: Come July, the garlic in the market has lost much of its moisture, but I found that this dish still works. I simply add a bit of liquid—either olive oil or a touch of chicken stock—to the gratin dish and roast the garlic covered with foil to retain moisture.

LAMB'S LETTUCE PURÉE

Purée de Mâche

Lamb's lettuce, or *mâche,* is more than a salad green. This perky, crisp vegetable is equally at home in soups and in this gorgeous, deep green purée. Nutmeg is a secret flavor here, a spice that always manages to add another haunting dimension to cooked greens. 4 servings

EQUIPMENT: A 10-quart pasta pot fitted with a colander; a food processor or a blender.

3 tablespoons coarse sea salt
2 pounds lamb's lettuce, thoroughly washed, drained, and trimmed
¼ cup Homemade Chicken Stock (page 294)
¼ cup light cream
Freshly grated nutmeg
Fine sea salt

1. In a 10-quart pasta pot fitted with a colander, bring 8 quarts water to a rolling boil over high heat. Add the coarse salt and plunge the lamb's lettuce leaves into the boiling water. Blanch, uncovered, just until softened, 2 to 3 minutes. Drain, leaving the leaves in the colander, and rinse under cold running water. Drain thoroughly, pressing down on the lamb's lettuce to remove any excess liquid.

2. Transfer the lamb's lettuce to a food processor or a blender. Add enough chicken stock and cream just to make a smooth, light mixture and purée. Season with nutmeg and salt. The purée can be prepared up to 6 hours in advance and stored in an airtight container in the refrigerator. Reheat at serving time.

77 calories per serving ⁕ 4 g fat ⁕ 5 g protein ⁕ 5 g carbohydrates

The Anti-Stress Vegetable

Lamb's lettuce is considered the best anti-stress green. It contains plenty of folic acid, known as the "wellness vitamin," which prevents irritability and fatigue and helps one sleep. Lamb's lettuce is a member of the valerian family, from which the tranquilizer Valium gets its name.

STEAMED LEEKS IN MUSTARD
AND CAPER VINAIGRETTE

Poireaux Vinaigrette

The French love leeks and give them the respect they are due. When shopping, I always glance to see what my neighbors are adding to their market baskets. Invariably there is a tall, slender, shiny leek or two, for putting in salads, soups, stews. But leeks can be treated badly, especially when they are cooked to death and their gorgeous alabaster and spring green colors turn to dull army-drab gray-green. Here the elegant *poireau* is simply steamed, then immediately bathed in a lively sauce of vinegar, mustard, capers, and oil, so it absorbs all those delicious flavors, maintaining both color and integrity. For this dish, choose the smallest, freshest leeks you can find. I use only the tender white portion here, reserving the green portions for soups and stocks. 4 servings

EQUIPMENT: **A steamer.**

The Vinaigrette
1 tablespoon sherry-wine vinegar
½ teaspoon fine sea salt
2 teaspoons imported French mustard
1 tablespoon capers in vinegar, drained
¼ cup extra-virgin olive oil

8 small fresh leeks (about 1 pound), white portion only, trimmed and rinsed
½ cup finely minced fresh chives or flat-leaf parsley leaves

1.   Prepare the vinaigrette: In a small bowl, combine the vinegar and salt and whisk to dissolve the salt. Add the mustard, capers, and oil and whisk to blend. Taste for seasoning. Set aside.

2.   Bring 1 quart water to a simmer in the bottom of a steamer. Place the leeks on the steaming rack. Place the rack over the simmering water, cover, and steam until the leeks are soft and cooked through, about 10 minutes.

3.   Drain the leeks and transfer to a platter. Immediately cover with the vinaigrette while the leeks are warm, so they soak up the sauce. Sprinkle with chives or parsley and serve.

160 calories per serving ❋ 14 g fat ❋ 2 g protein ❋ 9 g carbohydrates

WILD MOREL MUSHROOMS IN CREAM

Morilles à la Crème

Meaty, fragrant morels assisted by a touch of cream and lemon juice make for a truly special trio of flavors. These can be used as a side dish or as a pasta sauce or a garnish for Fresh White Bean Soup with Morels in Cream (page 65). 12 servings

EQUIPMENT: Dampened cheesecloth; a medium skillet with a lid.

2 cups (4 ounces) dried morel mushrooms
3 tablespoons unsalted butter, at room temperature
Fine sea salt
2 shallots, trimmed, peeled, and finely minced
2 cups light cream
About 2 teaspoons freshly squeezed lemon juice, or to taste
Freshly ground white pepper

1. If any of the morels are extremely large, halve them lengthwise. Place the morels in a colander and rinse well under cold running water to rid them of any grit. Transfer them to a heat-proof measuring cup. Pour boiling water over the mushrooms to cover. Set aside for 20 minutes to plump them up. With a slotted spoon, carefully remove the mushrooms from the liquid, leaving behind any grit that may fall to the bottom.

2. Place a piece of dampened cheesecloth in a colander set over a large bowl. Carefully spoon the soaking liquid into the colander, leaving behind any grit at the bottom of the measuring cup. You should have 1 1/2 cups liquid. Set aside. (You will not need all the soaking "bouillon" for this recipe. I like to freeze the remaining liquid to enhance a mushroom soup.)

3. In a medium skillet, combine the butter, a pinch of salt, and the shallots and sweat—cook, covered, over moderate heat until soft but not browned—for 2 to 3 minutes. Add the drained morels and about 1/2 cup of the strained soaking liquid. Cook, uncovered, over moderate heat until the liquid is reduced to 2 to 3 tablespoons, about 5 minutes. Add the cream and simmer, still uncovered, over low heat until the morels have lost most of their firmness, 8 to 10 minutes. Add lemon juice to taste. Season generously with white pepper. Taste for seasoning. Serve.

116 calories per serving ⁕ 11 g fat ⁕ 2 g protein ⁕ 4 g carbohydrates

AUTUMN VEGETABLE RAGOUT WITH WILD MUSHROOMS

Ragoût d'Automne aux Champignons

Early one September we sat on the sunlit terrace of Tina and Guy Julien's La Beaugravière, one of our favorite restaurants in Provence. That day Guy outdid himself with a memorable vegetable medley that was outstanding all on its own. Yet he embellished it with a healthy dose of fresh wild mushrooms, turning the dish into a meal of its own. Make all or part of it, depending upon your menu, mood, and pocketbook. 8 servings

> EQUIPMENT: A large heavy-bottomed saucepan with a lid; a 6-quart pasta pot fitted with a colander; a steamer; a 12-inch skillet; a large skillet; 8 warmed dinner plates.

¼ cup extra-virgin olive oil

5 plump, moist cloves garlic, peeled, halved, green germ removed

1 pound small fresh white beans in the pod, shelled, or 8 ounces dried white beans

2 fresh or dried bay leaves

About 2½ cups Homemade Chicken Stock (page 294)

Fine sea salt

3 tablespoons coarse sea salt

About 5 ounces snow peas

About 5 ounces baby leeks

About 5 ounces cauliflower florets

About 5 ounces baby fennel, trimmed

About 5 ounces spring onions, trimmed

1 pound large fresh cèpe or porcini mushrooms, cleaned, trimmed, and sliced

2 tablespoons unsalted butter

2 tablespoons minced fresh chervil or parsley, or more to taste

Freshly ground white pepper

1.   For fresh beans: In a large heavy-bottomed saucepan, combine 2 tablespoons olive oil and garlic and stir to coat the garlic with the oil. Place over moderate heat and cook until the garlic is fragrant and soft, about 2 minutes. Do not let it brown. Add the beans, stir to coat with oil, and cook for 1 minute more. Add the bay leaves and about 2 cups of the stock, enough to just cover the beans. Cover, bring to a simmer

over moderate heat, and simmer for 15 minutes. Season with fine sea salt. Continue cooking at a gentle simmer until the beans are tender, about 15 minutes more. Stir from time to time to make sure the beans are not sticking to the bottom of the pan. Add stock or water if necessary. Taste for seasoning. Remove and discard the bay leaves.

2.   For dried beans: Rinse the beans, picking them over to remove any pebbles. Place the beans in a large bowl, add boiling water to cover, and set aside for 1 hour. Drain the beans, discarding the water. In a large heavy-bottomed saucepan, combine 2 tablespoons olive oil and garlic and stir to coat the garlic with the oil. Cook over moderate heat until the garlic is fragrant and soft, about 2 minutes. Do not let it brown. Add the beans, stir to coat with oil, and cook for 1 minute more. Add about 2 cups of the stock, enough to just cover the beans. Cover, bring to a simmer over moderate heat, and simmer for 30 minutes. Season with fine sea salt. Continue cooking at a gentle simmer until the beans are tender, about 30 minutes more. Stir from time to time to make sure the beans are not sticking to the bottom of the pan. Add stock or water if necessary. (Cooking time will vary according to the freshness of the beans.) Taste for seasoning. Remove and discard the bay leaves.

3.   Prepare a large bowl of ice water.

4.   Prepare the snow peas and the baby leeks: Fill a 6-quart pasta pot fitted with a colander with 5 quarts water and bring to a boil over high heat. Add the coarse salt and the snow peas. Boil, uncovered, until the snow peas are crisp-tender, about 3 minutes. Immediately remove the colander holding the snow peas and pour the peas into the ice water so they cool down as quickly as possible and retain their crispness and bright green color. (The snow peas will cool in 1 to 2 minutes. After that, they will soften and begin to lose crispness and flavor.) Transfer the snow peas to the colander, drain, and wrap in a thick towel to dry. (The snow peas can be cooked up to 2 hours in advance. Keep them wrapped in the towel and hold at room temperature.) Repeat for the baby leeks, using fresh water in the pasta pot fitted with a colander.

5.   Prepare the cauliflower, baby fennel, and spring onions: Bring about 2 cups water to a simmer in the bottom of a vegetable steamer. Place the cauliflower florets, the baby fennel, and the spring onions on the steaming rack. Place the rack over the simmering water, cover, and steam until the vegetables are soft, 3 to 4 minutes. Drain.

6.   Prepare the mushrooms: Heat the remaining 2 tablespoons oil in a 12-inch skillet over moderate heat until hot but not smoking. Add the mushrooms, season lightly with fine sea salt, and sauté just until they begin to give up their juices, 1 to 2 minutes. Using a slotted spoon, transfer the mushrooms to a platter to drain. With paper towels, wipe out the skillet. Melt the butter over moderate heat and return the mushrooms to the skillet. Season lightly with fine sea salt. Cook for 2 minutes more. Off the heat, sprinkle the mushrooms with chervil and toss to coat with the herb. Season with freshly ground white pepper and transfer to warmed dinner plates.

7.   In a large skillet, combine all the reserved vegetables with enough of the remaining stock to moisten. Heat just to warm through, stirring gently, about 1 to 2 minutes. Taste for herbs and white pepper. Serve immediately with the mushrooms.

✴C 216 calories per serving ❋ 8 g fat ❋ 12 g protein ❋ 26 g carbohydrates

✴ Variation: For a winter ragout, blanch and refresh turnips and baby leeks; steam carrots, fennel, spring onions, and slices of pumpkin.

WILD MUSHROOMS IN PARCHMENT WITH WILD MINT

Champignons en Papillote à la Menthe

This is a most versatile, easy, and satisfying dish. Whether you use domestic or wild mushrooms or a combination of both, this makes for warming cold-weather fare. Make a giant batch and declare it lunch or dinner. As a side dish, this fragrant, wholesome dish is right at home with roast chicken or duck or seared duck breasts. I use fresh wild mint, or nepeta, which grows like a weed on our property in Provence. Any domestic mint or fresh oregano works just as well here. 4 servings

EQUIPMENT: Parchment paper; a baking sheet; 4 warmed salad plates.

1 pound large fresh *cèpes* or *porcini* mushrooms (or a mix of chanterelles or girolles, cremini, portobello, or standard cultivated mushrooms), cleaned, trimmed, and cut into ½-inch slices
3 tablespoons fresh wild mint, mint, or oregano
4 plump, moist cloves garlic, peeled, halved, green germ removed, slivered
Fine sea salt
Freshly ground black pepper
1 tablespoon best-quality walnut oil or extra-virgin olive oil

1. Preheat the oven to 425 degrees F.

2. Prepare 4 pieces of parchment, each about 12 inches square.

3. In a large bowl, combine the sliced mushrooms, mint, garlic, salt, pepper, and oil and toss gently to blend. With a large spoon, transfer the mushrooms to the square of parchment. Fold the top half of the parchment over and seal with several staples.

4. Place the parchment packages on a baking sheet. Place in the center of the oven and roast until the mushrooms are soft and fragrant, about 25 minutes. Carefully open the mushroom packages and transfer the mushrooms to warmed salad plates.

67 calories per serving ❖ 4 g fat ❖ 3 g protein ❖ 7 g carbohydrates

Folklore: Since wild mushrooms seem to grow out of nowhere, the vegetable has always been suspect. Mushrooms growing in a circle—known as a circle of witches—mark the spot where there was a meeting of very bad fairies. In Brittany, they were known as "venoms of the soil."

WINTER KALEIDOSCOPE:
CARROTS, JERUSALEM ARTICHOKES, TURNIPS, AND RADISHES

Méli-Mélo de Légumes d'Hiver

The doorbell rang just a few minutes after 7:00 one dark, dreary, gray Paris morning in February. It was my first order from the vegetable home delivery service Le Haut du Panier, and when I opened the door, there was Antoine Meyssonnier holding a giant cardboard box filled with treasures picked only hours earlier, in the gardens of market gardener Joël Thiebault. I gasped as I opened the box, for every single vegetable beamed with a healthy glow, a panorama of colors, including such heirloom specialties as yellow carrots and green radishes, as well as firm, purple-tinged Jerusalem artichokes, slender yellow parsnips, firm brownish gold potatoes, gorgeous bundles of spinach as well as lamb's lettuce, parsley, and leeks. I hesitated, not wanting to unpack the box, but knew the jewels would be happier hanging out in the refrigerator until I got to them later in the day. To top it off, Antoine had included a recipe, entitled *Poêlée de Petits Légumes-Racines du 18 Février.* So here it is, in all its glory. When I cooked up the colorful mélange of root vegetables, I couldn't believe the kaleidoscope of colors. What a way to brighten up a winter's day! My husband, Walter, loved the dish and commented, "It's like a delicious vegetable soup without the liquid." 8 servings

EQUIPMENT: A mandoline or a very sharp knife; a large, heavy-duty, flame-proof casserole; 8 warmed dinner plates.

16 plump, moist cloves garlic, peeled, halved, green germ removed

2 parsnips, trimmed and peeled

2 carrots, trimmed and peeled

6 Jerusalem artichokes, rinsed

2 turnips, trimmed and peeled

2 green radishes, trimmed and peeled (or additional parsnips and turnips)

3 tablespoons extra-virgin olive oil

1 teaspoon fine sea salt

1 teaspoon cumin seeds

1 teaspoon ground *piment d'Espelette* or dried Anaheim chilies (or ground mild chili pepper)

1 tablespoon best-quality walnut oil or pistachio oil

1.   Using a mandoline or a very sharp knife, slice all the vegetables into thin rounds. If the turnips are large, quarter each slice so all the vegetables remain about the same size.

2.   Place the olive oil in the casserole and heat over low heat. Add all the vegetables, the salt, cumin, and pepper, and cook, covered, just until the vegetables are cooked through but still a bit crunchy, about 20 to 25 minutes. Taste for seasoning.

3.   Transfer to warmed dinner plates. Drizzle each serving with a few drops of walnut or pistachio oil.

✣ᴄ 197 calories per serving ❈ 7 g fat ❈ 4 g protein ❈ 32 g carbohydrates

FRESH PEAS WITH MINT AND SPRING ONIONS

Petits Pois à la Menthe et Oignons Nouveaux

Few dishes say spring like this bright, aromatic vegetable dish. Mint and peas are a marriage made in heaven: I love the green on green, with the haunting sweetness of the peas, the vibrant fragrance of the mint. I like to serve this with roasted poultry as well as the creamy alabaster Cauliflower Purée (page 172). 8 servings

EQUIPMENT: A 5-quart pasta pot fitted with a colander; a large skillet.

3 tablespoons coarse sea salt
3 pounds fresh peas in the pod, shelled, or 1 pound frozen peas (3½ cups)
1 tablespoon unsalted butter
Fine sea salt
2 spring onions (or 4 scallions), trimmed and cut into thin rings
½ cup fresh mint leaves, cut into chiffonade

1.   In a 5-quart pasta pot fitted with a colander, bring 3 quarts water to a rolling boil over high heat. Add the coarse salt and the peas and cook for just 1 minute, so they remain crisp and retain their bright green color. Immediately remove them from the heat, drain, and rinse under cold running water to stop the cooking and help preserve the bright green color. Drain well and set aside. (The peas can be prepared up to 2 hours in advance, reserved at room temperature.)

2.   At serving time, in a large skillet, melt the butter over low heat. Add the peas and gently warm them, tossing to coat with the butter. Taste and add fine sea salt. Add the spring onions and mint, tossing gently to coat the peas. Serve immediately.

73 calories per serving ⁑ 2 g fat ⁑ 4 g protein ⁑ 11 g carbohydrates

OVEN-ROASTED RED PEPPERS IN OLIVE OIL

Poivrons Rouges au Four

Beautiful as well as versatile, these roasted peppers can be served warm or at room temperature, as a side vegetable dish, or tossed into an omelet, a pasta sauce, or a salad. 6 servings

EQUIPMENT: A small, oven-proof casserole with a lid.

3 red bell peppers
¼ cup extra-virgin olive oil
2 teaspoons coarse sea salt
1 tablespoon best-quality red-wine vinegar

1.   Preheat the oven to 425 degrees F.

2.   Wash the peppers, quarter them, and remove and discard the seeds and membranes. Cut lengthwise into thin slices. Place in a small oven-proof casserole. Toss with the oil and the salt.

3.   Cover and place in the center of the oven. Roast for 30 minutes, turning the peppers from time to time. Remove from the oven and toss with the vinegar. Taste for seasoning. Serve warm or at room temperature. Store in an airtight container in the refrigerator for up to two days.

90 calories per serving ⁕ 9 g fat ⁕ trace of protein ⁕ 3 g carbohydrates

RED PEPPERS, TOMATOES, ONIONS, CUMIN, AND ESPELETTE PEPPER

Poivrons Rouges et Tomates au Piment d'Espelette

With just the right amount of spice, and the slightly haunting flavor of the Espelette pepper from France's Basque country, this lovely vegetable dish is eminently flexible: I like to serve it alongside polenta, but it can be used as a sauce for pasta or rice or can stand all on its own as a side dish. It's delicious warm or at room temperature and seems to hit a chord with everyone. "Can I please have the recipe?" guests ask as I serve it. 10 servings

EQUIPMENT: A small skillet; a large, heavy-duty skillet with a lid.

2 tablespoons cumin seeds
4 red bell peppers
2 tablespoons extra-virgin olive oil
1 teaspoon fine sea salt
2 medium onions, peeled, halved, and thinly sliced
1 teaspoon ground *piment d'Espelette* or dried Anaheim chilies (or ground mild chili pepper)
2 pounds garden fresh tomatoes, cored and cubed (do not peel)

1.   Toast the cumin: Place the cumin in a small, dry skillet over moderate heat. Shake the pan regularly until the cumin seeds are fragrant and evenly toasted, about 2 minutes. Watch carefully! They can burn quickly. Transfer the cumin to a large plate to cool. Set aside.

2.   Wash the bell peppers, quarter them lengthwise, and remove and discard the seeds and membranes. Cut each quarter lengthwise into ⅛-inch-thick slices. Set aside.

3.   In a large, heavy-duty skillet, combine the oil, salt, onions, cumin seeds, and *piment d'Espelette* and toss to evenly coat all the ingredients. Sweat—cook, covered, over low heat until soft—for 3 to 4 minutes.

4.   Add the bell peppers and tomatoes to the onion mixture and cook, covered, over low heat until the peppers are soft and meltingly tender, about 30 minutes. Serve warm or at room temperature.

❋ᴄ 46 calories per serving ❋ 1 g fat ❋ 2 g protein ❋ 10 g carbohydrates

PUMPKIN GRATIN WITH PISTACHIOS AND PISTACHIO OIL

Gratin de Potiron à la Pistache

Come Thanksgiving, come Christmas, this festive, brilliant orange gratin finds its way to our family table. The French menagerie of pumpkin-style squash—including the giant *courge muscade* and the smaller *potimarron*—are densely flavored, rich, and fragrant and are always a welcome part of our diet. Butternut squash, which the French endearingly call just that, *butternut*, is a worthy substitute. 8 servings

EQUIPMENT: A food processor or a blender; a 1-quart gratin dish.

3 cups cooked pumpkin or squash (see page 62)
About ¹/₂ cup Homemade Chicken Stock (page 294)
2 tablespoons best-quality pistachio, hazelnut, or walnut oil
¹/₂ teaspoon fine sea salt
¹/₂ cup freshly grated Parmigiano-Reggiano cheese
¹/₂ cup whole salted pistachio nuts, coarsely chopped

1. Preheat the broiler.

2. In a food processor or a blender, combine the squash, stock, oil, and salt and purée. Taste for seasoning.

3. Transfer the purée to the gratin dish, smoothing it out with the back of a spoon. Sprinkle with cheese. Sprinkle with pistachio nuts.

4. Place under the broiler just until the cheese is melted and the nuts are toasted, 2 to 3 minutes.

≫c 132 calories per serving ⁂ 9 g fat ⁂ 5 g protein ⁂ 10 g carbohydrates

✣ Variation: Replace the pistachios and pistachio oil with hazelnuts and hazelnut oil, walnuts and walnut oil, or roasted peanuts and toasted peanut oil.

The *courge muscade* is a summer specialty of the family gardens of Provence. This nutty, almost nutmeg-flavored and highly perfumed pumpkin requires a minimum of 120 days of sunshine to ripen into a giant, deep orange squash.

JUST SPINACH!

Des Épinards, Rien de Plus!

If I could cook spinach only one way, this would be it! Nothing but healthy-looking green spinach, seasoned with just a touch of salt and nutmeg. My husband Walter's eyes light up when he sees me tossing this into the skillet. If you've never cooked a huge batch of spinach like this, don't be surprised at how it "disappears." I once had a novice cook in my class who, when he lifted the pan lid, shouted in disbelief, "What happened to my spinach?!" 4 servings

EQUIPMENT: A large, deep skillet with a lid.

2 pounds spinach leaves, stemmed, washed, and spun dry
Fine sea salt
Freshly grated nutmeg

Place the spinach in the skillet, adding a few tablespoons of water to the pan. Cover and cook over high heat until the spinach is completely wilted, 3 to 4 minutes. Drain well in a colander. Serve with a slotted spoon, draining off any remaining liquid. Season with salt and nutmeg. Serve warm.

50 calories per serving ⊛ 1 g fat ⊛ 7 g protein ⊛ 8 g carbohydrates

SPICY SWEET POTATO "FRIES"

"Frites" de Patates Douces

Spicy, golden, wholesome, and delicious, these are a great fall or winter treat. Serve with roasted poultry or as part of a vegetarian buffet. 8 servings

EQUIPMENT: A baking sheet lined with parchment or a silicone mat.

2 pounds sweet potatoes
¼ cup extra-virgin olive oil
2 teaspoons coarse sea salt
1 teaspoon ground cumin
1 teaspoon ground *piment d'Espelette* or dried Anaheim chilies (or ground mild chili pepper)
Fleur de sel

1. Preheat the oven to 500 degrees F.

2. Peel the sweet potatoes and cut into thick fries, ½ inch wide and 3½ inches long. Place the sweet potatoes in a bowl and add the oil, salt, and spices. Carefully toss to evenly coat the potatoes.

3. Arrange the potatoes in a single layer on the baking sheet. Place the baking sheet in the oven and bake—turning so they brown evenly—until the potatoes are crisp and a deep golden brown, 15 to 20 minutes. Remove from the oven, season generously with *fleur de sel,* and serve immediately.

166 calories per serving ❋ 6 g fat ❋ 2 g protein ❋ 28 g carbohydrates

SWISS CHARD LEAF PURÉE WITH BACON LA BEAUGRAVIÈRE

La Purée de Feuilles de Bettes au Bacon de La Beaugravière

For more than twenty-five years, chef Guy Jullien has wooed family, friends, and students at his homey Provençal restaurant, La Beaugravière, in the village of Mondragon. Several years ago he offered this super-simple but totally delicious purée of Swiss chard leaves. He wisely blanches and refreshes the leaves, so they retain their deep green color and tart, tangy flavor. The gentle hint of smokiness from the bacon is a welcome addition. 12 servings

EQUIPMENT: A 10-quart pasta pot fitted with a colander; a food processor or a blender; a medium saucepan; a large skillet.

4 pounds Swiss chard
About ¼ cup Homemade Chicken Stock (page 294)
About ¼ cup light cream
Freshly grated nutmeg
Fine sea salt
¾ cup (2½ ounces) smoked bacon, rind removed, cut into ¼-inch cubes

1.   Wash and drain the Swiss chard, reserving the ribs for another recipe. You should have about 1½ pounds of leaves.

2.   Prepare a large bowl of ice water.

3.   In a 10-quart pasta pot fitted with a colander, bring 8 quarts of water to a rolling boil over high heat. Plunge the leaves into the boiling water and blanch, uncovered, just until softened, 2 to 3 minutes. Drain and plunge the leaves into the bowl of ice water. Once cooled, drain thoroughly.

4.   Transfer the leaves to a food processor or a blender. Add enough chicken stock and cream just to make a smooth, light mixture. Season with nutmeg and salt. Transfer the purée to a medium saucepan. Set aside.

5.   In a large, dry skillet, brown the bacon over moderate heat until crisp and golden, about 5 minutes. With a slotted spoon, transfer the bacon to several layers of paper towel to absorb the fat. Blot the top of the bacon with several layers of paper towel to absorb any additional fat. Set aside.

6.   Stir the bacon into the purée in the saucepan. Taste for seasoning. (The purée can be prepared up to 4 hours in advance and reheated at serving time. Stir the bacon in at the very last minute.) Serve warm.

56 calories per serving ☸ 4 g fat ☸ 3 g protein ☸ 2 g carbohydrates

YANNICK ALLÉNO'S SWISS CHARD RIB GRATIN WITH PINE NUTS AND PARMESAN

Le Gratin de Bettes de Yannick Alléno

Several years ago I spent the morning in the grand kitchens of Paris's Hotel Meurice, where the lean, muscular chef Yannick Alléno had just taken over. Alléno's food has a real style—lots of rounds upon rounds, squares upon squares—and while ingredients are generally soft in texture, there is always a touch of crunch at the end, fulfilling our natural desire for a bit of snap, crackle, and pop on the palate. That morning, I snapped up some home-style recipes to incorporate into my own repertoire, including this winning gratin of Swiss chard ribs: Alléno poached matchstick-sized ribs in chicken stock, layered them in a gratin dish with sprinklings of grated Parmesan, heated the gratin beneath a broiler, then finished it all with miniature cubes of Parmesan, tiny bits of celery leaf and basil leaf, and a shower of well-toasted pine nuts. 12 servings

EQUIPMENT: A small skillet; a large saucepan with a lid; a 2-quart gratin dish.

4 pounds Swiss chard
1 lemon, scrubbed
1/4 cup pine nuts
2 cups Homemade Chicken Stock (page 294)
1 cup freshly grated Parmigiano-Reggiano cheese
1/4 cup celery leaves, minced
1/2 cup 1/4-inch cubes of Parmigiano-Reggiano cheese
1/4 cup fresh basil leaves, cut into chiffonade

1.   Wash and drain the Swiss chard, reserving the leaves for another recipe. You should have about 2 pounds ribs.

2.   Preheat the broiler.

3.   Halve the lemon, squeeze the juice, and add the juice and the lemon halves to a large bowl of cold water. Trim and remove any large, fibrous strings from each rib of chard. Cut the ribs crosswise (against the grain of the rib, much as you would cut celery) into even, thin slices. Drop the slices into the bowl of acidulated water. Set aside.

4.   Place the pine nuts in a small, dry skillet over moderate heat. Toast, shaking the pan regularly until the nuts are fragrant and evenly browned, about 2 minutes. Watch carefully! They can burn quickly. Transfer the nuts to a large plate to cool. Set aside.

5.   Drain the ribs and place in a large saucepan. Cover with chicken stock and cook, covered, over moderate heat until tender, about 10 minutes. With a slotted spoon, transfer the ribs to a gratin dish. Cover with grated cheese. Place under the broiler and cook until the cheese is golden and bubbling, about 5 minutes. Remove from the oven and sprinkle with celery leaves, pine nuts, cubed cheese, and basil. Return to the broiler just until the pine nuts and cheese are browned, 1 to 2 minutes more. Serve immediately.

    ✳c 81 calories per serving ❋ 5 g fat ❋ 7 g protein ❋ 4 g carbohydrates

OVEN-ROASTED CHERRY TOMATOES

Confit de Tomates-Cerises

Come September, I have an overabundance of cherry tomatoes in the garden. This is when I roast them long and slow in a low oven, to help bring out their intense sweetness and dense tomato flavor. These are an integral part of my Eggplant, Tomato, Basil, and Cheese Timbales (page 253). **12 servings**

EQUIPMENT: A baking sheet.

2 pounds fresh cherry tomatoes, rinsed and halved
Fine sea salt
Freshly ground white pepper
Pinch of confectioners' sugar
2 sprigs fresh thyme, stemmed

1.   Preheat the oven to the lowest possible setting, about 200 degrees F.

2.   Arrange the tomato halves, cut side up, side by side on a baking sheet. Sprinkle lightly with salt, pepper, and confectioner's sugar. Scatter the thyme leaves over the tomatoes. Place in the oven and roast until the tomatoes are very soft, about 1 hour. Turn the tomatoes, baste with the juices, and cook until meltingly tender and reduced to about half their size, about 2 hours total. Check the tomatoes from time to time: they should remain moist and soft. Remove from the oven and allow to cool thoroughly.

3.   Transfer the tomatoes to a jar, cover with the cooking juices, cover securely, and refrigerate for up to 1 week. Use in salads, on sandwiches, for pasta, or anywhere you want a rich, pure tomato flavor.

15 calories per serving ⁘ trace of fat ⁘ 1 g protein ⁘ 3 g carbohydrates

PROVENÇAL ROAST TOMATOES WITH LIGHT BASIL PURÉE

Tomates au Four à la Purée de Basilic

This versatile tomato dish shows up often on my summer table. Try making a colorful, flavorful first-course trio that includes these tomatoes, Zucchini Blossoms Stuffed with Goat Cheese and Basil (page 216), and Eggplant, Tomato, Basil, and Cheese Timbales (page 175). 12 servings

EQUIPMENT: A large skillet; a large oval baking dish (about 10 × 16 inches).

3 tablespoons extra-virgin olive oil
12 garden-fresh tomatoes, cored and halved lengthwise (do not peel)
Fine sea salt
1 tablespoon best-quality sherry-wine vinegar
¼ cup mixed minced fresh herbs, such as parsley, basil, and mint
¼ cup Light Basil Purée (page 301)

1. Preheat the oven to 425 degrees F.

2. In a large skillet, heat the oil over moderate heat until hot but not smoking. When hot, place as many tomatoes in the pan as will fit easily, cut side down. (If you crowd the pan, the tomatoes will steam, not sear.) Sear, without moving the tomatoes, until they are dark and almost caramelized, 3 to 4 minutes. With a slotted spatula, transfer the tomatoes, seared side up, to a baking dish large enough to hold them in one layer, overlapping slightly, since they will reduce as they bake. Continue until all the tomatoes are seared. Season the tomatoes lightly with salt. Remove the skillet from the heat. Deglaze the pan with the vinegar. Return the pan to moderate heat, scraping the bottom of the pan to loosen drippings into the liquid. Pour over the tomatoes. Sprinkle with the fresh herbs.

3. Place the baking dish in the center of the oven and bake, uncovered, until the tomatoes are soft, shriveled, and even a bit dark around the edges, about 30 minutes. Place a dollop of basil purée in the center of each tomato. Serve warm or at room temperature.

*c 84 calories per serving * 6 g fat * 1 g protein * 8 g carbohydrates

TOMATO TARTARE

Tomate Tartare

If a dish can win points on visual appeal alone, this tomato tartare gets a ten out of ten. I first sampled a version of this dish as part of a tomato menu at Christian Etienne's in Avignon. Glistening towers of red, yellow, and green tomatoes, chopped and well seasoned, make a quintessential summer dish. 4 servings

EQUIPMENT: A 1½-inch-diameter ring mold or round cutter, at least 1½ inches high (or use a small tomato paste can, with both ends removed).

⅔ pound garden-fresh heirloom red tomatoes
⅔ pound garden-fresh heirloom green tomatoes
⅔ pound garden-fresh heirloom yellow or orange tomatoes
2 shallots, trimmed, peeled, and finely minced
½ cup fresh flat-leaf parsley leaves, finely minced
½ cup fresh basil leaves, finely minced
2 plump, moist garlic cloves, peeled, halved, green germ removed, minced
Fine sea salt
Several tablespoons Classic Vinaigrette (page 296)
2 cups arugula leaves, washed and drained
Small fresh basil leaves for garnish

1.   Rinse, core, and peel the tomatoes. Halve them crosswise. Squeeze the halves to release excess juices and seeds. (The juice and seeds can be added to soups or sauces.) Cut the red tomatoes into ⅛-inch cubes and transfer them to a sieve set over a bowl. Repeat for the green and yellow tomatoes, keeping each color separate. (This can be done up to 2 hours in advance. Keep the tomatoes at room temperature.)

2.   At serving time, season each color of tomato with equal parts of the shallots, parsley, basil, and garlic. Season lightly with salt and a touch of vinaigrette.

3.   Place a mold on a plate. Using a small spoon, spoon the red tomato mixture into the mold. Carefully remove the mold. Repeat with the yellow and the green tomato mixture. Repeat for the remaining 3 plates. In a large bowl, toss the arugula with just enough vinaigrette to coat the leaves. Taste for seasoning. Place a small mound of salad on each plate. Garnish the tomatoes with the basil leaves. Serve immediately.

107 calories per serving * 5 g fat * 4 g protein * 17 g carbohydrates

TOMATO SORBET

Sorbet à la Tomate

This slightly sweet yet tangy tomato sorbet goes well with just about any course. Sometimes I place a small scoop in the center of a bowl of icy gazpacho; at other times I serve it as a predessert in tiny bowls. Whenever it is served, it receives raves. 12 servings

> EQUIPMENT: A food processor or a blender; a food mill fitted with the finest blade; an ice-cream maker.
>
> 1 1/4 pounds garden-fresh heirloom tomatoes
> 2/3 cup sugar
> 1 tablespoon freshly squeezed lemon juice
> 1/2 teaspoon fine sea salt
> Several drops Tabasco sauce

Rinse, core, and quarter the tomatoes. Do not peel. In a food processor or a blender, purée the tomatoes. Set the food mill over a large bowl. Transfer the purée to the food mill. Pass the purée through the food mill into the bowl. Stir in the sugar, lemon juice, 3/4 cup cold water, salt, and Tabasco. Taste for seasoning. Chill thoroughly. Transfer to an ice-cream maker and freeze according to the manufacturer's directions.

52 calories per serving ◦ trace of fat ◦ trace of protein ◦ 13 g carbohydrates

Customs: After the potato, the tomato is the second-most-consumed vegetable in France.

THAI MEDLEY:
SPICY TURNIPS, SQUASH, CARROTS, AND POTATOES

Mélange de Légumes Thaï

I sampled a variation on this dish years ago, during one of my semiannual visits to the Golden Door spa north of San Diego. The dish is full of color and spices and is a warming wintertime treat. Delicious any time of day, it's a great way to get an essential number of varied vegetables together in a single dish. 8 servings

EQUIPMENT: A large, heavy-duty skillet with a lid; a small saucepan.

2 teaspoons extra-virgin olive oil

1 tablespoon grated fresh ginger

2 medium onions, peeled and thinly sliced

1/2 teaspoon fine sea salt

1 1/2 cups 1-inch cubes of butternut squash

2 medium turnips, cut into 1-inch cubes

2 medium carrots, peeled and thinly sliced

4 small yellow-fleshed potatoes (such as Yukon Gold), scrubbed and cut into 1-inch cubes

2 medium zucchini, trimmed and cut into 1-inch cubes

2 tomatoes, cored, halved, seeded, and cut into 1-inch cubes (do not peel)

2 cups Homemade Chicken Stock (page 294)

1 cup canned coconut milk, shaken to blend

1 1/2 tablespoons freshly squeezed lime juice

1/4 cup fresh cilantro leaves

Thai Curry Paste (page 309) to taste

In a large, heavy-duty skillet, combine the oil, ginger, onions, and salt and sweat—cook, covered, over low heat until soft but not browned—for about 3 minutes. Add the vegetables and stock. Cover and simmer until the vegetables are tender but not overcooked, about 20 minutes. Meanwhile, in a small saucepan, reduce the coconut milk by half. Add the coconut milk to the vegetable mixture and simmer gently for 5 minutes. At serving time, add the lime juice and stir to blend. Serve over steamed rice. Garnish with cilantro leaves and curry paste.

175 calories per serving ◦ 11 g fat ◦ 6 g protein ◦ 16 g carbohydrates

ZUCCHINI SPAGHETTI WITH CREAMY LEMON-CHIVE DRESSING

Spaghettis de Courgette

I don't know when and where I first sampled this nonspaghetti spaghetti, but I think it's a brilliant way to trick our minds into thinking we're eating pasta when it's really raw zucchini. I could live on this in the summer months, for the fine texture makes this light and oh-so-digestible. Be sure to follow to the letter the amount of salt: too much and the dish is just too salty, too little and the zucchini will not give off enough of its liquid. 4 servings

EQUIPMENT: A mandoline with a julienne blade.

1 pound small fresh zucchini, rinsed, dried, and trimmed at both ends
1 teaspoon fine sea salt
¼ cup Creamy Lemon-Chive Dressing (page 299)
Fleur de sel

1. Using the julienne blade of a mandoline, slice the zucchini into long julienne strips. Transfer the zucchini to a colander set over a mixing bowl. Toss the zucchini with the salt. Set aside for 15 minutes at room temperature.

2. Gently squeeze the zucchini to extract excess water. Transfer to a bowl and toss with just enough dressing to evenly coat the zucchini. Season with *fleur de sel*. Serve.

37 calories per serving ❊ 2 g fat ❊ 5 g protein ❊ 4 g carbohydrates

ZUCCHINI CARPACCIO WITH AVOCADO, LEMON THYME, AND PISTACHIO OIL

Carpaccio de Courgette et d'Avocat

I love the play of color and texture as the smooth bright green strips of zucchini lie side by side with the equally fine-textured slices of ripe avocado. A touch of brilliant green pistachio oil and a few sprigs of lemon thyme make for an ideal summer first course. 4 servings

EQUIPMENT: A small jar with a lid; a mandoline or a very sharp knife.

1 tablespoon freshly squeezed lemon juice
½ teaspoon fine sea salt
¼ cup best-quality pistachio oil, almond oil, or extra-virgin olive oil
4 small fresh zucchini (each about 4 ounces), rinsed, dried, and trimmed
1 ripe avocado, peeled and very thinly sliced
¼ cup salted pistachio nuts
4 sprigs fresh lemon thyme, with flowers if possible
Zesty Lemon Salt (page 310)

1. In a small jar, combine the lemon juice and salt and stir to blend. Add the oil, cover the jar, and shake to blend.

2. With a mandoline or a very sharp knife, slice the zucchini lengthwise as thinly as possible. Place the slices on a platter and pour the lemon mixture over the zucchini. Tilt the platter back and forth to evenly coat the slices. Cover with plastic wrap and let marinate for at least 30 minutes and up to 1 hour so the zucchini absorbs the sauce and does not dry out.

3. At serving time, carefully arrange the slices of marinated zucchini on individual salad plates, alternating with the avocado slices, slightly overlapping each slice. Sprinkle with the pistachio nuts. Season with thyme and lemon salt. Serve.

237 calories per serving ◦ 22 g fat ◦ 4 g protein ◦ 10 g carbohydrates

ZUCCHINI BLOSSOMS STUFFED WITH
GOAT CHEESE AND BASIL

Fleurs de Courgettes Farcies

Each morning in the summer months, I stroll through my zucchini and pumpkin patch to collect the color-ful golden blossoms that seem to multiply like rabbits. I gather them to steam and coat with tomato sauce, to add to any zucchini gratin that might be on the menu, and to use in this, an all-time favorite, tender blossoms stuffed with a mixture of young fresh goat's milk cheese blended with a touch of basil. 6 servings

EQUIPMENT: A demitasse spoon; a 10½-inch round baking dish.

8 ounces fresh young goat's milk cheese
¼ cup fresh basil leaves, cut into chiffonade
12 zucchini blossoms
Fine sea salt
2 tablespoons Basil Oil (page 312) or extra-virgin olive oil

1. Preheat the oven to 425 degrees F.

2. Place the cheese on a large, flat plate. Sprinkle with the basil and mash with a fork until the mixture is evenly blended.

3. With a sharp knife, carefully cut through one side of a zucchini blossom to slightly open it up. With a demitasse spoon, spoon the cheese into the blossom. Carefully close the blossom and arrange like spokes on a wheel in the baking dish. Repeat for the remaining blossoms. Season lightly with salt. Drizzle with 1 tablespoon of oil. Cover with aluminum foil.

4. Place in the center of the oven and bake until golden, 15 to 20 minutes. Remove from the oven. Drizzle with the remaining tablespoon of oil. Serve immediately.

74 calories per serving ◦ 7 g fat ◦ 2 g protein ◦ 1 g carbohydrates

ZUCCHINI LA PONCHE

Les Courgettes du Domaine de La Ponche

Over the past several years, Domaine de la Ponche has been one of our favorite dinner spots. Outgoing host Jean-Pierre Onimus is ably assisted by his wife, Ruth Spahn, and sister-in-law Madeleine Frauenknecht. Their food is totally simple, often surprising, and always appealing. They served this one night as an amuse-bouche, or quick starter. I like to serve it at home as a first course. 4 servings

EQUIPMENT: A mandoline or a very sharp knife.

4 small zucchini (each about 4 ounces), rinsed, dried, and trimmed
12 thin shavings of Parmigiano-Reggiano cheese
4 teaspoons best-quality balsamic vinegar
1/2 teaspoon *fleur de sel*
Freshly ground black pepper

With a mandoline or very sharp knife, slice the zucchini crosswise into very thin rounds. Arrange the rounds of zucchini, slightly overlapping, on each of 4 dinner plates. Arrange shavings of cheese over the zucchini. Drizzle with vinegar, then sprinkle with the *fleur de sel* and pepper. Let marinate for about 10 minutes before serving as a first course or a vegetable course.

49 calories per serving ✳ 2 g fat ✳ 4 g protein ✳ 4 g carbohydrates

Wine Suggestion
A chilled white from the Viognier grape.

POTATOES

Les Pommes de Terre

◈

POTATO GRATIN FROM THE SAVOY

Gratin Savoyard

Is there anything more French, more welcoming, than a golden potato gratin? This light and wholesome gratin comes bubbling from the oven, always gathering oohs and ahs. I realized a long time ago that if you want to please your guests (especially the men), serve them a potato gratin! 6 servings

EQUIPMENT: A mandoline or a very sharp knife; a small saucepan; a 1½-quart rectangular baking dish.

1¼ pounds firm yellow-fleshed potatoes (such as Yukon Gold)
1 cup Homemade Chicken Stock (page 294)
Butter for the baking dish
1 cup freshly grated Swiss Gruyère cheese
½ teaspoon freshly grated nutmeg
Fine sea salt

1.   Preheat the oven to 425 degrees F.

2.   Peel the potatoes, but do not rinse. The starch on the potatoes makes for a more flavorful gratin. With a mandoline or a very sharp knife, cut the potatoes into very thin slices.

3.   In a small saucepan, warm the stock over low heat.

4.   Lightly butter the baking dish. Carefully arrange half of the potatoes in an overlapping layer in the dish. Sprinkle with half of the cheese and nutmeg and season with salt. Arrange the remaining potatoes in an overlapping layer on top of the cheese. Sprinkle with the remaining cheese and nutmeg and season with salt. Pour the warm stock over all.

5.   Place in the center of the oven and bake until crisp and golden on top, about 1 hour. Serve immediately.

153 calories per serving ◦ 7 g fat ◦ 9 g protein ◦ 13 g carbohydrates

GOLDEN ROASTED POTATOES WITH GRUYÈRE, SMOKED BACON, AND CHIVES

Pommes de Terre au Four

My friend Catherine O'Neill is the greatest potato lover I know. When she walks into a restaurant, the first thing she asks is "What kind of potatoes do you have?" Boiled, roasted, seared, or fried, she loves them all. The first time I prepared this dish, Catherine was invited to inaugurate the creation. Thank goodness, she loved it and asked for seconds. 8 servings

EQUIPMENT: A baking sheet; a large skillet.

4 large (each about 6 ounces) yellow-fleshed potatoes (such as Yukon Gold)
1 teaspoon fine sea salt
1 tablespoon extra-virgin olive oil
2½ ounces smoked bacon, rind removed, cut into ¼-inch cubes (¾ cup)
½ cup freshly grated Swiss Gruyère cheese
Freshly ground black pepper
¼ cup minced fresh chives

1.   Preheat the oven to 425 degrees F.

2.   Scrub the potatoes, but do not peel. Halve them lengthwise. In a large bowl, combine the potatoes, salt, and olive oil. Place the potatoes, cut side down, on a baking sheet. Roast until the potatoes are golden, puffy, and tender when pierced with a fork, about 40 minutes.

3.   While the potatoes roast, cook the bacon: In a large, dry skillet, brown the bacon over moderate heat until crisp and golden, about 5 minutes. With a slotted spoon, transfer the bacon to several layers of paper towel to absorb the fat. Blot the top of the bacon with several layers of paper towel to absorb any additional fat. Set aside.

4.   When the potatoes are golden and tender, remove them from the oven. Turn the potatoes cut side up. Score them lightly, 4 diagonal cuts in 2 directions. Sprinkle with the cheese and bacon. Season generously with pepper. Return to the oven and bake until the cheese is melted, 2 to 3 minutes. Garnish with the chives and additional pepper if desired. Serve warm.

*c 145 calories per serving * 8 g fat * 6 g protein * 12 g carbohydrates

JO AND GEORGE'S POTATO CRISPIES

Les Crisps de Pommes de Terre de Jo et George

What more can you ask of a potato than to arrive on your plate golden, crisp, and glistening? Ever since my friends Johanne Killeen and George Germon shared this recipe with me, it's been a family favorite. 6 servings

EQUIPMENT: A baking sheet; a large saucepan; a meat mallet or a cast-iron skillet.

¼ cup extra-virgin olive oil
2 pounds yellow-fleshed potatoes (such as Yukon Gold), scrubbed
Coarse sea salt

1.   Preheat the oven to 375 degrees F.

2.   Brush the baking sheet with 1 tablespoon of the oil.

3.   Place the potatoes in a large saucepan. Cover with water. Add 1 tablespoon salt. Bring to a boil over high heat and cook until tender, about 20 minutes. Drain the potatoes and dry them on paper towels.

4.   With a meat mallet or a cast-iron skillet, press down on each potato to flatten it. It should be ¼ to ³⁄₈ inch thick. With a spatula, transfer the potatoes to a baking sheet. Drizzle with the remaining oil. Sprinkle lightly with salt.

5.   Place in the center of the oven and bake until golden and crispy, 30 to 40 minutes. Serve immediately.

 169 calories per serving ⊛ 9 g fat ⊛ 2 g protein ⊛ 20 g carbohydrates

---

Folklore: When you taste the first new potato of the year, be sure to make a wish.

POTATOES IN CHICKEN STOCK WITH MINT AND BUTTER

Pommes de Terre au Bouillon de Menthe

Simple, yet out of the ordinary, this golden, refreshing potato dish lets each ingredient star, even the touch of butter used to sear the potatoes in the end. Bathed gently in rich chicken stock, seasoned with a bundle of fresh, fragrant mint, the potatoes are then browned in butter and garnished with another touch of the sweet mint. 8 servings

EQUIPMENT: A large, heavy-duty, flame-proof casserole with a lid.

2 pounds firm yellow-fleshed potatoes (such as Yukon Gold)
1½ quarts Homemade Chicken Stock (page 294)
4 fresh or dried bay leaves
1 bunch of fresh mint leaves
1 tablespoon coarse sea salt
2 tablespoons unsalted butter
¼ cup finely minced fresh mint leaves for garnish
Fleur de sel

1. Scrub the potatoes, but do not peel. Halve them lengthwise. Place them in the casserole. Cover with the stock, the bay leaves, the bunch of mint, and the salt. Bring to a simmer over moderate heat and cook, covered, until cooked through when pierced with the tip of a knife, about 20 minutes. Drain and set aside. Discard the bay leaves and mint. (Strain the stock and reserve for soups or sauces.)

2. In the same casserole, heat the butter over moderate heat until hot but not smoking. Add the potatoes, cut side down, and cook until beautifully browned, about 3 minutes. Garnish with mint and season with *fleur de sel*. Serve immediately.

158 calories per serving ⁎ 5 g fat ⁎ 11 g protein ⁎ 18 g carbohydrates

"Vouloir le beurre et l'argent du beurre." To want to have one's cake and eat it too.

POTATO SALAD WITH SPRING ONIONS, CAPERS, AND MINT

Salade de Pommes de Terre, Sauce Printanière

This simple yet elegant potato salad appears on our table with great frequency. The tangy mustard and caper dressing adds punch and crunch, while the delicate young onions and fresh mint add a springlike dimension.
6 servings

EQUIPMENT: A steamer.

1 pound firm yellow-fleshed potatoes (such as Yukon Gold)
¼ cup extra-virgin olive oil
2 tablespoons freshly squeezed lemon juice
1 tablespoon imported French mustard
3 spring onions (or 6 scallions), trimmed, peeled, and cut into very thin slices
¼ cup capers in vinegar, drained
Fine sea salt
¼ cup fresh mint leaves, cut into chiffonade

1. Scrub the potatoes, but do not peel. Bring 1 quart water to a simmer in the bottom of a steamer. Place the potatoes on the steaming rack. Place the rack over the simmering water, cover, and steam just until the potatoes are fully cooked, about 25 minutes.

2. While the potatoes are cooking, prepare the dressing: In a large salad bowl, combine the oil, lemon juice, and mustard and whisk to blend. Add the onions and capers and toss to blend. Taste for seasoning. Set aside.

3. Once the potatoes are cooked, cut them crosswise into thin slices, tossing the slices directly into the dressing. Do this while the potatoes are still warm so they quickly absorb the dressing. Toss to thoroughly coat the potatoes with the dressing. Add the mint chiffonade and toss again. Taste for seasoning. Serve warm.

139 calories per serving ◦ 9 g fat ◦ 2 g protein ◦ 13 g carbohydrates

"Il se prend pour le premier moutardier du pape!" He thinks he's the first mustard maker to the pope, or He thinks he's the cat's whiskers!

POTATO-CHIVE WAFFLES WITH SMOKED SALMON, CAPERS, AND CRÈME FRAÎCHE

Gaufres de Pommes de Terre au Saumon Fumé

To my mind, this is an ideal Sunday lunch dish, one that is quick and easy, festive, and cries out for a chilled glass of Chenin Blanc, of which my favorite is a golden aged Vouvray. 4 servings

EQUIPMENT: An electric waffle iron; a box grater.

¼ cup finely minced fresh chives

2 large eggs

1 large egg white

1 cup *crème fraîche* or sour cream

½ teaspoon fine sea salt

1 pound firm baking potatoes (such as Russet)

4 slices best-quality smoked salmon

2 tablespoons capers in vinegar, drained

Several fresh fennel or dill fronds for garnish

1. Preheat the waffle iron.

2. In a small bowl, combine the chives, eggs, egg white, ½ cup of the *crème fraîche*, and the salt. Stir to blend.

3. Peel the potatoes, but do not rinse. Using the largest holes of the grater, grate the potatoes onto a large plate. Squeeze the potatoes with your hands to remove as much liquid as possible. Transfer the grated potatoes to the bowl of *crème fraîche* and eggs and stir to blend thoroughly.

4. Using a large spoon, drop half of the batter onto the waffle iron. Cook according to the manufacturer's instructions. Repeat with the remaining batter.

5. To serve, place half a waffle on each of 4 large dinner plates. Drape a slice of smoked salmon on top of the waffle. Sprinkle with capers and arrange a few fennel or dill fronds on top of the salmon. Place a dollop of *crème fraîche* alongside. Serve.

315 calories per serving ◦ 21 g fat ◦ 13 g protein ◦ 20 g carbohydrates

BOULEVARD RASPAIL POTATO GALETTES

Les Galettes de Pommes de Terre du Boulevard Raspail

Whenever I am in Paris on weekends, I awaken with anticipation on Sunday morning, wondering what delights I will discover at the organic market along Boulevard Raspail. Right at the beginning of the market, there's always a stand where they hawk fragrant potato galettes. The cook told my friend Steven Rothfeld—a true potato addict—that on a good day he sold eight hundred potato cakes! At the market, they are consumed out of hand, wrapped in a napkin. At home, they make a nice "side" to a green salad. Eight 5-inch galettes

EQUIPMENT: A steamer; a box grater; a nonstick crêpe pan; a baking sheet.

1 pound firm baking potatoes (such as Russet)
1/2 teaspoon fine sea salt
3 tablespoons extra-virgin olive oil

1. Peel the potatoes, but do not rinse. Bring 1 quart water to a simmer in the bottom of a steamer. Place the potatoes on the steaming rack. Place the rack over the simmering water, cover, and steam just until the potatoes are partially cooked, 12 to 15 minutes. Cut one of the potatoes in half crosswise. If there is a raw central core, steam for 2 or 3 minutes more. Let cool uncovered. The potatoes must be thoroughly cold before you grate them. (This can be done a day in advance. Store the potatoes, whole, wrapped in plastic wrap, in the refrigerator.)

2. Preheat the oven to 250 degrees F.

3. Using the largest holes of the grater, grate the potatoes onto a large plate. Toss with the salt. Set aside.

4. In a nonstick crêpe pan, heat 1 tablespoon of the oil over moderate heat until hot but not smoking. Spread about 1/2 cup of grated potatoes onto the pan, pressing down with the back of a spatula. Sauté until golden, continuing to press the potatoes lightly with a spatula, until the bottom is crusted and brown, 4 to 5 minutes. Flip the galette over and brown the other side, 2 to 3 minutes more. With the spatula, carefully transfer the galette to a baking sheet and keep warm. Repeat for the remaining potatoes. (Once the pan is heated, only a small amount of additional oil is necessary to brown the galettes.)

78 calories per serving ◦ 5 g fat ◦ 1 g protein ◦ 8 g carbohydrates

LEMON-ROASTED POTATOES WITH BAY LEAVES

Pommes de Terre au Four au Citron et au Laurier

Fragrant, gorgeous, delicious, this simple potato dish combines the tang of fresh lemons, the intensity of a fine walnut oil, and the woodsy aroma of bay leaves and oregano. Serve them with Sautéed Quail with Mustard and Fennel (page 113). 8 servings

EQUIPMENT: A large roasting pan.

2 pounds firm yellow-fleshed potatoes (such as Yukon Gold)
2 bay leaves, preferably fresh
2 lemons, preferably organic, scrubbed and cut lengthwise into 8 slices
3 tablespoons freshly squeezed lemon juice
2 tablespoons best-quality walnut oil or extra-virgin olive oil
1 teaspoon coarse sea salt
1 teaspoon dried oregano

1.   Preheat the oven to 425 degrees F.

2.   Scrub the potatoes, but do not peel. Halve them lengthwise. In a large bowl, combine the potatoes, bay leaves, lemons, lemon juice, oil, and salt. Toss to evenly coat the potatoes. Transfer to a roasting pan large enough to hold them in a single layer. Roast until the potatoes are soft and golden, turning the potatoes regularly, about 40 minutes. Remove from the oven and remove and discard the bay leaves. Season generously with oregano, rubbing the herb with your palms to intensify the oregano flavor.

 103 calories per serving ∗ 4 g fat ∗ 2 g protein ∗ 18 g carbohydrates

EGGS, CHEESE, AND FRIENDS

Les Oeufs, les Fromages et leurs Amis

❖

GOAT CHEESE "OREOS" WITH TRUFFLES

Mini-Toasts au Chèvre et à la Truffe

This is the first truffle taste of my January truffle week. I hand the students a pair of these toasty warm, melted goat cheese appetizers as they pass through the doors of our farmhouse. I call them "reverse Oreos," for the slice of fresh black truffles is layered between two slices of goat's milk cheese. During my last class, this was voted "Best Taste of the Week," winning out over some forty different truffle creations. 10 servings (2 "Oreos" per serving)

> EQUIPMENT: A mandoline or a very sharp knife; unflavored dental floss; a 1½-inch round pastry cutter; a baking sheet.
>
> 1 fresh black truffle (about 2 ounces)
> 8 ounces 1½-inch cylinders of semisoft goat's milk cheese
> About 7 slices whole wheat sourdough bread
> 1 tablespoon Truffle Butter (page 314)
> 1 teaspoon Truffle Oil (page 313)
> *Fleur de sel*

1. Preheat the broiler.

2. With a mandoline or a very sharp knife, cut the truffle into very thin slices. You should have about 20 slices. With unflavored dental floss or a very sharp knife, cut the cheese into slices about ¼ inch thick. You should have about 40 rounds of cheese. Begin making 20 "reverse Oreos" by placing a slice of cheese on a plate. Top with a slice of truffle, then a slice of cheese. Set aside.

3. With a 1½-inch round pastry cutter, cut the bread into rounds. You will need 20 rounds of bread. Place the rounds of bread side by side on a baking sheet. Butter them lightly with Truffle Butter. Place them beneath the broiler to toast lightly. Remove the baking sheet from the oven and place the truffle "Oreos" on top of the toast.

4. Return the baking sheet to the oven and broil just until the cheese is soft, just 1 to 2 minutes. Remove from the oven and drizzle lightly with Truffle Oil and *fleur de sel*. Serve immediately.

106 calories per serving ❋ 8 g fat ❋ 6 g protein ❋ 6 g carbohydrates

> *"Ménager la chèvre et le chou."* To sit on the fence.

PARMESAN, PINE NUT, AND TRUFFLE GRATINS

Truffes aux Pignons de Pin et Parmesan

I like to serve these tasty little cheese gratins at the end of a meal, in place of a cheese course, alongside a nice big arugula salad. If truffles are not available, either make the gratins without truffles or substitute fresh mushrooms, lightly sautéed in olive oil. The marriage of Parmigiano-Reggiano and pine nuts is one that is heavenly. 4 servings

EQUIPMENT: A mandoline or a very sharp knife; a small jar with a lid; a small skillet; four ¼-cup ramekins; a baking sheet.

1 fresh black truffle (about 2 ounces) or fresh mushrooms
2 teaspoons extra-virgin olive oil
¼ cup pine nuts
½ cup freshly grated Parmigiano-Reggiano cheese

1. With a mandoline or a very sharp knife, cut the truffles into very thin slices. Place them in the jar, cover with oil, and seal. Marinate at room temperature for at least 15 minutes.

2. Preheat the broiler.

3. Toast the pine nuts: Place the pine nuts in a small, dry skillet over moderate heat. Shake the pan regularly until the nuts are fragrant and evenly toasted, about 2 minutes. Watch carefully! They can burn quickly. Transfer the nuts to a small plate to cool. Set aside.

4. Place the ramekins on a baking sheet. Place a sprinkling of cheese in each of the ramekins. Sprinkle with pine nuts. Top with truffle slices. Top with the remaining cheese.

5. Place under the broiler until the cheese is golden and bubbly, about 1 minute. Serve immediately, with a large green salad alongside.

❦ 140 calories per serving ✸ 10 g fat ✸ 7 g protein ✸ 5 g carbohydrates

Wine Suggestion

The last time I prepared these, we sampled a lovely white Côtes de Provence, Château de Roquefort's Les Genêts, an elegant yet not overly sophisticated wine that's a southern blend of Clairette and Rolle, making for a sunny wine with a fine acidity and plenty of ripe fruit.

"You never know what is enough unless you know what is more than enough."

William Blake, British poet, painter, and mystic (1757–1827)

A Winter Truffle Feast

Goat Cheese "Oreos" with Truffles (page 243)
Parmesan, Pine Nut, and Truffle Gratins
Creamy Polenta with a Poached Egg (page 239)
Truffled Chaource (page 237)

TRUFFLED CHAOURCE

Chaource à la Truffe

Each January I hold an extravagant truffle workshop for my students. For four jam-packed days, we engage in the magic of the Provençal truffle hunt, visit the local truffle cannery, dine in restaurants with incredibly varied truffle menus, and of course manage to sneak truffles into everything from soups to salads to sorbets. Although truffles are found fresh only from November to March, I spend the entire year thinking of new truffle creations. A longtime favorite has been the Saint-Marcellin truffle sandwich: We take a disc of the perfectly aged local cow's milk cheese, cut it in half crosswise, layer the bottom half with slices of fresh truffles, reconstructing the cheese. Then we bake it until the cheese begins to melt. A few years ago Walter came up with this latest creation, using Chaource, a cow's milk cheese from the Champagne region. Cheese and truffles love one another, for the cheese virtually inhales and absorbs the intense truffle aroma, and the fat in the cheese fixes the flavor of the truffle. Chaource—weighing just 1 pound—is a double-cream cheese, with just a touch more butterfat, 50 percent as opposed to 45 percent for most cheeses. It appears as a beautiful white cylinder, with a soft rind and a creamy, delicate interior. It has an exhilarating aroma of mushrooms and fresh walnuts. Chaource cheese can be ordered from fromages.com. Fresh truffles can be ordered from plantin.com. 24 servings

EQUIPMENT: Unflavored dental floss or a very sharp knife.

1 Chaource cheese, chilled
1 fresh black truffle (about 2 ounces), thinly sliced

1. With unflavored dental floss or a very sharp knife, carefully cut the cheese crosswise into 3 even discs. Layer the truffle slices on the 2 bottom slices of cheese, reconstructing the cheese. Wrap securely with plastic wrap. Refrigerate for 24 to 48 hours to flavor the cheese with the truffles.

2. To serve, remove from the refrigerator and bring to room temperature. Unwrap and place on a cheese tray. Serve, cutting into thin wedges.

32 calories per serving ❋ 21 g fat ❋ 2 g protein ❋ 1 g carbohydrates

Wine Suggestion

The best white Châteauneuf-du-Pape you can afford! Favorites include offerings from Château du Beaucastel, Château La Nerthe, and Domaine de la Janasse.

POTATO AND CHIVE OMELET

Omelette de Pommes de Terre et à la Ciboulette

This hearty, golden baked omelet is at home on any table, any time of year. It's put together in a matter of minutes and is a favorite weeknight dinner, accompanied by a tossed green salad. 8 servings

EQUIPMENT: A steamer; a large omelet pan with an oven-proof handle.

1 pound firm baking potatoes (such as Russet), peeled
5 ultra-fresh large eggs
Fine sea salt
⅓ cup finely minced fresh chives, plus 1 tablespoon for garnish
2 tablespoons extra-virgin olive oil
Freshly ground black pepper

1.   Bring 1 quart water to a simmer in the bottom of a vegetable steamer. Place the potatoes on the steaming rack over the simmering water, cover, and steam until the potatoes are partially cooked, 12 to 15 minutes. Cut one of the potatoes in half crosswise: If there is a raw central core, steam for 2 or 3 minutes more. Let cool uncovered. The potatoes must be thoroughly cold before you slice them. (This can be done up to 6 hours in advance. Store the potatoes, wrapped in plastic wrap, in the refrigerator.)

2.   Preheat the broiler.

3.   Break the eggs into a small bowl. Season with salt and stir in the chives. Whisk to blend.

4.   Pour the oil into the omelet pan and swirl to evenly coat the bottom and sides of the pan. Slice the potatoes about ⅛ inch thick and arrange them in overlapping circles in the pan, seasoning each layer lightly with salt. Place the pan over moderately high heat and cook for 4 minutes. Reduce the heat to moderate and pour the eggs over the potatoes. Cook for 3 minutes more. With a spatula, loosen the omelet from the pan, to prevent sticking later on.

5.   Transfer the pan to the broiler, placing it about 5 inches from the heat. Broil until the omelet browns lightly and becomes puffy and firm, about 2 minutes. (Watch carefully: A minute can make the difference between an omelet that is golden brown and one that is overcooked.) Remove the pan from the broiler and let cool in the pan for 2 minutes. Place a large flat plate over the top of the pan and invert the omelet onto it. Season liberally with black pepper and the remaining chives. Serve warm or at room temperature.

111 calories per serving ✳ 7 g fat ✳ 5 g protein ✳ 8 g carbohydrates

CREAMY POLENTA WITH
A POACHED EGG

Crème de Polenta à l'Oeuf Poché

This golden, creamy polenta dish is a wintertime favorite in our house. Although the dish is quick and easy, it takes careful coordination, for the polenta and the poached eggs cook quickly but need to be eaten right away. I make the polenta, arrange it in bowls, and keep the bowls warm in the oven while the eggs poach. 4 servings

EQUIPMENT: A large saucepan; a mandoline or a very sharp knife; 4 warmed shallow soup bowls; a large, deep skillet with a lid; 4 ramekins.

1 quart 1% milk
1 teaspoon fine sea salt
1/2 teaspoon freshly grated nutmeg
3/4 cup instant polenta
1 cup freshly grated Parmigiano-Reggiano cheese
1 tablespoon distilled vinegar
4 ultra-fresh large eggs
Fleur de sel

1.   Preheat the oven to 250 degrees F.

2.   In a large saucepan, bring the milk, salt, and nutmeg to a boil over high heat. (Watch carefully, for milk will boil over quickly.) Add the polenta in a steady stream and, stirring constantly with a wooden spoon, cook until the mixture begins to thicken, about 3 minutes.

3.   Remove from the heat. Stir in the cheese, stirring to blend thoroughly. The polenta should be very creamy and pourable. Divide among 4 warmed soup bowls. Place the bowls in the oven to keep them warm.

4.   In a large, deep skillet, bring 2 inches of water to a boil. Reduce the heat to maintain a simmer and add the vinegar. Break the eggs into ramekins and, one by one, carefully lower the lip of the ramekin 1/2 inch into the water. Let the eggs flow out. Immediately cover the skillet. Poach the eggs until the whites are firm but the yolks are still runny and are covered with a thin, translucent layer of white, about 3 minutes for medium-firm yolks and 5 minutes for firm yolks. With a slotted spoon, carefully lift the eggs from the water, drain, and place on the polenta. Season with *fleur de sel*. Serve immediately.

✤ᶜ 379 calories per serving ✼ 15 g fat ✼ 25 g protein ✼ 35 g carbohydrates

Wine Suggestion

This is the moment to take out your best white Châteauneuf-du-Pape. My favorite is the 100 percent Roussanne from Château de Beaucastel, the white Vieilles Vignes. It's stunning, singular, and loves the company of eggs and polenta.

Words on Wine: "Don't judge a wine; appreciate it and search for what it has to share."

Fabrice Langlois, sommelier at Château de Beaucastel in Châteauneuf-du-Pape

SAFFRON, PEAR, AND PRUNE COMPOTE FOR CHEESE

Compote de Poires et Pruneaux au Safran

Over the past few years, this has been one of the most popular recipes in my cooking school. We have cheese at the end of most meals, and I like to expand the pleasure by offering a fruity or nutty accompaniment. This sweet-and-sour compote is a winner: rich with the haunting aroma and flavor of saffron and sweet with the addition of pears, prunes, and a touch of honey. 16 servings

EQUIPMENT: A large saucepan.

Pinch of saffron threads
½ cup best-quality sherry-wine vinegar
1 cup heather honey
8 ounces (about 20) prunes, pitted
3 firm pears, peeled, halved, cored, and cut lengthwise into sixteenths

1.   Place the saffron threads in a small bowl and cover with 1 tablespoon hottest tap water. Set aside.

2.   In a large saucepan, combine the vinegar and honey. Cook over low heat until the honey has melted, about 3 minutes. Add the prunes and the pears and simmer until the fruit is soft, about 15 minutes. Stir in the saffron and saffron liquid. Refrigerate, covered. Serve slightly chilled, with the cheese course. The relish can be stored, covered and refrigerated, for up to 6 weeks.

*c 113 calories per serving ⁂ trace of fat ⁂ trace of protein ⁂ 30 g carbohydrates

FENNEL AND FIG SALAMI FOR BLUE CHEESE

Salami de Figues aux Graines de Fenouil

Guests love these thin, flavorful slices of fig and fennel, a sweet accompaniment to a platter of blue cheeses. Why not do an all-blue platter, including the delicate cow's milk Fourme d'Ambert and Bleu des Causses, along with the pungent sheep's milk Roquefort? 3 logs, 12 slices per log

EQUIPMENT: A food processor or a blender.

24 dried figs (about 2 cups)
2 tablespoons sweet wine such as a red *Vin Doux Naturel*
1 tablespoon fennel seeds

In a food processor or a blender, process the figs and wine until the mixture is a coarse purée and forms a soft ball. Transfer the mixture to a work surface and knead in the fennel seeds. Form the mixture into three 4-inch logs, each about 1 inch in diameter. Wrap the logs loosely in foil and let stand in a cool, dry place for 3 to 4 days to dry slightly. Once dried, wrap tightly in foil and refrigerate for up to 2 weeks. To serve, cut into very thin slices and serve with blue cheese and toasted walnuts.

30 calories per slice ⁕ trace of fat ⁕ trace of protein ⁕ 8 g carbohydrates

Wine Suggestion

I serve these little treats with a tiny glass of the sweet, fortified wine known as a Vin Doux Naturel. The wine is fortified with alcohol so the sweetness is "natural." One of the best comes from the village of Rasteau in Provence, where winemakers André and Frédéric Romero of Domaine la Soumade make an astonishing red, one that's earthy, smoky, and made for curling up with a snack and book by the winter's fire.

FRESH FIGS ON ROSEMARY SKEWERS

Brochettes de Figues au Romarin

Figs and rosemary are great partners. The haunting, woodsy aromas of each make a lovely pair, with flavors accentuated when heated over an open fire. Serve a branch of these with the cheese course, as a salad accompaniment, or with slices of good Spanish ham. (If you do not have good, firm fresh rosemary branches, use regular metal or wooden skewers, soaking wooden ones in water for 30 minutes before using.) 8 servings

EQUIPMENT: A pastry brush.

8 thick, firm branches fresh rosemary, each about 6 inches long
8 large ripe, firm figs, any variety, stems trimmed, halved lengthwise
½ cup honey
2 tablespoons freshly squeezed lemon juice
Freshly ground black pepper

1.   Start a charcoal or gas grill or preheat a broiler; the fire should be moderately hot and the rack about 4 inches from the heat source.

2.   Strip the leaves from all but the top inch of each of the rosemary branches. Reserve about 1 tablespoon of the leaves and mince them. Place the stems in a bowl and add cold water to cover. Soak for 30 minutes. Drain the stems and blot them dry.

3.   Skewer 2 fig halves lengthwise on each rosemary stem. Arrange the skewers, figs cut sides up, on a plate. In a small bowl, combine the honey and lemon juice. Brush the cut side of the figs with the honey mixture.

4.   Grill or broil the figs until they are lightly browned and softened, 1 to 2 minutes per side. Sprinkle evenly with the rest of the rosemary leaves and some black pepper. Serve, on skewers, while still warm.

113 calories per serving ❀ trace of fat ❀ trace of protein ❀ 30 g carbohydrates

Folklore: Always add rosemary to a dish to help improve your memory.

BREADS

Les Pains

◆

DATE AND WALNUT BREAD

Pain aux Dattes et aux Noix

This bread is a lightened, updated bread from my childhood. My mother's repertoire included all sorts of dates and figs, and I have always loved the dense chewiness of the two. Walnuts are one of the most versatile ingredients, playing a starring role in so many dishes, from sweet to savory. This dense bread is always found on our table come time for the cheese course. It's a good make-ahead bread, since it stores well. 1 loaf, 24 slices

EQUIPMENT: A nonstick 1-quart rectangular bread pan.

1 teaspoon best-quality walnut oil
2 cups dates (about 18; 12 ounces), pitted and cubed
1 cup walnut halves, coarsely chopped
½ teaspoon baking soda
½ teaspoon fine sea salt
½ cup honey
¾ cup hottest possible tap water
2 large eggs, lightly beaten
1 teaspoon vanilla extract
1½ cups unbleached all-purpose flour

1.   Preheat the oven to 375 degrees F. Coat the pan with the walnut oil. Set aside.

2.   In a large bowl, combine the dates, walnuts, baking soda, salt, and honey. Add the hot water and stir to blend. Add the eggs and vanilla extract to the date mixture and stir to blend thoroughly and evenly. Slowly add the flour, stirring to blend thoroughly. The batter will be fairly thick.

3.   Pour the batter into the bread pan, evening out the top with the back of a spatula. Place the pan in the center of the oven and bake until a toothpick inserted into the center of the bread comes out clean, 40 to 50 minutes.

4.   Remove the pan from the oven. Turn the loaf out and place it on a rack to cool. Do not slice the bread for at least 1 hour, for it will continue to bake as it cools. The bread can be stored for up to three days, tightly wrapped in plastic. Serve in very thin slices.

123 calories per slice ◦ 5 g fat ◦ 3 g protein ◦ 18 g carbohydrates

QUICK WALNUT BREAD

Pain aux Noix

This is actually a quick bread made with yeast. It demands no kneading or extra rising, and the result is a dense, flavorful bread that I slice very thinly, toast, and serve with the cheese course. Toasting the walnuts makes a world of difference in flavor! 2 loaves, 18 slices each

EQUIPMENT: 2 nonstick 1-quart rectangular bread pans; a large skillet.

2 teaspoons best-quality walnut oil
2 cups walnut halves
2 envelopes (1½ tablespoons) active dry yeast
½ cup light brown sugar, lightly packed
1¼ cups lukewarm 1% milk
2 large eggs, lightly beaten
2½ cups bread flour
2 teaspoons fine sea salt

1. Preheat the oven to 425 degrees F. Coat each pan with 1 teaspoon of the oil. Set aside.

2. In a large, dry skillet, toast the walnuts over moderate heat, stirring frequently, until golden and fragrant, about 5 minutes. Transfer to a plate to cool.

3. In a large bowl, combine the yeast, brown sugar, and warm milk and stir to blend. Cover and set aside until the mixture is bubbly, about 15 minutes. Stir in the eggs, flour, and salt, mixing until all of the flour has been absorbed. Stir in the walnuts, being sure to distribute them evenly throughout the dough.

4. Spoon the dough—dividing it evenly—into the two bread pans. Cover with a clean cloth and let rise until doubled in bulk, about 1 hour.

5. Place the bread pans in the center of the oven and bake until the bread is firm and golden and a toothpick inserted into the center of the loaves comes out clean, about 1 hour.

6. Remove the bread pans from the oven and let the bread cool for 10 minutes. Remove the bread from the pans and transfer the loaves to a rack, laying them on their side to cool. Serve toasted, with cheese. The bread can be stored for up to three days, tightly wrapped in plastic. Serve in very thin slices.

96 calories per slice ❀ 4 g fat ❀ 4 g protein ❀ 11 g carbohydrates

ROSEMARY-SCENTED WHOLE WHEAT BRIOCHE

Brioche Complète au Romarin

Making brioche fills me with a great sense of satisfaction. This recipe is quite foolproof and always makes two gorgeous golden loaves. I have altered my traditional recipe here, adding a touch of whole wheat flour and minced rosemary. During our truffle week in Provence, we serve this with cow's milk Fourme d'Ambert cheese and sweet cherries in cherry eau-de-vie. 2 loaves, 22 slices each

EQUIPMENT: A heavy-duty electric mixer fitted with a whisk; two nonstick 1-quart rectangular bread pans; a pastry brush; a scissors; an instant-read thermometer.

The Sponge
1/3 cup warm whole milk
1 envelope (2 1/4 teaspoons) active dry yeast
1 teaspoon sugar
2 cups unbleached all-purpose flour
1 large egg, lightly beaten

The Dough
1/3 cup sugar
1 teaspoon fine sea salt
4 large eggs, lightly beaten
About 1 1/2 cups whole wheat flour
12 tablespoons (1 1/2 sticks) unsalted butter, at room temperature
1 tablespoon minced fresh rosemary
Butter for the bread pans
1 large egg, beaten with 1 tablespoon cold water

1.   In the bowl of a heavy-duty mixer fitted with a dough hook, combine the milk, yeast, and sugar and mix to blend. Let stand until foamy, about 5 minutes. Stir in 1 cup of the flour and the egg and mix to blend. The sponge will be sticky and fairly dry. Sprinkle with the remaining 1 cup flour to cover the sponge. Set aside to rest, uncovered, for 30 to 40 minutes. The sponge should erupt slightly, cracking the flour.

2.   Add the sugar, salt, eggs, and 1 cup of the whole wheat flour to the sponge. With the dough hook attached, mix at low speed for 1 or 2 minutes, just until the ingredients come together. Still mixing, sprinkle in ½ cup additional flour. When the flour is incorporated, increase the mixer speed to medium and beat for 15 minutes, scraping down the hook and bowl as needed.

3.   Incorporate the butter into the dough: The butter should be the same consistency as the dough. To prepare the butter, place the butter on a flat work surface and, with a dough scraper, smear it bit by bit across the surface. When it is ready, the butter should be smooth, soft, and still cool—not warm, oily, or greasy.

4.   With the mixer on medium-low, add the butter a few tablespoons at a time, along with the rosemary. When all of the butter has been added, increase the mixer speed to medium-high for 1 minute, then reduce the speed to medium and beat the dough for 5 minutes. The dough will be soft and sticky.

First rise: Cover the bowl tightly with plastic wrap. Let rise at room temperature until doubled in bulk, 2 to 2½ hours.

Second rise and chilling: Punch down the dough. Cover the bowl tightly with plastic wrap and refrigerate the dough overnight, or for at least 4 to 6 hours, during which time it will continue to rise and may double in size again.

After the second rise, the dough is ready to use. If you are not going to use the dough after the second rise, deflate it, wrap it airtight, and store in the freezer. The dough can remain frozen for up to 1 month. Thaw the dough, still wrapped, in the refrigerator overnight and use it directly from the refrigerator.

To Make Two Rectangular Loaves

1 recipe brioche dough, chilled

1.   Butter the bread pans. Divide the dough into 12 equal pieces, each weighing about 2½ ounces. Roll each piece of dough tightly into a ball and place 6 pieces side by side in each of the buttered bread pans. Cover the pans with a clean cloth and let rise until doubled in bulk, about 1 to 1½ hours.

2.   Preheat the oven to 375 degrees F.

3.   With a pastry brush, lightly brush the brioche with the egg wash. Working quickly, use the tips of a pair of sharp scissors to snip several crosses along the top of the dough. (This will help the brioche

rise evenly as it bakes.) Place in the center of the oven and bake until deeply golden and an instant-read thermometer plunged into the center of the bread reads 200 degrees F., 30 to 35 minutes. Remove from the oven and place on a rack to cool. Turn out once cooled.

Note: The brioche is best eaten the day it is baked. It can be stored for a day or two, tightly wrapped. To freeze, wrap tightly and store for up to one month. Thaw, still wrapped, at room temperature.

✴c 79 calories per slice ✲ 4 g fat ✲ 2 g protein ✲ 9 g carbohydrates

"Etre bon comme du bon pain." To have a heart of gold.

PUMPKIN BREAD WITH TOASTED PUMPKIN SEEDS

Cake au Potiron et ses Graines Grillées

My two modest pumpkin patches yield more pumpkins than I can consume in a season, as well as an almost daily crop of squash blossoms for stuffing or folding into vegetable dishes. When I have time, I roast the squash, purée it, and freeze the purée in small containers so I always have squash on hand. This bread has an exotic, almost Asian quality, even though it is little more than standard bread dough with the pumpkin purée and seeds added. If you have access to top-quality pistachio oil, use it here in place of olive oil. This is particularly delicious when toasted and served warm. 2 loaves, 12 slices each

EQUIPMENT: A heavy-duty electric mixer fitted with a dough hook; a pastry scraper; 2 nonstick 1-quart rectangular bread pans; a razor blade; an instant-read thermometer.

1 teaspoon active dry yeast

1 teaspoon sugar

1 ⅓ cups lukewarm water

1 tablespoon extra-virgin olive oil or top-quality pistachio oil

2 teaspoons fine sea salt

½ cup Pumpkin Purée (page 62)

½ cup Toasted, Seasoned Pumpkin Seeds (page 2)

About 4½ cups (1¼ pounds) bread flour

1. In the bowl of a heavy-duty electric mixer fitted with a dough hook, combine the yeast, sugar, and lukewarm water and mix to blend. Let stand until foamy, about 5 minutes. Stir in the oil and the salt.

2. Add the pumpkin purée, the pumpkin seeds, and the flour, a bit at a time, mixing at medium-low speed until most of the flour has been absorbed and the dough forms a ball. Continue to mix at medium-low speed until soft and satiny but still firm, 4 to 5 minutes, adding flour to keep the dough from sticking.

3. Cover the bowl tightly with plastic wrap and place in the refrigerator. Let the dough rise until doubled or tripled in bulk, 8 to 12 hours.

4. Remove the dough from the refrigerator. Punch down the dough, cover securely with plastic wrap, and let rise until doubled in bulk, about 1 hour. Punch down the dough and let rise again until doubled in bulk, about 1 hour.

5.   Punch down again. Divide the dough in half. Form each half into a tight rectangle. Place each half in a nonstick 1-quart rectangular bread pan. Cover with a clean cloth and let rise until doubled in bulk, about 1 hour.

6.   Preheat the oven to 425 degrees F.

7.   With a razor blade, slash the top of the dough several times so it can expand regularly during baking. Place the bread pans on the bottom shelf of the oven. Once the bread is lightly browned and nicely risen— about 15 minutes—reduce the heat to 375 degrees F. Rotate the loaf so that it browns evenly. Bake until the crust is firm and golden brown and the bread sounds hollow when tapped on the bottom, about 40 minutes more, for a total baking time of 55 minutes, or until an instant-read thermometer plunged into the center of the bread reads 200 degrees F. Remove the pans from the oven. Turn the loaves out and place on a rack to cool. Do not slice the bread for at least 1 hour, for it will continue to bake as it cools. The bread can be stored for up to three days, tightly wrapped in plastic. Serve in very thin slices.

❧ 107 calories per slice ✳ 1 g fat ✳ 3 g protein ✳ 20 g carbohydrates

"Oter à quelqu'un le pain de la bouche." To deprive someone of his means of existence.

TOMATO-QUINOA BREAD

Pain de Quinoa à la Tomate

This summery tomato-quinoa bread is fine in texture, tinged with a sunny orange hue, and bursting with warm-weather energy. The quinoa grains add a nice touch of crunch and improve its healthy glow. It's hard to beat the flavors of this bread, slathered with mayonnaise, topped with crisp bacon and slices of garden-fresh tomato. It's often present at my vegetable buffets, cut into thin, elegant slices. 1 loaf, 12 slices

EQUIPMENT: A heavy-duty electric mixer fitted with a dough hook; a pastry scraper; a nonstick 1-quart rectangular bread pan; a razor blade or a sharp knife; an instant-read thermometer.

1 teaspoon active dry yeast

1 teaspoon sugar

⅓ cup lukewarm water

1 tablespoon extra-virgin olive oil

2 teaspoons fine sea salt

1 cup seasoned vegetable juice (such as V-8)

½ cup quinoa

About 3¾ cups (1 pound) bread flour

1.   In the bowl of a heavy-duty electric mixer fitted with a dough hook, combine the yeast, sugar, and lukewarm water and mix to blend. Let stand until foamy, about 5 minutes. Stir in the oil, salt, juice, and quinoa.

2.   Add the flour a bit at a time, mixing at medium-low speed until most of the flour has been absorbed and the dough forms a ball. Continue to mix at medium-low speed until soft and satiny but still firm, 4 to 5 minutes, adding flour to keep the dough from sticking.

3.   Cover the bowl tightly with plastic wrap and place in the refrigerator. Let the dough rise in the refrigerator until doubled or tripled in bulk, 8 to 12 hours. (The dough can be kept for two days in the refrigerator. Simply punch it down as it doubles or triples.)

4.   At least 40 minutes before baking the bread, preheat the oven to 450 degrees F.

5.   Remove the dough from the refrigerator. Punch down the dough and form it into a ball again. Cover the bowl securely with plastic wrap. Let the dough rise until doubled in bulk, about 1 hour.

6.   Punch down the dough again. Form the dough into a tight rectangle. Place the dough in a nonstick 1-quart rectangular bread pan. Cover with a clean cloth and let rise until doubled in bulk, about 1 hour.

7.   With a razor blade or a sharp knife, slash the top of the dough several times so it can expand regularly during baking. Place the oven rack in the center of the oven. Place the bread pan in the center of the rack. Bake until the crust is firm and golden brown and the bread sounds hollow when tapped on the bottom, about 45 minutes, or until an instant-read thermometer plunged into the center of the bread reads 200 degrees F. Remove the pan from the oven. Turn the loaf out and place it on a rack to cool. Do not slice the bread for at least 1 hour, for it will continue to bake as it cools. The bread can be stored for up to three days, tightly wrapped in plastic. Serve in very thin slices.

❧ 179 calories per slice ❋ 2 g fat ❋ 6 g protein ❋ 34 g carbohydrates

---

"Faute de grives, on mange des merles." If we don't have thrush, we'll eat blackbirds, or Half a loaf is better than none.

Folklore: Make a cross over a loaf of bread before you slice it to chase away the devil.

JALAPEÑO-POLENTA BREAD

Pain à la Polenta Epicée

Here's a golden, crusty polenta bread with a kick! I am a bona fide jalapeño lover (I have hot peppers for breakfast every morning, with light cheese and crackers). This bread goes with everything, and in the summer months it can take the place of polenta in a main dish, served with tomato sauce or a lusty batch of Red Peppers, Tomatoes, Onions, Cumin, and Espelette Pepper (page 200). 12 servings

EQUIPMENT: A 10-inch round baking dish.

1 teaspoon extra-virgin olive oil for the dish
1¼ cups instant polenta
½ teaspoon baking soda
¾ teaspoon fine sea salt
1 large egg, lightly beaten
1 cup buttermilk, shaken to blend
¼ cup canned jalapeño pepper slices, drained
½ cup freshly grated Parmigiano-Reggiano cheese

1.   Preheat the oven to 425 degrees F. Oil the dish and set aside.

2.   In a medium bowl, combine the polenta, baking soda, and salt and stir to blend. In another bowl, combine the egg, the buttermilk, and the peppers and whisk lightly to blend. Combine the polenta mixture with the egg mixture and stir until well combined.

3.   Pour the batter into the prepared baking dish. Sprinkle with the cheese. Place the dish in the center of the oven and bake until firm and a cake tester inserted in the center comes out clean, about 15 minutes. Let sit for 5 minutes. Cut into wedges and serve warm or at room temperature.

87 calories per serving ❋ 2 g fat ❋ 4 g protein ❋ 13 g carbohydrates

"Avoir du pain sur la planche!" To have one's work cut out.

QUICK WHOLE WHEAT PIZZA WITH ARTICHOKES, CAPERS, AND FRESH TOMATOES

Pizza de Blé Complet aux Artichauts, Câpres et Tomates

At our house, pizza is on the menu on a regular basis. Like many people, we can't ever get enough of it. I adore this quick, wholesome dough that can be prepared in a matter of minutes. In fact I keep "pizza kits" in my cupboard, zippered bags filled with the premeasured flours, salt, and sugar. Come dinnertime, I just add yeast, water, and oil, and by the time the oven is heated, the pizza is ready to bake. I prefer my pizza toppings to be limited so that you can actually taste each ingredient: favorites here include a spicy homemade tomato sauce, mozzarella or *scamorza* cheese, capers, artichokes, and fresh tomatoes. Two 12-inch pizzas, 8 slices each

EQUIPMENT: A pizza stone; a food processor; a rolling pin; a wooden pizza peel or a rimless baking sheet; a metal pizza peel or a large metal spatula.

¾ cup whole wheat flour
¾ cup unbleached all-purpose flour
1 envelope (2¼ teaspoons) quick-rising yeast
¾ teaspoon fine sea salt
¼ teaspoon sugar
⅔ cup lukewarm water
2 teaspoons extra-virgin olive oil
Coarse cornmeal for the peel
1½ cups Chunky Fresh Tomato Sauce (page 305)
10 canned artichoke hearts, drained and thinly sliced
¼ cup capers in vinegar, drained
10 ounces mozzarella or *scamorza* cheese, broken into bite-sized pieces
4 small fresh tomatoes, cored and cubed
Hot red pepper flakes to taste

1. Place a pizza stone on the bottom rack of the oven. Preheat the oven to 500 degrees F.

2. In a food processor, combine the whole wheat flour, all-purpose flour, yeast, salt, and sugar and pulse to mix. In a measuring cup, combine the lukewarm water and the oil. With the motor running, gradually add enough of the warm liquid until the mixture forms a ball. The dough should be soft. If it is dry, add

1 to 2 tablespoons of water and process to form a ball. If it is sticky, add 1 to 2 tablespoons of flour and process until it forms a ball. Transfer to a clean surface and knead by hand for 1 minute. Cover with a cloth and let rest for 10 minutes before rolling. (The dough can be kept in an airtight container for two to three days. Simply punch it down as it doubles or triples.) Divide the dough in half. Shape each piece into a ball. On a generously floured work surface, roll each portion of the dough into a 12-inch round.

3.   Sprinkle a wooden pizza peel (or a rimless baking sheet) with coarse cornmeal and place a round of dough on the peel or baking sheet. Working quickly to keep the dough from sticking, assemble the pizza: Brush the dough with half of the tomato sauce, then dot with half of the artichokes, half of the capers, half of the cheese, and half of the fresh tomatoes. Season to taste with hot pepper flakes.

4.   Slide the pizza off the peel and onto the baking stone or place the baking sheet on a rack in the oven. Bake until the dough is crisp and golden and the top bubbly, about 10 minutes. With a metal pizza peel (or large metal spatula), remove the pizza from the oven. Transfer to a cutting board and cut into 8 wedges. Serve immediately, passing a shaker of red pepper flakes for seasoning. Repeat with the second round of dough and the remaining toppings.

✤c 144 calories per slice ❋ 5 g fat ❋ 8 g protein ❋ 19 g carbohydrates

Wine Suggestion

I like a wine from the sunny south of France with pizza. Why not one of the bold, racy reds from Provence? A favorite from my wine cellar is Château Roquefort's Côtes de Provence Les Mûres, a hearty blend of Grenache, Syrah, Cinsault, and Carignan, a spicy wine that matches the energy of a well-seasoned pizza.

"Long comme un jour sans pain." Long as a day without bread.

PARSLEY, MINT, LEMON, AND ORANGE FLATBREAD

Pain Arabe aux Parfums d'Agrumes

Colorful, tangy, and crispy, this savory flatbread finds a home at many meals. It is delicious as an appetizer, served with a series of spreads or dips, as a simple bread accompaniment to any meal, or embellished with cubes of cheese and turned into an instant meal. 8 servings

EQUIPMENT: A food processor or a blender.

1 cup fresh parsley leaves
1 cup fresh mint leaves
Grated zest of 2 lemons, preferably organic
Grated zest of 2 oranges, preferably organic
3 tablespoons extra-virgin olive oil
4 whole wheat pita breads (each about 3 ounces)
Fleur de sel

1.   Preheat the oven to 450 degrees F.

2.   In a food processor or a blender, mince the parsley and mint leaves.

3.   In a small bowl, combine the parsley, mint, lemon and orange zests, and 2 tablespoons of the oil. Stir to blend. Brush the mixture onto the pita breads, going all the way to the edges. Place in the center of the oven and bake until golden and firm, about 10 minutes. Out of the oven, drizzle with the remaining oil and season with *fleur de sel*. To serve, cut each pita in half.

103 calories per serving ⊛ 1 g fat ⊛ 4 g protein ⊛ 21 g carbohydrates

Variation: To make a meal out of this flatbread, simply dot the dressed flatbread with cubes of goat's milk cheese or feta cheese—3 to 4 ounces—and bake. It makes a lovely quick lunch accompanied by a tossed green salad.

> *"Ça se vend comme des petits pains!"* It sells like hotcakes!

LEBANESE FLATBREAD WITH FETA AND MINT

Pain Arabe à la Feta et à la Menthe

On Thursdays and Saturdays in Paris I love to make a ritualistic visit to the Avenue de Breteuil market in the shadow of the Eiffel Tower. I always begin at one end, working my way past the exquisite vegetable stands, the home-grown-poultry shop, my apple lady, and on around, up and down the aisles, all the while anticipating the treat that comes at the very end, a tangy Lebanese flatbread laden with creamy feta cheese and a healthy hit of fresh mint. I make my own version with traditional pizza dough and often serve it in wedges, like a pizza, as a warming appetizer. 18 appetizer servings

EQUIPMENT: A heavy-duty electric mixer fitted with a dough hook; a food processor or a blender; a rolling pin; a nonstick baking sheet.

The Bread Dough
½ teaspoon active dry yeast
½ cup lukewarm water
½ teaspoon fine sea salt
About 2 cups bread flour

The Feta-Mint Topping
8 ounces feta cheese
½ cup low-fat cottage cheese
20 fresh mint leaves, cut into chiffonade

Cornmeal for dusting the baking sheets

1.   In the bowl of a heavy-duty electric mixer fitted with a dough hook, combine the yeast and lukewarm water and mix to blend. Let stand until foamy, about 5 minutes. Stir in the salt.

2.   Add the flour all at once, mixing at medium speed until most of the flour has been absorbed and the dough forms a ball. Continue to mix until soft and satiny but still firm, 2 to 3 minutes, adding flour as necessary to keep the dough from sticking. Transfer the ball of dough to a clean work surface and knead by hand for 1 minute. The dough should be smooth and should spring back when you indent it with your fingertip.

3. Place the dough in a large bowl and cover it tightly with plastic wrap. Place in the refrigerator. Let the dough rise until doubled or tripled in bulk, 8 to 12 hours. (The dough can be kept for up to two days in the refrigerator. Simply punch down the dough as it doubles or triples.)

4. At baking time, preheat the oven to 500 degrees F.

5. In a food processor or a blender, combine the feta cheese, cottage cheese, and mint leaves. Process until smooth. Set aside.

6. Divide the dough into 3 even portions. Roll each into a ball and let the dough relax for 15 minutes. Roll each ball of dough into a 6-inch round. The dough should be quite thin.

7. Place the rolled-out dough on a baking sheet dusted with cornmeal. With a spatula, spread the feta-mint mixture on top of the dough, working it all the way to the edge. Place the baking sheets in the oven and bake until crisp and brown, about 5 minutes. Remove the bread from the oven and cut into 6 wedges. Eat while still warm.

❧ 129 calories per serving ❀ 3 g fat ❀ 9 g protein ❀ 16 g carbohydrates

"Faire passer à quelqu'un le goût du pain!" To teach someone a lesson he won't forget!

LEMON AND ROSEMARY FLATBREAD

Fougasse au Citron et au Romarin

Here the faint tang of lemon and the rustic, resinous rosemary team up for an unusual flatbread. The first time I made this, my husband, Walter, exclaimed: "Just add sugar, and you've got dessert." Once it's baked, I also like to slice this paper-thin on an electric slicer, then rebake it in the oven, making for lean and crispy toasts to use at appetizer time with all manner of spreads and dips. *Fougasse* is a flatbread from Provence, similar to Italian focaccia. 1 bread, 24 thin slices

EQUIPMENT: A heavy-duty electric mixer fitted with a dough hook; a pastry scraper; a rolling pin; a baking sheet.

1 teaspoon active dry yeast
1 teaspoon sugar
1⅓ cups lukewarm water
1 tablespoon extra-virgin olive oil
2 teaspoons fine sea salt
Zest of 1 lemon, preferably organic
¼ cup finely minced fresh rosemary
About 3¾ cups (1 pound) bread flour

The Topping
1 tablespoon extra-virgin olive oil
About 2 teaspoons coarse sea salt
¼ cup coarsely chopped fresh rosemary

1.   In the bowl of a heavy-duty electric mixer fitted with a dough hook, combine the yeast, sugar, and lukewarm water and mix to blend. Let stand until foamy, about 5 minutes. Stir in the oil and the salt.

2.   Add the lemon zest, the rosemary, and the flour a bit at a time, mixing at medium-low speed until most of the flour has been absorbed and the dough forms a ball. Continue to mix at medium-low speed until soft and satiny but still firm, 4 to 5 minutes, adding flour to keep the dough from sticking.

3.   Cover the bowl tightly with plastic wrap and place in the refrigerator. Let the dough rise in the refrigerator until doubled or tripled in bulk, 8 to 12 hours. (The dough can be kept for two to three days in the refrigerator. Simply punch it down as it doubles or triples.)

4.   At least 40 minutes before placing the dough in the oven, preheat the oven to 450 degrees F.

5.   Punch down the prepared dough. On a lightly floured surface, roll or simply stretch the dough into a neatly formed rectangle measuring about 10 by 15 inches. Carefully transfer the dough to the baking sheet. Prick the dough all over with a fork. Drizzle with the oil. Sprinkle with the coarse salt and rosemary.

6.   Place the baking sheet in the oven and bake until the bread is firm and golden, 20 to 25 minutes. Remove from the oven and let cool about 10 minutes before serving. The bread can be eaten warm or at room temperature.

   ❧ 76 calories per slice ✳ 1 g fat ✳ 2 g protein ✳ 15 g carbohydrates

DESSERTS

Les Desserts

◈

ROSEMARY-APPLE-CRANBERRY GALETTE

Galette Fine aux Pommes, Airelles et Romarin

This thin-crust galette is a showstopper. The tender whole wheat crust is rolled paper-thin, topped with delicate slices of baking apple, and showered with a vibrant mix of minced rosemary, dried cranberries, sugar, and cinnamon. 12 servings

EQUIPMENT: An apple corer; a mandoline, an electric slicer, or a very sharp knife; a pastry brush.

2 tablespoons minced rosemary
1 teaspoon ground cinnamon
1 teaspoon sugar
½ cup dried cranberries
1 large baking apple (Newton Pippin, Fuji, Criterion, Macoun, Jonagold, or Northern Spy)
2 tablespoons apricot jam, melted
Buttermilk Sorbet (page 271)
One 4 × 13-inch unbaked Light, Flaky Whole Wheat Pastry sheet (page 270) on a baking sheet

1. Preheat the oven to 425 degrees F.

2. In a small bowl, combine 1 tablespoon of the rosemary, the cinnamon, sugar, and cranberries. Toss to blend. Set aside.

3. Trim and discard a very thin slice of apple at both the stem and bottom ends. (This makes the apple easier to peel and creates more uniform slices.) Peel and core the apple. Using a mandoline, an electric slicer, or a very sharp knife, slice the apples crosswise into paper-thin rings.

4. Arrange the apple rings on the pastry shell: Beginning on the outside edge of a long side of the rectangle, arrange a row of overlapping rings from top to bottom. Repeat for 2 more rows to completely cover the pastry shell. Sprinkle evenly with the rosemary-cinnamon mixture.

5. Place the baking sheet in the center of the oven and bake the tart until the pastry shell is puffy and browned and the apples are a deep golden brown, 35 to 40 minutes. Remove the baking sheet from the oven and brush gently with the apricot jam. Sprinkle with the remaining tablespoon of rosemary. This tart is best served slightly warm. Cut the tart crosswise into 12 thin slices. Serve with a scoop of sorbet.

58 calories per serving ❋ 3 g fat ❋ 1 g protein ❋ 9 g carbohydrates

LIGHT, FLAKY WHOLE WHEAT PASTRY

Pâte Brisée Légère

This wholesome whole wheat crust has little butter but still manages to render a tender, flaky texture. Use it as an all-purpose dough. I like to use it as a base for the Rosemary-Apple-Cranberry Galette (page 268). Pastry for 2 rimless tarts, 12 slices per tart

EQUIPMENT: A food processor; a rolling pin; a baking sheet.

½ cup unbleached all-purpose flour

½ cup whole wheat flour

¼ teaspoon fine sea salt

5 tablespoons unsalted butter, chilled and cut into cubes

¼ cup ice water

1.   Place the flours and salt in a food processor and process to blend. Add the butter and process until well blended, about 10 seconds. With the machine running, add the water and process just until the mixture resembles fine curds of cheese and almost begins to form a ball, about 10 seconds more. Transfer to a clean work surface and, with your palm, smear the dough bit by bit across the work surface until the dough is thoroughly incorporated. (This is called *fraisage,* the practice of mixing all the ingredients until every trace of water and flour has disappeared, at which point the mass becomes dough.) Divide the dough into 2 even portions. Form each into a flattened round. Cover with plastic wrap and refrigerate for at least 1 hour and up to 48 hours.

2.   On a lightly floured surface, roll each portion of dough into a 9-inch circle or into a 4 × 13-inch rectangle. Place on a baking sheet and refrigerate until ready to use.

39 calories per slice of pastry ⁕ 3 g fat ⁕ 1 g protein ⁕ 4 g carbohydrates

BUTTERMILK SORBET

Sorbet au Lait Fermenté

I confess to a severe weakness for anything with a slightly lactic tang, and buttermilk is among those light, refreshing, delicate flavors that appeal to my palate. Buttermilk, which the French market as *lait fermenté*, is to my thinking an underused ingredient. It offers the pleasures of richer ingredients such as cream with much less of the fat. This sorbet goes with just about everything, so I serve it often. 12 servings

EQUIPMENT: A medium saucepan; an ice-cream maker.

⅓ cup freshly squeezed lemon juice
1 cup sugar
¼ cup light corn syrup
2 cups buttermilk, shaken to blend

1.   In a medium saucepan, combine the lemon juice, sugar, and corn syrup. Simmer over medium heat until the sugar is dissolved. Cool to room temperature.

2.   Combine the lemon syrup and the buttermilk and stir to blend. Chill thoroughly. Transfer to an ice-cream maker and freeze according to the manufacturer's instructions. The sorbet should be served as soon as it is made.

102 calories per serving ※ trace of fat ※ 1 g protein ※ 24 g carbohydrates

What I Learned: Be sure to wash the lid and the top edge of the bottle of corn syrup before putting it back in the pantry. Or else next time you'll need a sumo wrestler to help you open it!

INDIVIDUAL CHOCOLATE CUSTARDS WITH ESPELETTE PEPPER

Petit Pots de Crème au Chocolat au Piment d'Espelette

For years, chef Guy Jullien of the restaurant La Beaugravière in Mondragon has served these tiny treats as a "predessert" at the end of his usual banquet meals. I always look forward to the tiny thimble-sized servings of smooth and creamy chocolate. On one visit—during our annual truffle extravaganza—I asked if he might ever share the recipe. A few seconds later he returned from the kitchen with the recipe scribbled on the back of the day's menu. I have sampled chocolates from the Pays Basque that were seasoned with a touch of the local chili pepper, *piment d'Espelette*, and so have added a touch of that pepper here. The flavor is mysterious, and one won't immediately recognize it as spicy pepper, but it is intriguing as well as satisfying. 8 servings

EQUIPMENT: A double boiler; eight ¼-cup vodka or shot glasses.

5 ounces bittersweet chocolate (preferably Valrhona Manjari 64%)
¾ cup light cream
2 tablespoons unsalted butter
Generous ¼ teaspoon ground *piment d'Espelette* or dried Anaheim chili (or ground mild chili pepper)
Fleur de sel

1.   Break the chocolate into small pieces. Set aside.

2.   In the top of a double boiler set over, but not touching, boiling water, heat the cream and ¼ cup water just until warm. Add the chocolate pieces, stirring until the chocolate is melted. Add the butter and stir to melt and combine. Stir in the *piment d'Espelette*. Pour the mixture into the glasses. Refrigerate until firm, about 20 minutes. At serving time, sprinkle lightly with additional *piment d'Espelette* and *fleur de sel*.

147 calories per serving ※ 15 g fat ※ 3 g protein ※ 6 g carbohydrates

Frenchwoman Chloé Doutre-Roussel is known as the Chocolate Lady. She travels the world in search of the finest chocolates, and this slender young blonde consumes as much as a pound of chocolate a day. Whenever possible, I invite her to lead a tasting of chocolates during my cooking weeks in Paris. It was during one of those tastings that she helped me decide that Valrhona's Manjari, made from the finest cocoa beans from Madagascar, is ideal for this preparation, with its fruity, almost berrylike flavor, vibrancy, and gentle touch of acid.

CRUNCHY ALMOND-PEAR CAKE

Gâteau aux Poires et Amandes, Sucre Amande

Golden and fragrant, this fall and winter specialty is quick, easy, and appealing. The sugar and egg topping gives it a nice glow, and the almond-sugar mixture adds a pleasant crunch. This is a variation on simple apple and pear cakes that have been part of my repertoire for years. Serve it, for sure, with a scoop of Almond-Buttermilk Sorbet (page 283), also topped with that crunchy almond topping. Do not be alarmed by the small amount of batter: there is more fruit than cake, since the batter really serves to hold the pears together. 12 servings

EQUIPMENT: A 9½-inch springform pan; a small skillet; a food processor or a blender.

Unsalted butter and flour for the pan
½ cup all-purpose flour
⅓ cup sugar
1 tablespoon baking powder
⅛ teaspoon fine sea salt
½ teaspoon almond extract
2 large eggs, lightly beaten
1 tablespoon vegetable oil
⅓ cup nonfat yogurt
1 tablespoon pear eau-de-vie
Grated zest of 1 lemon, preferably organic
4 large pears (about 2 pounds)

The Egg Topping
⅓ cup sugar
1 large egg, lightly beaten
1 tablespoon pear eau-de-vie
½ teaspoon almond extract
Grated zest of 1 lemon, preferably organic

The Almond-Sugar Topping
½ cup unblanched almonds
¼ cup sugar

1. Preheat the oven to 425 degrees F.

2. Butter and flour the pan and set aside.

3. In a large bowl, combine the flour, sugar, baking powder, and salt and stir to blend. In another bowl, combine the almond extract, eggs, oil, yogurt, eau-de-vie, and lemon zest and stir until well blended. Add to the flour mixture and stir until thoroughly combined. Peel, halve, and core the pears. Cut each pear lengthwise into 16 thin slices, dropping them into the batter as they are sliced. Stir to thoroughly coat the fruit with the batter.

4. Spoon the mixture into the prepared cake pan. Place the pan in the center of the oven and bake until fairly firm and golden, about 40 minutes.

5. Meanwhile, prepare the egg topping: In a small bowl, combine the sugar, egg, eau-de-vie, almond extract, and lemon zest and stir to blend. Set aside.

6. Prepare the almond-sugar topping: Place the almonds in a small, dry skillet over moderate heat. Shake the pan regularly until the nuts are fragrant and evenly toasted, about 2 minutes. Watch carefully! They can burn quickly. Transfer the nuts to a large plate to cool. Once cooled, combine the almonds and sugar in a food processor or a blender and process to a powder. Set aside.

7. Once the cake is firm and golden, remove it from the oven, leaving the oven on, and pour the egg topping over the cake, evening it out with a spatula. Top with the almond-sugar mixture. Return the cake to the oven and bake until the top is a deep golden brown and the cake feels quite firm when pressed with a fingertip, about 10 minutes more, for a total baking time of 50 minutes.

8. Transfer to a rack to cool. After 10 minutes, run a knife around the edges of the pan. Release and remove the side of the springform pan, leaving the cake on the pan base. Serve at room temperature, cut into thin wedges. The cake should be served the day it is baked.

✲ 183 calories per serving ⁕ 6 g fat ⁕ 4 g protein ⁕ 30 g carbohydrates

Wine Suggestion
A tiny glass of pear eau-de-vie makes for a perfect marriage.

Folklore: Keep an almond or an almond leaf with you at all times, to ward off lightning.

"Couper la poire en deux." To cut the pear in two, or to split the difference.

HAZELNUT AND HEATHER HONEY CAKE

Gâteau aux Noisettes et Miel de Bruyère

As soon as fresh hazelnuts arrive in the market in early fall, I get this cake together and into the oven. Heather honey has a distinctive, intense flavor that marries well with the elegant flavor of hazelnuts. If heather honey is not available, use a strong, full-flavored honey such as buckwheat. 12 servings

EQUIPMENT: A 9½-inch springform cake pan; a small saucepan; a food processor or a blender.

5 tablespoons unsalted butter, plus butter for the pan
3 tablespoons heather or buckwheat honey
1½ cups hazelnuts
¼ cup sugar
½ cup plus 2 tablespoons unbleached all-purpose flour
½ teaspoon fine sea salt
3 large eggs, lightly beaten
Several tablespoons *crème fraîche* for garnish

1.   Butter the cake pan and set aside. Preheat the oven to 325 degrees F.

2.   In a small saucepan, combine the butter and honey and melt over low heat. Set aside to cool.

3.   In a food processor or a blender, combine the hazelnuts and sugar and process until the nuts and sugar are well blended and the nuts are chopped to the size of lentils.

4.   In a large mixing bowl, combine the flour and salt. Stir to blend with a wooden spoon. Stir in the eggs. Stir in the butter-honey mixture until the mixture is smooth and homogenous. Stir in the hazelnut-sugar mixture until the mixture is homogenous.

5.   Pour the batter into the prepared cake pan, smoothing out the top with a spatula. Place in the center of the oven and bake until the cake is an even golden brown and a toothpick inserted in the center comes out clean, 25 to 30 minutes.

6.   Remove from the oven and transfer to a rack to cool. After 10 minutes, run a knife around the edges of the pan. Release and remove the side of the springform pan, leaving the cake on the pan base. Serve at room temperature, cut into wedges, with *crème fraîche*. The cake should be served the day it is baked.

230 calories per serving * 17 g fat * 5 g protein * 16 g carbohydrates

Folklore: In former times, newlyweds were showered with hazelnuts as they left the church, for hazelnuts were believed to encourage fertility.

LEMON ZEST SORBET

Sorbet au Zeste de Citron

This quick and easy sorbet is a favorite in my cooking classes. The tang of lemon goes with just about everything. 12 servings

EQUIPMENT: A food processor or a blender; an ice-cream maker.

Grated zest of 1 lemon, preferably organic
1 cup sugar
1/8 teaspoon salt
2/3 cup freshly squeezed lemon juice
2 teaspoons vodka
2/3 cup nonfat yogurt

In a food processor or a blender, process the zest, sugar, and salt. With the machine running, add the juice in a slow, steady stream, processing until the sugar is fully dissolved, about 1 minute. Transfer to a large bowl. Whisk in 1 1/2 cups water, the vodka, and the yogurt. Transfer to an ice-cream maker and freeze according to the manufacturer's instructions. The sorbet should be served as soon as it is made.

77 calories per serving ⁕ 0 g fat ⁕ 1 g protein ⁕ 19 g carbohydrates

PISTACHIO-CHERRY CAKE WITH CHERRY SORBET

Gâteau Pistache-Cerises, Sorbet aux Cerises

We have several ancient cherry trees in Provence, with a brief, three-week window of opportunity to harvest the fruits in May. During that period I am a whirling dervish in the kitchen, making jams and jellies, packing bags full of pitted fruit for the freezer, and making cherry desserts and sorbets. This cake is a current favorite, combining the rich flavor of pistachio nuts with the sweet, tender cherries. Serve it with Sweet Cherry Sorbet. 12 servings

EQUIPMENT: A 9½-inch springform pan; a cherry pitter; a heavy-duty electric mixer with 2 bowls, fitted with a whisk.

1 teaspoon best-quality almond oil for the pan
4 large eggs, separated
½ cup sugar
6 tablespoons bleached all-purpose flour
1 teaspoon vanilla extract
1 teaspoon almond extract
1 teaspoon kirsch or cherry eau-de-vie
¾ cup roasted, salted pistachio nuts (from 4 ounces pistachios in their shells), coarsely ground
1 pound (4 cups) fresh sweet cherries, rinsed, stemmed, and pitted (or raspberries or quartered, pitted apricots)
Sweet Cherry Sorbet (page 281)

1.   Preheat the oven to 350 degrees F.

2.   Brush the pan with the almond oil. Set aside.

3.   Prepare the batter: In the bowl of a heavy-duty electric mixer fitted with a whisk, combine the egg yolks and 6 tablespoons of the sugar and beat at highest speed until thick and pale, 2 to 3 minutes. Add ¼ cup of the flour, the vanilla extract, the almond extract, the kirsch, and the pistachios and stir with a wooden spoon to blend. Set aside.

4.   Rinse and dry the whisk. Place the egg whites in the second bowl of a heavy-duty electric mixer fitted with a whisk. Whisk at low speed until the whites are frothy. Gradually increase the speed to high. Slowly add the remaining 2 tablespoons sugar, whisking at high speed until stiff but not dry.

5.   Whisk a third of the egg white mixture into the batter and stir until the two are thoroughly blended. (This will lighten the batter and make it easier to fold in the remaining egg white mixture.) With a large rubber spatula, gently fold in the remaining egg white mixture. Do this slowly and patiently. Do not overmix, but be sure that the mixture is well blended and that no streaks of white remain.

6.   Spoon two-thirds of the combined mixture into the prepared pan. Carefully place the cherries on top. Cover with the remaining third of the batter. Place in the center of the oven and bake until golden and a toothpick inserted into the center of the cake comes out clean, about 40 minutes.

7.   Remove from the oven and transfer to a rack to cool. After 10 minutes, run a knife around the edges of the pan. Release and remove the side of the springform pan, leaving the cake on the pan base. Serve at room temperature, cut into wedges, with the sorbet. The cake should be served the day it is baked.

❧c 141 calories per serving ❀ 6 g fat ❀ 5 g protein ❀ 18 g carbohydrates

Wine Suggestion

A tiny glass of cherry eau-de-vie or kirsch, if baked with cherries. Otherwise the pleasantly sweet Muscat de Beaumes-de-Venise is a good choice.

SWEET CHERRY SORBET

Sorbet aux Cerises

This intense sorbet could be called a double-cherry sorbet, for the rich flavor of cherries comes through loud and clear. 12 servings

EQUIPMENT: A cherry pitter; a large saucepan; a fine-mesh sieve; a food processor or a blender; a coarse-mesh sieve; an ice-cream maker.

1½ pounds (6 cups) fresh sweet cherries
1½ cups dry white wine
1 cup sugar
2 tablespoons kirsch or cherry eau-de-vie
2 tablespoons freshly squeezed lemon juice

1.   Rinse, stem, and pit the cherries, reserving the pits.

2.   In a large saucepan, combine the wine, sugar, and cherry pits over high heat. Boil, uncovered, stirring frequently, until syrupy, about 4 minutes. Strain the liquid through a fine-mesh sieve, discarding the pits. Return the liquid to the pan. Add the cherries and return to a boil. Reduce the heat to medium and simmer, uncovered, stirring occasionally, until the cherries are very soft, about 15 minutes more.

3.   Remove the saucepan from the heat and stir in the kirsch and lemon juice.

4.   In a food processor or a blender, purée the mixture. As a precaution, strain through a coarse sieve to catch any cherry pits that may have been left behind. (The food processor or blender will let you know!) Cover and refrigerate until thoroughly chilled.

5.   Transfer to an ice-cream maker and freeze according to the manufacturer's instructions. The sorbet should be served as soon as it is made.

118 calories per serving ❋ trace of fat ❋ 1 g protein ❋ 26 g carbohydrates

ALMOND MACAROONS

Macarons aux Amandes

These light, delicate, golden cookies are a fragrant favorite in our house, especially when served with a soothing scoop of Almond-Buttermilk Sorbet (page 283). Since a precise quantity of egg whites is important here, be sure to measure the whites. 30 cookies

> EQUIPMENT: A large skillet; a food processor or a blender; 2 baking sheets lined with parchment paper or silicone mats.
>
> 1 cup unblanched almonds
> ¾ cup sugar
> ⅓ cup egg whites (from 2 large eggs)
> ½ teaspoon pure vanilla extract
> ¼ teaspoon almond extract
> ⅛ teaspoon fine sea salt

1.   Preheat the oven to 375 degrees F.

2.   Toast the almonds: Place the almonds in a large, dry skillet over moderate heat. Shake the pan regularly until the nuts are fragrant and evenly toasted, about 2 minutes. Watch carefully! They can burn quickly. Transfer the nuts to a large plate to cool.

3.   In a food processor or a blender, combine the cooled almonds and sugar and process just until the mixture is quite fine. Do not overprocess. Add the egg whites, vanilla extract, almond extract, and salt and pulse to blend. The batter will be thick and sticky, and you should be able to shape it with your hands.

4.   With a teaspoon, drop the batter onto the prepared baking sheets. Leave enough room for the batter to spread out as the cookies bake. The final cookie will be flat and thin. You should have 15 cookies per baking sheet. Place in the center of the oven and bake until lightly browned and slightly firm, 12 to 15 minutes. Remove the baking sheets from the oven and allow the cookies to firm up and cool completely, at least 5 minutes. Using a thin metal spatula, very carefully remove the cookies and transfer to a plate or a rack. Store in an airtight container, at room temperature, for up to one week.

♣c 49 calories per cookie ❋ 2.5 g fat ❋ 1 g protein ❋ 6 g carbohydrates

ALMOND-BUTTERMILK SORBET

Sorbet Amande–Lait Fermenté

This creamy white dessert always brings raves and a request for the recipe. Serve it with Almond Macaroons (page 282). 12 servings

EQUIPMENT: A medium saucepan; a small skillet; a food processor or a blender; an ice-cream maker.

1/3 cup freshly squeezed lemon juice
1 cup sugar
1/4 cup light corn syrup
2 cups buttermilk, shaken to blend
1/2 teaspoon almond extract

The Topping
1/2 cup unblanched almonds, toasted
1/4 cup sugar

1.   In a medium saucepan, combine the lemon juice, sugar, and corn syrup. Simmer over moderate heat until the sugar is dissolved. Cool to room temperature.

2.   Toast the almonds: Place the almonds in a small, dry skillet over moderate heat. Shake the pan regularly until the nuts are fragrant and evenly toasted, about 2 minutes. Watch carefully! They can burn quickly. Transfer the nuts to a large plate to cool.

3.   In a food processor or a blender, combine the almonds and sugar and process to a powder. Set aside.

4.   Combine the lemon syrup, buttermilk, and almond extract and stir to blend. Chill thoroughly. Transfer to an ice-cream maker and freeze according to the manufacturer's instructions. Serve in small bowls, sprinkled with the almond and sugar topping. The sorbet should be served as soon as it is made.

153 calories per serving ⁕ 4 g fat ⁕ 3 g protein ⁕ 30 g carbohydrates

Customs: In France, almonds are eaten fresh during the month of June, before the shell has hardened. The fruit is soft, silken, and delicate.

ALMOND CAKE WITH CARROTS, WITH LEMON THYME SORBET

Gâteau aux Amandes et Carottes, Sorbet Thym Citron

It's worth preparing this moist, dense cake just to appreciate the sweet, nutty aroma that wafts from the kitchen as it bakes. The cake takes just minutes to prepare and has become a wintertime favorite. I love it as an afternoon snack, with a cup of almond tea. For dessert, pair it with a scoop of Lemon Thyme Sorbet. 16 servings

EQUIPMENT: A 9½-inch springform pan; a small skillet; a food processor or a blender; a small saucepan.

1 teaspoon best-quality almond oil for the pan
1¼ cups unblanched almonds
¾ cup sugar
½ cup unbleached all-purpose flour
1 teaspoon baking powder
⅛ teaspoon fine sea salt
3 large eggs, lightly beaten
2½ cups grated carrots (from about 4 carrots, weighing 10 ounces)

Lemon Sauce
⅓ cup freshly squeezed lemon juice
3 tablespoons sugar

Lemon Thyme Sorbet (page 286)

1.   Preheat the oven to 425 degrees F.

2.   Drizzle the oil into the cake pan and, using paper towels, rub it all over the bottom and sides of the pan. Set aside.

3.   Toast the almonds: Place the almonds in a small, dry skillet over moderate heat. Shake the pan regularly until the nuts are fragrant and evenly toasted, about 2 minutes. Watch carefully! They can burn quickly. Transfer the nuts to a large plate to cool.

4.   In a food processor or a blender, combine the sugar and almonds and chop until fairly fine. Add the flour, baking powder, and salt and blend. Transfer the mixture to a large bowl. Add the eggs and stir to blend. Add the carrots and stir to blend. The batter will be fairly thick but should not be dry.

5.   Transfer the batter to the prepared pan. Smooth out the top with a spatula. Place the pan in the center of the oven and bake until golden and firm and a toothpick inserted into the center of the cake comes out clean, 40 to 45 minutes.

6.   Transfer to a rack to cool. After 10 minutes, run a knife around the edges of the pan. Release and remove the side of the springform pan, leaving the cake on the pan base.

7.   While the cake cools, prepare the sauce: Combine the lemon juice and sugar in a small saucepan and simmer over low heat until the sugar is dissolved, 2 to 3 minutes.

8.   Serve the cake at room temperature: Cut it into thin wedges and top with the warm lemon sauce and a scoop of sorbet. The cake should be served the same day it is baked.

❧ᶜ 141 calories per serving ✳ 7 g fat ✳ 4 g protein ✳ 17 g carbohydrates

Origins: Almonds are actually stone fruits related to cherries, plums, and peaches, though we consider them a nut.

LEMON THYME SORBET

Sorbet au Thym-Citron

Lemon thyme grows profusely in my country garden. I like to use it in sweet dessert treats such as this one. 12 servings

EQUIPMENT: A large saucepan with a lid; a fine-mesh sieve; an ice-cream maker.

1 cup sugar
¼ cup lemon thyme leaves
Juice and zest of 2 lemons, preferably organic

1. In a large saucepan, combine the sugar, thyme, and 2 cups water and bring to a boil over high heat. Remove from the heat, cover, and set aside to steep for 1 hour.

2. Strain through a fine-mesh sieve, discarding the thyme leaves. Stir in the lemon juice and zest. Cover and refrigerate until thoroughly chilled. Transfer to an ice-cream maker and freeze according to the manufacturer's instructions. The sorbet should be served as soon as it is made.

70 calories per serving ※ trace of fat ※ trace of protein ※ 18 g carbohydrates

PUMPKIN FLAN WITH LEMON SAUCE

Flan de Potimarron, Sauce Citron

Each summer my gardener plants two little pumpkin patches in my garden, growing several varieties of pumpkins known for their dense, sunset-orange flesh. This soufflélike flan is light but full of the rich, nutty, almost spicy flavor of the fresh squash known as *potimarron*. Butternut squash is a worthy substitute. 12 servings

EQUIPMENT: A 9½-inch springform pan; a food processor or a blender; a small saucepan.

Butter and flour for the pan
3 cups squash or pumpkin purée (see page 62)
¾ cup 1% milk
⅓ cup sugar
⅓ cup unbleached all-purpose flour
Grated zest of 1 lemon, preferably organic
¼ teaspoon fine sea salt
½ teaspoon vanilla extract
3 large eggs, lightly beaten

Lemon Sauce
Grated zest of 1 lemon, preferably organic
3 tablespoons sugar
⅓ cup freshly squeezed lemon juice

1. Preheat the oven to 425 degrees F. Butter and flour the pan and set aside.

2. In a food processor or a blender, combine the squash or pumpkin purée, milk, sugar, flour, lemon zest, salt, vanilla, and eggs. Process to blend.

3. Pour the mixture into the prepared pan. Place the pan in the center of the oven and bake until golden and firm and a toothpick inserted into the center of the flan comes out clean, 35 to 45 minutes.

4. Transfer to a rack to cool. After 10 minutes, run a knife around the edges of the pan. Release and remove the side of the springform pan, leaving the flan on the pan base.

5. While the flan cools, prepare the sauce: Combine the lemon zest, sugar, and lemon juice in a small saucepan and simmer over low heat until the sugar is dissolved, 2 to 3 minutes.

6.   Serve the flan warm or at room temperature: Cut it into thin wedges and top with the warm lemon sauce.

    ❋c 69 calories per serving ❋ 1 g fat ❋ 2 g protein ❋ 12 g carbohydrates

What I Learned: It's often a mess and a hassle to lightly dust a baking pan with flour. The task is eased if you put superfine flour (such as Wondra) in a small sugar shaker. Then when you need to dust a pan or dust a work surface when rolling out pastry or pizza dough, you'll have it at hand.

RHUBARB-BERRY COMPOTE IN GRENADINE

Compote de Rhubarbe aux Fruits Rouges

I love the sharp tang of rhubarb, and here it is offset by the sweetness of grenadine (which also gives a ruby color to the rhubarb) and pairs well with the texture of fresh raspberries or strawberries. 6 servings

EQUIPMENT: A large saucepan.

1 cup grenadine
1 pound rhubarb, rinsed and cut into 2-inch pieces (peeled if the rhubarb is very thick)
1 pound raspberries, rinsed, or strawberries, rinsed, hulled, and quartered

In a large saucepan, combine the grenadine and the rhubarb and cook just until the rhubarb is soft, 2 to 3 minutes. Set aside to cool. At serving time, stir in the raspberries or strawberries. Serve in small glass bowls.

❧ 150 calories per serving ◦ trace of fat ◦ 1 g protein ◦ 38 g carbohydrates

❧ Variation: When fresh figs are in season, I substitute figs for the berries, adding them to the rhubarb as soon as it is cooked. This allows the flavors of the fruits to blend and mellow.

SEASONAL FRUITS ROASTED WITH HONEY-LEMON SAUCE AND FRESH LEMON VERBENA

Fruits d'Eté au Four à la Verveine Odorante

Fresh lemon verbena is a godsend in the garden. The tangy, sharp, lemony flavor of this perennial herb will intensify the flavors of just about any dish. Here I take seasonal fresh summer fruits and roast them in the wood-fired bread oven, garnishing with fresh lemon verbena leaves at the very last moment. Serve with Sheep's Milk Yogurt Sorbet. 6 servings

EQUIPMENT: A small saucepan; a 10-inch round porcelain baking dish.

½ cup lavender honey, melted

2 tablespoons freshly squeezed lemon juice

24 ripe black figs, rinsed, stemmed, and halved lengthwise

2 cups raspberries, rinsed

Fresh lemon verbena leaves for garnish

1 recipe Sheep's Milk Yogurt Sorbet (page 291)

1. Preheat the oven to 375 degrees F.

2. In a small saucepan, combine the honey and lemon juice over low heat, stirring until the honey has totally dissolved with the juice. Set aside.

3. Arrange the fruits in the baking dish. Drizzle with the honey-lemon sauce and place in the oven. Bake just until warmed through, about 10 minutes. Remove from the oven. Spoon the fruits into small bowls and garnish with fresh lemon verbena leaves and a scoop of sorbet.

254 calories per serving ✶ 1 g fat ✶ 2 g protein ✶ 66 g carbohydrates

Wine Suggestion
A tiny glass of chilled Muscat de Beaumes-de-Venise.

SHEEP'S MILK YOGURT SORBET

Sorbet au Yaourt de Brebis

I eat yogurt in some form every day. This is a very tasty way to get a bit of calcium in the form of a light and creamy sorbet. Serve this with the Seasonal Fruits Roasted with Honey-Lemon Sauce and Fresh Lemon Verbena (page 295). 12 servings

EQUIPMENT: A heavy-duty electric mixer fitted with a whisk; an ice-cream maker.

2 cups low-fat sheep's milk yogurt
3 large egg whites
⅔ cup sugar

1. Place the yogurt in a large bowl and whisk to blend. Set aside.

2. Place the egg whites in the bowl of a heavy-duty mixer fitted with a whisk. Whisk at low speed until the whites are frothy. Gradually increase the speed to high. Slowly add the sugar, whisking at high speed until stiff but not dry. Gradually fold the yogurt into the beaten egg whites. Transfer to an ice-cream maker and freeze according to the manufacturer's instructions. The sorbet should be served as soon as it is made.

75 calories per serving ❋ 1 g fat ❋ 1 g protein ❋ 13 g carbohydrates

What I Learned: Remember, eggs separate most easily when cold, but the whites whip better at room temperature. So plan ahead when making this sorbet.

THE PANTRY

Au Garde-Manger

❖

HOMEMADE CHICKEN STOCK

Fond de Volaille Maison

Nothing gives me a greater sense of contentment than the aroma of chicken stock wafting from my kitchen. Chicken stock also gives me a sense of empowerment, knowing that no matter how bare the cupboard may be, I can always fashion a meal in a jiffy, using the rich and golden stock as the base. In this recipe, I use a whole raw chicken and simmer it for one hour. The bird is then removed from the pot, the cooked meat removed from the bones, and the carcass and skin returned to the pot to simmer for another few hours. The resulting stock is rich and fragrant, and this preparation also means that I have plenty of super-tender poached chicken for making salads. 3 quarts

> EQUIPMENT: A 10-quart pasta pot fitted with a colander; a fine-mesh skimmer; dampened cheesecloth.
>
> 2 large onions, halved but not peeled
> 4 whole cloves
> 1 farm-fresh chicken, about 5 pounds
> Pinch of salt
> 4 carrots, scrubbed but not peeled, cut into 1-inch pieces
> 1 head of garlic, halved but not peeled
> 4 ribs celery
> 1 leek (white and tender green parts), halved lengthwise, washed, and cut into 1-inch pieces
> 1 ounce trimmed and peeled fresh ginger
> 12 whole white peppercorns
> Bouquet garni: several bay leaves, celery leaves, sprigs of thyme, and parsley, encased in a wire mesh tea infuser

1. Spear the onion halves with a long-handled, two-pronged fork and hold them directly over a gas flame (or directly on an electric burner) until scorched. Stick a clove into each of the onion halves. (Scorching the onions will give the broth a richer flavor. The onion skin also serves to "dye" the stock a rich golden color.)

2. Place the chicken in the pasta pot and fill with 5 quarts cold water. Add the remaining ingredients, including the onions. Bring to a gentle simmer, uncovered, over medium heat. Skim to remove any scum

that rises to the surface. Add additional cold water to replace the water removed and continue skimming until the broth is clear.

3.   After about 1 hour, remove the chicken from the pot. Remove the chicken meat, removing the skin. Return the skin and the carcass to the pot. Continue cooking at a gentle simmer for 2½ hours more.

4.   Line a large colander with a double layer of dampened cheesecloth and place the colander over a large bowl. Ladle—do not pour—the liquid into the colander, to strain off any remaining fat and impurities. Discard the solids. Measure. If the stock exceeds 3 quarts, return to moderate heat and reduce. Transfer the stock to covered containers.

5.   Immediately refrigerate the stock and spoon off all traces of fat that rise to the surface. The stock may be refrigerated safely for three days or can be frozen for up to three months.

❧c 22 calories per cup ❈ 1 g fat ❈ 1 g protein ❈ 1 g carbohydrates

❧ Variation: Use 2 whole chicken carcasses rather than a whole raw chicken. The resulting stock will not have the same clean, fresh flavor, but it is worthy nonetheless. One can also use about 4 pounds of inexpensive chicken necks and backs to prepare the stock.

Tips for Stock Making

• For a clear stock, begin with cold water and bring it slowly to a simmer. Never allow a stock to boil or it will be cloudy, since the fat will emulsify. Cold water also aids in extracting greater flavor.

• For the first 30 minutes of cooking, skim the impurities that rise to the surface as the stock simmers.

• Use a tall pot, for it will limit evaporation. I always use a large pasta pot fitted with a colander, which makes it easy to remove the stock ingredients and begin to filter the stock.

Is It Stock, Broth, or Consommé? Generally, a stock is cooked for a long time, up to 4 hours, while a broth— usually lighter—is cooked for a short time, usually around 40 minutes. A consommé is a stock that has been clarified, usually with egg whites. Sometimes stock is also referred to as *bouillon,* but generally this term is used in reference to a court bouillon, usually of fish or vegetables.

"Indeed, stock is everything in cooking. Without it, nothing can be done."
Georges-Auguste Escoffier, French chef, 1846–1935

CLASSIC VINAIGRETTE

Vinaigrette Classique

This complex, classic vinaigrette can always be found in my pantry. Use two different vinegars and top-quality oil to create deep, intense flavors. 1¼ cups

EQUIPMENT: A small jar with a lid.

2 tablespoons best-quality sherry-wine vinegar
2 tablespoons best-quality red-wine vinegar
Fine sea salt
1 cup extra-virgin olive oil

Place the vinegars and salt in a small jar. Cover and shake to dissolve the salt. Add the oil and shake to blend. Taste for seasoning. The vinaigrette can be stored at room temperature or in the refrigerator for several weeks. Shake again at serving time to create a thick emulsion.

128 calories per tablespoon ⚬ 14 g fat ⚬ trace of protein ⚬ trace of carbohydrates

Origins: Salads have been eaten since antiquity but were generally served very salty and with a warm sauce. It was not until the fifteenth century that vinaigrette became the main salad seasoning.

BASIL-LEMON DRESSING

Sauce Basilic-Citron

About ¼ cup

EQUIPMENT: A small jar with a lid.

¼ cup Basil Oil (page 312)
1 tablespoon freshly squeezed lemon juice
Fine sea salt to taste

Place the Basil Oil and lemon juice in a small jar. Cover and shake to blend. Taste for seasoning. The dressing can be used immediately or stored, covered and refrigerated, for up to one week. Shake again at serving time to create a thick emulsion.

❄c 65 calories per tablespoon ❋ 7 g fat ❋ trace of protein ❋ trace of carbohydrates

BUTTERMILK-THYME DRESSING

Sauce au Lait Fermenté au Thym

This light and creamy dressing can be used on any salad but is particularly nice with Steamed Eggplant (page 182). 10 tablespoons

EQUIPMENT: A small jar with a lid.

¼ teaspoon fine sea salt
2 teaspoons extra-virgin olive oil
1 tablespoon imported French mustard
1 teaspoon fresh thyme leaves
½ cup buttermilk, shaken to blend

Combine all the ingredients in a small jar. Cover and shake to blend. Let sit for 1 hour to blend the flavors. Store, covered and refrigerated, for up to one week. At serving time, shake to blend once again.

14 calories per tablespoon ⁜ 1 g fat ⁜ 1 g protein ⁜ 1 g carbohydrates

CREAMY LEMON-CHIVE DRESSING

Sauce au Citron et à la Ciboulette

This light, tangy dressing finds its way into many dishes at my table. I love it with a simple green salad or a medley of heirloom tomatoes. 1¼ cups

EQUIPMENT: A small jar with a lid.

2 tablespoons freshly squeezed lemon juice
½ teaspoon fine sea salt
1 cup light cream
⅓ cup finely minced fresh chives

In a small jar, combine the lemon juice and the salt. Cover and shake to dissolve the salt. Add the cream and chives. Shake to blend. Taste for seasoning. Store, covered and refrigerated, for up to one week. Shake to blend again before using.

16 calories per tablespoon * 2 g fat * trace of protein * trace of carbohydrates

But Will It Curdle? Given the right circumstances, any milk or cream product will curdle (meaning the curd protein coagulates and forms clumps). Acid and heat can cause curdling, while the greater the fat content of the milk or cream, the more it will resist curdling. I use a light cream with a 12 percent fat content, much like what is also called *half-and-half*, and have never had a problem with curdling when adding lemon juice to the cream.

SHALLOT VINAIGRETTE

Vinaigrette aux Echalotes

The sweet and tender flavor of shallot gives it a place of royalty in the onion family. This vinaigrette goes particularly well with any salad. About ⅔ cup

EQUIPMENT: A small jar with a lid.

⅓ cup minced shallot (about 2 large)
2 tablespoons best-quality sherry-wine vinegar
2 tablespoons freshly squeezed lemon juice
Grated zest of 1 lemon, preferably organic
Fine sea salt
⅓ cup extra-virgin olive oil

Place the shallot, sherry-wine vinegar, lemon juice, lemon zest, and salt in a jar. Cover and shake to dissolve the salt. Add the oil and shake to blend. Taste for seasoning. The vinaigrette can be prepared up to one day in advance, covered, and refrigerated. Shake again at serving time to create a thick emulsion.

✣C 54 calories per tablespoon ❋ 6 g fat ❋ trace of protein ❋ 1 g carbohydrates

LIGHT BASIL PURÉE

Sauce Basilic Légère

This is a light, peppy version of the traditional pesto, here made with an abundance of fragrant, fresh basil and just a bit of tasty extra-virgin olive oil. 12 tablespoons

EQUIPMENT: A mortar and pestle; a food processor fitted with a small bowl or a blender.

4 plump, moist garlic cloves, peeled, halved, green germ removed, minced

1/8 teaspoon fine sea salt

4 cups loosely packed fresh basil leaves and flowers

6 tablespoons extra-virgin olive oil

1. By hand: Place the garlic and salt in a mortar and mash with a pestle to form a paste. Be patient and work slowly and evenly. Add the basil, little by little, pounding and turning the pestle with a grinding motion to form a paste. Slowly add the oil, turning the pestle with a grinding motion until all the oil has been used. The sauce will not form an emulsion, like a mayonnaise, but rather the basil leaves will remain suspended in the oil. Taste for seasoning. Stir again before serving.

In a food processor or a blender: Place the garlic, salt, and basil in the small bowl of a food processor or in a blender and process to a paste. With the machine running, slowly pour the oil through the tube and process again. Taste for seasoning. Stir again before serving.

2. The sauce can be stored, covered and refrigerated, for three days, or frozen up to six months. Bring to room temperature and stir again before serving.

63 calories per tablespoon ∗ 7 g fat ∗ trace of protein ∗ 1 g carbohydrates

"Pounding fragrant things—particularly garlic, basil, parsley—is a tremendous antidote to depression. But it applies also to juniper berries, coriander seeds, and the grilled fruits of the chili pepper. Pounding these things produces an alteration in one's being—from sighing with fatigue to inhaling with pleasure."

Patience Gray (1917–2005), author of Honey from a Weed

FRESH CILANTRO SAUCE

Sauce à la Coriandre

This quick and easy sauce is versatile and ideal for when you find yourself with a bounty of fresh herbs. This version marries particularly well with my Lamb Couscous with Chickpeas and Zucchini (page 124), when I pass a small bowl of this as a condiment. I use the same technique for dill (delicious as a dipping sauce for steamed cauliflower) and chervil (wonderful with *crudités* such as carrots and celery). ½ cup

EQUIPMENT: A large saucepan; a fine-mesh sieve; a food processor or a blender; a small jar with a lid.

3 tablespoons coarse sea salt
2 cups loosely packed fresh cilantro leaves
¼ cup extra-virgin olive oil
½ teaspoon fine sea salt

1. Prepare a large bowl of ice water.

2. In a large saucepan, bring 1 quart water to a rolling boil over high heat. Add the salt and the cilantro leaves and blanch for 15 seconds. Transfer the cilantro leaves to a fine-mesh sieve. Dip the sieve into the ice water to refresh the cilantro and help it keep its bright green color. Transfer the cilantro leaves to a thick clean towel. Roll the towel and squeeze to dry the leaves.

3. In a food processor or a blender, combine the drained leaves, the oil, and the salt and process until puréed and well blended. The mixture should be fairly thick but not chunky. Transfer to a small airtight jar. Store, refrigerated, for up to ten days. Remove from the refrigerator several minutes before using. Shake to blend again before using.

61 calories per tablespoon ∗ 7 g fat ∗ trace of protein ∗ trace of carbohydrates

WATERCRESS PESTO

Pesto au Cresson

I first sampled this peppery, vibrant watercress pesto at the hands of Chef Frédéric Anton of Paris's restaurant Le Pré Catelan. The pesto served as a sauce for delicate steamed turbot, joined by a buttery serving of penne pasta. It's a brilliant change from a basil pesto, one that's big on color and zest. I like the fact that you can savor the distinct flavors of each ingredient. It's great as a sauce for fish and poultry, as well as pasta. 2 cups

EQUIPMENT: A food processor or a blender.

2 bunches (8 cups loosely packed) watercress, washed and dried (do not stem)
¾ cup freshly grated Parmigiano-Reggiano cheese
2 tablespoons extra-virgin olive oil
2 plump, moist garlic cloves, peeled, halved, green germ removed
½ teaspoon fine sea salt

In a food processor or a blender, combine all the ingredients and purée until smooth. Taste for seasoning. Store in an airtight container in the refrigerator for up to two days.

12 calories per tablespoon ❋ 1 g fat ❋ 1 g protein ❋ trace of carbohydrates

SPICY GARLIC MAYONNAISE

Aïoli

I can't imagine a summer season without at least one hit of the pungent Provençal garlic mayonnaise known as *aïoli*. In this version, it gets spiced up just another level with a touch of Espelette pepper or hot pepper of your choice. 1¼ cups

EQUIPMENT: A large mortar and pestle; a food processor fitted with a small bowl or a blender.

6 plump, moist garlic cloves, peeled, halved, green germ removed, minced
½ teaspoon fine sea salt
2 large egg yolks, at room temperature
1 cup extra-virgin olive oil
1 teaspoon *piment d'Espelette* or other hot pepper, or to taste

1.   By hand: Pour boiling water into a large mortar to warm it; discard the water and dry the mortar. Place the garlic and salt in the mortar and mash together evenly with a pestle to form as smooth a paste as possible. (The fresher the garlic, the easier it will be to crush.) Add the egg yolks. Stir, pressing slowly and evenly with the pestle, always in the same direction, to thoroughly blend the garlic paste and yolks. Continue stirring, gradually adding just a few drops of the oil, whisking until thoroughly incorporated. Do not add too much oil in the beginning or the mixture will not emulsify. As soon as the mixture begins to thicken, add the remaining oil in a slow and steady stream, whisking constantly. Add the *piment d'Espelette*. Taste for seasoning.

In a food processor or a blender: In the small bowl of a food processor or in a blender, combine the garlic, salt, and egg yolks and process until well blended. With the motor running, very slowly add several tablespoons of oil, processing until the mixture thickens. With the motor still running, slowly add the remaining oil in a slow and steady stream. Add the *piment d'Espelette*. Taste for seasoning.

2.   Transfer to a small bowl. Cover and refrigerate for at least 1 hour to allow the flavors to blend. The aïoli can be stored, covered and refrigerated, for up to three days.

171 calories per tablespoon ❋ 19 g fat ❋ 1 g protein ❋ 1 g carbohydrates

CHUNKY FRESH TOMATO SAUCE

Sauce aux Tomates du Jardin

This is a quick, rustic tomato sauce that can be put together in a matter of minutes yet tastes as though you have labored for hours. Just use the ripest, most flavorful tomatoes you can find. 5 cups

EQUIPMENT: A large, heavy-duty saucepan; a food mill fitted with the coarsest blade.

1 tablespoon extra-virgin olive oil
3 pounds garden-fresh tomatoes, rinsed, cored, and quartered (do not peel)
1 tablespoon coarse sea salt
Several celery leaves
Several fresh or dried bay leaves
1 head of plump, moist garlic, cloves separated and peeled
Hot red pepper flakes to taste (optional)

1.   In a large, heavy-duty saucepan, combine all the ingredients. Cook, uncovered, over moderate heat, stirring regularly, until the tomatoes have collapsed and are cooking in their own juices, about 15 minutes. Taste for seasoning. Remove and discard the celery leaves and bay leaves.

2.   Place the food mill over a large bowl. Using a large ladle, transfer the sauce to the food mill and purée into the bowl. Store, covered, in the refrigerator for one week or in the freezer for six months.

89 calories per cup ◦ 4 g fat ◦ 3 g protein ◦ 14 g carbohydrates

What I Learned: This makes a rather rustic sauce that will have seeds. If you prefer a more refined sauce, pass through the fine blade of the food mill.

RUSTIC OVEN-ROASTED TOMATO SAUCE

Sauce aux Tomates Cuites au Four

When tomatoes are plentiful in the garden or market, I make batches of this versatile sauce, one that I use on pastas and in gratins, thin to make a creamy warm or cold soup, and add to varied purées such as a chunky eggplant purée. 6 servings

EQUIPMENT: A baking sheet; a food processor or a blender.

3 pounds garden-fresh tomatoes, rinsed, cored, and halved crosswise (do not peel)
Fine sea salt
About 2 teaspoons dried oregano

1. Preheat the oven to 425 degrees F.

2. Arrange the tomato halves, cut side up, side by side on a baking sheet. Sprinkle lightly with salt. Rub the oregano between your palms, showering the tomatoes with the fragrant herb.

3. Place the baking sheet in the center of the oven and roast until the tomatoes are very soft, about 40 minutes.

4. Transfer the tomatoes and any juices to a food processor or a blender and purée until smooth.

43 calories per serving ⁕ 1 g fat ⁕ 2 g protein ⁕ 10 g carbohydrates

ESPELETTE PEPPER JELLY

Gelée de Piment d'Espelette

Espelette pepper is the mildly spicy pepper grown all over the Basque region of France's Southwest. This colorful, fragrant jelly has a nice bite but it is not designed to blow your head off. Rather it subtly complements everything with which it comes in contact, from a touch of soft cheese to a glaze for seared duck breast, or *magret de canard*. Three 8-ounce jars

> EQUIPMENT: A food processor or a blender; a copper jam pot or a large saucepan; three 8-ounce sterilized canning jars with lids.
>
> 3 red bell peppers, stemmed, seeded, and quartered
> 4 cups sugar
> 1 cup cider vinegar
> 1 tablespoon ground *piment d'Espelette* or dried Anaheim chilies (or ground mild chili pepper)
> 2 tablespoons finely ground dried red chili pepper
> 1/4 cup liquid pectin (1/2 packet)

In a food processor or a blender, pulse the red peppers to a coarse purée. Transfer the purée to a copper jam pot or a large saucepan. Add the sugar, vinegar, *piment d'Espelette*, and chili powder and bring to a simmer over moderate heat, stirring constantly until the mixture begins to thicken, 6 to 8 minutes. Remove from the heat and stir in the pectin. Return to the heat and stir constantly for 1 minute. Ladle into the sterilized jars to within 1/8 inch of the tops. Wipe the jar rims and threads. Cover and screw in the tops tightly. Invert the jars for 5 minutes, then turn them upright. Let stand at room temperature for 24 hours. Store unopened jars in a cool, dry place for up to one year. Refrigerate opened jars for up to three weeks.

67 calories per tablespoon ❋ 0 fat ❋ trace of protein ❋ 17 g carbohydrates

What I Learned: For this recipe, I prefer that the jelly be loose, almost pourable. It will have a nice consistency but not be so firm that a spoon will stand up in the jar. If you prefer a firmer jelly, double the amount of liquid pectin. Any kind of hot pepper can be used here. For instance, fresh jalapeño can be substituted for half of the red bell pepper, or use any dried hot pepper of choice.

CURRY POWDER

Poudre de Curry

Homemade curry powder is so much fresher and tastier than a store-bought mix and can be put together in minutes. ⅓ cup

EQUIPMENT: A small skillet; a spice grinder or a coffee mill.

2 small whole dried red chili peppers
2 tablespoons whole coriander seeds
1 tablespoon whole cumin seeds
½ teaspoon black mustard seeds
1 teaspoon whole black peppercorns
1 teaspoon whole fenugreek seeds
½ teaspoon ground ginger
½ teaspoon ground turmeric

In a small, dry skillet, combine the chili peppers, coriander, cumin, mustard, and peppercorns over medium heat and toast—shaking the pan often to prevent burning—for 2 to 3 minutes. Remove from the heat, transfer to a bowl, and let cool to room temperature. Add the whole fenugreek seeds. In a spice grinder or coffee mill, grind to a fine powder. Transfer to a small container. Stir in the ground ginger and turmeric. Store in an airtight container in a cool place for up to three months.

40 calories per tablespoon * 1 g fat * 2 g protein * 8 g carbohydrates

Turmeric is an East Indian perennial herb of the ginger family. The name is a modification of the fourteenth-century French words for it, *terra merité*, or "deserved earth."

THAI CURRY PASTE

Pâte à Curry Thaï

Like curry powder, homemade curry paste has a fresher, more authentic flavor. I like to spoon this on the Thai Medley (page 212). ½ cup

EQUIPMENT: A small skillet; a spice grinder or a coffee mill; a food processor or a blender.

2 teaspoons whole coriander seeds
1 teaspoon whole cumin seeds
1 teaspoon whole fennel seeds
1 teaspoon whole black peppercorns
½ cup tightly packed cilantro leaves
Two ¼-inch slices fresh ginger, peeled
1 stalk lemon grass, bottom third only, chopped
1 tablespoon finely ground dried red chili peppers
2 shallots, peeled and chopped
4 plump, moist garlic cloves, peeled, halved, green germ removed
Grated zest of 1 lime, preferably organic
1 teaspoon Thai shrimp paste (optional)
1½ teaspoons fine sea salt
1 teaspoon freshly grated nutmeg
⅓ cup canola oil

1.   In a small, dry skillet, combine the coriander, cumin, fennel, and peppercorns over moderate heat and toast—shaking the pan often to prevent burning—for 2 to 3 minutes. Remove from the heat and let cool to room temperature. In a spice grinder or a coffee mill, grind to a fine powder. Transfer to a small bowl.

2.   In a blender or a food processor, combine the cilantro, ginger, lemon grass, chili, shallots, garlic, lime zest, shrimp paste (if using), salt, and nutmeg and process until very finely chopped. Add the toasted spices and, with the machine running, slowly pour in the oil. Cover and refrigerate until ready to use. The paste will keep, covered and refrigerated, for up to one week.

 95 calories per tablespoon ◦ 9 g fat ◦ 1 g protein ◦ 3 g carbohydrates

ZESTY LEMON SALT

Sel au Zeste de Citron

This mélange of lemon zest and *fleur de sel* is a great combination, made for adding a touch of zest to everything in your kitchen. ¼ cup

EQUIPMENT: A small jar with a lid.

Grated zest of 1 lemon, preferably organic
¼ cup *fleur de sel*

In a small jar, combine the zest and salt. Cover and shake to blend. Keep covered when not using the salt to help the condiment retain its freshness. The lemon flavor will dissipate, so use within one month.

Fleur de Sel, Caviar of the Ocean

It is an ingredient as old as the Romans, but how is it that elementary sea salt—nothing more than seawater evaporated by the sun and the wind—has become one of the modern world's gastronomic treasures?

The story of *fleur de sel* actually begins in the windswept Guérande peninsula in the Brittany region of France. Since the Middle Ages it is here on this jagged body of marshy land jutting out into the Atlantic Ocean that man has captured the saline water in an intricate series of winding canals and tiny ponds until it is decanted and evaporated into one of the world's most precious commodities, *sel marin,* or sea salt. Although France's salt trade has been important for centuries, the practice in Brittany had all but died out in recent times, with increasing competition from large commercial salt operations in the Mediterranean, and ports and salt marshes in poor repair. In hopes of rescuing their dying craft, a small number of salt marsh workers—called *paludiers* and *paludières*—banded together in the late 1970s, and today there are about 220 artisans harvesting from mid-June to mid-September a total of 10,000 tons of sea salt each year in Brittany. Trapping the ocean water at high tide, the salt marsh workers store the seawater in giant reservoirs for up to one month. Then, pushed by an iodine rich wine, the increasingly saline water is directed into a labyrinth of smaller and smaller pools or basins, square reservoirs known as *oeillets*. The salt that crystallizes on the surface is carefully raked off and piled into giant alabaster mounds, what we know commonly as *sel gris,* or coarse gray salt, *sel de mer.* A *paludier,* working with as many as sixty to eighty *oeillets,* can gather up to 100 pounds of salt. This natural product—a source of sodium, potassium, calcium, magnesium, copper, and zinc—is totally unrefined and unwashed.

ESPELETTE PEPPER SALT

Sel au Piment d'Espelette

I love condiments! My cupboard and refrigerator are filled with all sorts of pick-me-ups, and this is one of my favorites. The lightly fiery salt is delicious on everything, even Individual Chocolate Custards with Espelette Pepper (page 272). ¼ cup

EQUIPMENT: A small jar with a lid.

1 tablespoon ground *piment d'Espelette* or dried Anaheim chili (or ground mild chili pepper)
¼ cup *fleur de sel*

In a small jar, combine the *piment d'Espelette* and salt. Cover and shake to blend. Keep covered when not using the salt to help the condiment retain its freshness.

At certain times of the year, when the temperature is just right, a dry wind blows in from the east, and a very, very fine film of crystals settles at the very edge of those small pools. This, the caviar of the ocean, *fleur de sel,* is traditionally harvested by women, whose delicate job it is to rake off only the *fleur de sel,* taking none of the larger crystals of *gros sel* with it. The practice is not only a delicate one, but dependent on the vagaries of nature, for the entire day's harvest can be destroyed by a sudden change in the weather. With a faint aroma of iodine—some even say violets—this precious commodity accounts for only 5 percent of the total Brittany sea salt production. The French like to call it *la fille du vent et du soleil,* daughter of the wind and the sun, for the moist, delicate, shiny crystals are set in wicker baskets to dry naturally, in the sun.

Fleur de sel is the darling of chefs and bakers. The famed chef Joël Robuchon likes to use both *gros sel* and *fleur de sel* to season his French fry potatoes, since each salt imparts its own flavor and texture. However one utilizes this gift from the sea, there is one solid rule: *fleur de sel* is never actually cooked; it is added only as a last-minute seasoning, for everything from a green salad to a resting roasted leg of lamb.

While the *fleur de sel* from Brittany's Guérande peninsula is the most famous in France, there are other excellent small-production salts that come from both the Ile de Noirmoutier and the Ile de Ré on the Atlantic Coast and from the Camargue region along the Mediterranean. Today, creative packaging (some are even dated and signed by the salt rakers) has rocketed sea salt into the realm of French gastronomic treasures.

Both coarse and fine sea salt are essential to any larder. To my palate, sea salt makes food taste seasoned, while table salt (refined and plumped up with additives to prevent clumping) makes food taste salty.

TRUFFLE BUTTER

Beurre de Truffe

I like to use coarse sea salt in this truffle butter: The crunch of the truffle and the sea salt makes this a truly memorable condiment. Use it with everything: on toast, as a pasta sauce, in a risotto, in omelets, in lentils, on fish and poultry. 6 tablespoons

EQUIPMENT: A small ramekin.

4 tablespoons (½ stick) unsalted butter, at room temperature
2 tablespoons minced truffle peelings
½ teaspoon coarse sea salt

On a small plate, mash the softened butter with a fork. Sprinkle with the truffles and salt, distributing as evenly as possible. Transfer the butter to a ramekin. Cover securely. Refrigerate for up to three days or freeze for up to one month. Serve at room temperature.

82 calories per tablespoon ⁕ 8 g fat ⁕ trace of protein ⁕ 2 g carbohydrates

"Il n'a pas inventé le fil à couper le beurre!" He is not very bright!

⊱INDEX⊰

Les Abeilles, Sablet, 49, 82, 183

L'Aile de Raie de La Cagouille, Sauce Gribiche, 94–95

Aïoli, 304

Yannick Alléno's Swiss Chard Rib Gratin with Pine Nuts and Parmesan, 206–7

Almond:
-Buttermilk Sorbet, 283
Cake with Carrots, with Lemon Thyme Sorbet, 284–85
Macaroons, 282
-Pear Cake, Crunchy, 273–74

L'Angle du Faubourg, Paris, 41

L'Angle's Vegetable Salad: Carrots, Fennel, Radishes, Beets, and Onions, 41–42

Anton, Frédéric, 303

Frédéric Anton's Heirloom Tomato Salad, 29

Appetizers, Starters, and First Courses, 2–19
Artichoke and White Bean Dip, 19
Beet Tartare with Capers, Mustard, and Shallots, 14
Chickpea and Basil Purée, 16
Chickpea Dip with Fresh Cilantro, 18
Chorizo with Sherry Vinegar and Thyme, 9
Eggplant-Cumin Spread, Chunky, 12
Evergreen Tomato Cooler, 5
Gazpacho, Tomato and Strawberry, 10
Polenta-Cheese Crackers, Spicy, 7
Pumpkin Seeds, Toasted, Seasoned Toasted, 2–3
Savory Mixed Herb and Goat Cheese Sorbet, 6
Smoked Salmon with Dill-Mustard Sauce, 4
Squid Squares Stewed in Tomatoes and White Wine, 8

Apple-Rosemary-Cranberry Galette, 268

Artichauts Grillés à l'Aïoli, 158

Artichoke(s):
Baby, with Avocado, Pine Nuts, and Parmesan, 156–57
and Lemons, Grilled, with Spicy Garlic Mayonnaise, 158
and Parmesan Soup, 48
Quick Whole Wheat Pizza with Capers, Fresh Tomatoes and, 259–60
Rabbit with Pistou and, 117–18

Roasted Chickpeas, Mushrooms, Tomatoes and, 146

and Warm Goat Cheese Cannelloni the Lancaster, 136–37

and White Bean Dip, 19

Arugula, Roasted Asparagus with Shallot Vinaigrette and, 162

Asparagus, 57
Braised with Fresh Rosemary and Bay Leaves, 160
with Gruyère and Smoked Ham, 159
Roasted, with Arugula and Shallot Vinaigrette, 162
Tomato Coulis with Mint and, Guy Savoy's, 56

Asperges:
Braisées au Romarin, 160
au Four, Vinaigrette à l'Échalote, 162
Vertes au Jambon Fumé, 159

Astrance, Paris, 80, 131

Aubergines:
au Four à la Sauce Tomate, 177–78
du Pique-nique de Johannes, 183
et Tomates, Marché de Velleron, 181
Vapeur au Thym, 182

Aubéry-Clément, Michèle, 116

Autumn Celeriac, Celery, and Chestnut Soup with Parmesan and Rosemary, 70

Autumn Vegetable Ragout with Wild Mushrooms, 190–93

Avocado:
Baby Artichokes with, Pine Nuts, Parmesan and, 156–57
and Crab "Ravioli," 80
Spring Onion, Tomato, and Basil Salad with Basil-Lemon Dressing, 32
Zucchini Carpaccio with Lemon Thyme, Pistachio Oil and, 214

Baby Squid:
Salad with Garlic, Olives, Tomatoes, and Parsley, 97
Seared, with Parsley and Garlic, 96

Bacon:
Smoked, Golden Roasted Potatoes with Gruyère, Chives and, 224
Steamed Brussels Sprouts with Cream and, 170

Swiss Chard Leaf Purée with, La Beaugravière, 205

Watercress Salad with Creamy, and Poached Egg, Bistrot Paul Bert's, 22–23

Barbot, Pascal, 80

Basil:
and Chickpea Purée, 16
Eggplant, Tomato, and Cheese Timbales, 175–76
-Lemon Dressing, 297
-Lemon Dressing, Spring Onion, Cucumber, and Basil Salad with, 31
-Lemon Dressing, Spring Onion, Tomato, Avocado, and Basil Salad with, 32
Oil, 312
Purée, Light, 301
Purée, Light, Provençal Roast Tomatoes with, 209
Purée, Penne with Fava Beans, Parmesan and, 138
Roasted Eggplant Towers with Tomato Sauce, Fresh Cheese and, 177–78
Spring Onion, and Cucumber Salad with Basil-Lemon Dressing, 31
Spring Onion, Tomato, and Avocado Salad with Basil-Lemon Dressing, 32
Zucchini Blossoms Stuffed with Goat Cheese and, 216
see also Pistou

Bay Leaves:
Asparagus Braised with Fresh Rosemary and, 160
Lemon-Roasted Potatoes with, 231

La Beaugravière, Provence, 190, 205, 272

La Beaugravière, Swiss Chard Leaf Purée with Bacon, 205

Beef, Braised, with Carrots, 119–20

Beet(s):
in L'Angle's Vegetable Salad, 41–42
Curried, Soup, 59–60
Gazpacho, Chilled, 58
Grated, Salad: the Red and the Gold, 40
Tartare with Capers, Mustard, and Shallots, 14

Berenger, Eliane, 76

Berry-Rhubarb Compote in Grenadine, 289

Beurre de Truffe, 314
Biscuits de Polenta au Poivre de Cayenne, 7
Bistrot Paul Bert's Watercress Salad with
    Creamy Bacon and Poached Egg, 22–23
Blake, William, 236
Blancs de Poulet à la Menthe, 110
Blot, Jacky, 87
Boeuf Braisé aux Carottes, 119–20
Bouillon de Tomates à l'Estragon, 50
Boulestin, Marcel, 169
Boulevard Raspail Potato Galettes, 230
Brana, Etienne, 99
Breads, 248–65
    Date and Walnut, 248
    Jalapeño-Polenta, 258
    Lebanese Flatbread with Feta and Mint,
        262–63
    Lemon and Rosemary Flatbread, 264–65
    Parsley, Mint, Lemon, and Orange Flatbread,
        261
    Pumpkin, with Toasted Pumpkin Seeds,
        254–55
    Quick Walnut, 250
    Quick Whole Wheat Pizza with Artichokes,
        Capers, and Fresh Tomatoes, 259–60
    Rosemary-Scented Whole Wheat Brioche,
        251–53
    Tomato-Quinoa, 256–57
Brioche, Rosemary-Scented Whole Wheat,
    251–53
Brioche Complète au Romarin, 251–53
Broccoli Purée with a Hint of Mint, 167
Brochettes de Figues au Romarin, 244
Bru, Gérard, 81
Brussels Sprouts:
    Sautéed, with Garlic and Olive Oil, 169
    Steamed, with Bacon and Cream, 170
Butter:
    Potatoes in Chicken Stock with Mint and,
        226
    Truffle, 314
    -Warmed Corn Kernels with Fresh Cilantro
        Leaves, 174
Butter Lettuce and Radish Salad with Radish
    Sandwiches, 24
Buttermilk:
    -Almond Sorbet, 283
    Sorbet, 271
    -Thyme Dressing, 298
    -Thyme Dressing, Steamed Eggplant with,
        182
Butternut Squash Soup, Spicy, 61–62

Cabbage:
    Carrots, and Celery: Grated Salad, 36
    Coleslaw, Tangy, 35
    Savoy, Susan's Monkfish with Spanish Ham
        and, 103–5
    Steamed, Creamy, 171
    and Veal Rolls with Parmesan, 130–31
Cabillaud Cuit à la Vapeur de Romarin, 76
La Cagouille's Poached Skate with Sauce
    Gribiche, 94–95
Cailles Poêlées à la Moutarde, 113–14
Cake au Potiron et ses Graines Grillées, 254–55
Cakes:
    Almond, with Carrots, with Lemon Thyme
        Sorbet, 284–85
    Almond-Pear, Crunchy, 273–74
    Hazelnut and Heather Honey, 276
    Pistachio-Cherry, with Cherry Sorbet,
        279–80
Dés de Calamar à la Tomate, 8
*Cannelloni de Chèvre Tiède et Artichauts Hôtel
    Lancaster*, 136–37
Caper(s):
    Beet Tartare with Mustard, Shallots and, 14
    Chicken Breasts with Mint, White Wine and,
        110
    Lemon, and Olive Sauce, Salmon Wrapped
        in Spinach Leaves with, 86–87
    and Mustard Vinaigrette, Steamed Leeks in,
        188
    Potato-Chive Waffles with Smoked Salmon,
        Crème Fraîche and, 228
    Potato Salad with Spring Onions, Mint and,
        227
    Quick Whole Wheat Pizza with Artichokes,
        Fresh Tomatoes and, 259–60
    Tuna Confit with Tomatoes, White Wine
        and, 100–101
Carpaccio de Courgettes et d'Avocat, 214
Carrots:
    Almond Cake with, and Lemon Thyme
        Sorbet, 284–85
    in L'Angle's Vegetable Salad, 41–42
    Braised Beef with, 119–20
    Cabbage, and Celery: Grated Salad, 36
    Spicy, in Thai Medley, 212
    in Winter (Vegetable) Kaleidoscope, 196–97
Cauliflower:
    Golden, and Rice Pilaf, 144
    Purée, 172
Les Caves Taillevent, Paris, 159
Caviar d'Aubergine au Cumin, 12

Celeriac:
    Celery, and Chestnut Soup with Parmesan
        and Rosemary, Autumn, 70
    Salad with Fresh Crabmeat, 78
Celery:
    Cabbage, and Carrots: Grated Salad, 36
    Celeriac, and Chestnut Soup with Parmesan
        and Rosemary, Autumn, 70
Cervelas Pistaché, Vinaigrette au Vin Rouge,
    128–29
Champignons, en Papillote à la Menthe, 194
Chaource à la Truffe, 237
La Chassagnette, Camargue, 37, 81
Cheese:
    Blue, Fennel and Fig Salami for, 242
    Chaource, Truffled, 237
    Eggplant, Tomato, and Basil Timbales,
        175–76
    Feta, Lebanese Flatbread with Mint and,
        262–63
    Fresh, Roasted Eggplant Towers with
        Tomato Sauce, Basil and, 177–78
    Gruyère, Asparagus with Smoked Ham and,
        159
    Gruyère, Golden Roasted Potatoes with
        Smoked Bacon, Chives and, 224
    -Polenta Crackers, Spicy, 7
    Saffron, Pear, and Prune Compote for, 241
    Sheep's Milk, Shaved Fennel and Parsley
        Salad with, 38
    see also Goat Cheese; Parmesan
Cherry:
    -Pistachio Cake with Cherry Sorbet, 279–80
    Sweet, Sorbet, 281
Chestnut, Celeriac, and Celery Soup with
    Parmesan and Rosemary, Autumn, 70
Chicken:
    Breasts with Mint, Capers, and White Wine,
        110
    Grilled, with Shallot Vinaigrette, 108–9
    Stock, Homemade, 294–95
Chickpea(s):
    and Basil Purée, 16
    Couscous, Grains and, 149
    Cumin-scented, with Roasted Eggplant and
        Rustic Tomato Sauce, 152
    Dip with Fresh Cilantro, 18
    Lamb Couscous with Zucchini and, 124–25
    Lentil, and Swiss Chard Stew, Curried, 63–64
    Mushrooms, Artichokes, and Tomatoes,
        Roasted, 146
Chidaine, François, 137

Child, Julia, 178
Chive(s):
  Golden Roasted Potatoes with Gruyère,
    Smoked Bacon and, 224
  -Lemon Dressing, Creamy, 299
  and Potato Omelet, 238
  -Potato Waffles with Smoked Salmon,
    Capers, and Crème Fraîche, 228
  Tuna, and Shallot Tartare, Le Kaiku's, 102
Chocolate Custards, Individual, with Espelette
  Pepper, 272
Chorizo:
  Mussels with Cilantro and, 81
  with Sherry Vinegar and Thyme, 9
Chorizo au Thym et au Vinaigre de Xérès, 9
Chou à la Crème, 171
Chou Cru Rapé, Sauce Piquante, 35
Choux de Bruxelles:
  à la Crème et au Bacon, 170
  Sautés à l'Ail, 169
Christian Etienne, Avignon, 210
Cilantro, Fresh:
  Chickpea Dip with, 18
  Chilled Heirloom Tomato, Corn, and
    Cucumber Soup with, 51
  Chunky Corn Soup with Smoked Spanish
    Paprika and, 52
  Leaves, Butter-Warmed Corn Kernels with,
    174
  Mussels with Chorizo and, 81
  Sauce, 302
Le Cinq Mars, Cucumber, Spring Onions, and
  Goat Cheese Salad, 26
Cod, Six-Minute Fresh, Steamed on a Bed of
  Rosemary, 76
Coleslaw, Tangy, 35
Compotes:
  Rhubarb-Berry, in Grenadine, 289
  Saffron, Pear, and Prune, for Cheese, 241
Compotes:
  de Poires et Pruneaux au Safran, 241
  de Rhubarbe aux Fruits Rouges, 289
Confit:
  de Thon aux Tomates, Câpres et Vin Blanc,
    100–101
  de Tomates-Cerises, 208
Coquilles Saint-Jacques, Fondue de Poireaux, 91–93
Corn:
  Heirloom Tomato, and Cucumber Soup,
    Chilled, with Fresh Cilantro, 51
  Kernels, Butter-Warmed, with Fresh
    Cilantro Leaves, 174

Soup, Chunky, with Cilantro and Smoked
    Spanish Paprika, 52
Cornillon, Ludovic, 129
Courgettes du Domaine de La Ponche, 217
Couscous:
  Grains, and Chickpeas, 149
  Lamb, with Chickpeas and Zucchini, 124–25
  Salad with Spinach, Parsley, and Spring
    Onions, 150
Couscous:
  d'Agneau aux Courgettes et Pois Chiches,
    124–25
  Pois Chiches et Flocons Variés, 149
Crab(meat):
  and Avocado "Ravioli," 80
  Fresh, Celeriac Salad with, 78
Cranberry-Rosemary-Apple Galette, 268
Cream(y):
  Cabbage, Steamed, 171
  Lemon-Chive Dressing, 299
  Sauce, Spicy, Warm Oysters with Spinach
    and, 84
  Steamed Brussels Sprouts with Bacon and,
    170
  Truffle, 313
  Wild Morel Mushrooms in, 189
Crème:
  de Concombre à l'Aneth et à la Menthe, 54
  Froide à la Tomate, 49
  de Poivrons Oranges, 68–69
  de Polenta à l'Oeuf Poché, 239–40
  de Topinambours, Huile de Noisette, 71
  de Truffe, 313
Crème Fraîche, Potato-Chive Waffles with
  Smoked Salmon, Capers and, 228
Crisps de Pommes de Terre de Jo et George, 225
Cucumber:
  and Dill Salad, 28
  Heirloom Tomato, and Corn Soup, Chilled,
    with Fresh Cilantro, 51
  Spring Onion, and Basil Salad with Basil-
    Lemon Dressing, 31
  Spring Onion, and Goat Cheese Salad Le
    Cinq-Mars, 26
  and Yogurt Soup, Chilled, with Dill and
    Fresh Mint, 54
Cumin:
  -Eggplant Spread, Chunky, 12
  Red Peppers, Tomatoes, Onions, and
    Espelette Pepper, 200
  -Scented Chickpeas with Roasted Eggplant
    and Rustic Tomato Sauce, 152

Curry(ied):
  Beet Soup, 59–60
  Chickpea, Lentil, and Swiss Chard Stew,
    63–64
  Paste, Thai, 309
  Powder, 308

Date and Walnut Bread, 248
"Daube," Definition of, 180
Daube d'Aubergines, 179
Delorme, Christophe, 98
Desserts, 268–91
  Almond-Buttermilk Sorbet, 283
  Almond Cake with Carrots, with Lemon
    Thyme Sorbet, 284–85
  Almond Macaroons, 282
  Almond-Pear Cake, Crunchy, 273–74
  Buttermilk Sorbet, 271
  Hazelnut and Heather Honey Cake, 276
  Individual Chocolate Custards with
    Espelette Pepper, 272
  Lemon-Thyme Sorbet, 286
  Lemon Zest Sorbet, 278
  Light, Flaky, Whole Wheat Pastry, 270
  Pistachio-Cherry Cake with Cherry Sorbet,
    279–80
  Pumpkin Flan with Lemon Sauce, 287–88
  Rhubarb-Berry Compote in Grenadine, 289
  Rosemary-Apple-Cranberry Galette, 268
  Seasonal Fruits Roasted with Honey-Lemon
    Sauce and Fresh Lemon Verbena, 290
  Sheep's Milk Yogurt Sorbet, 291
  Sweet Cherry Sorbet, 281
Dill:
  Cucumber and Yogurt Soup, Chilled, with
    Fresh Mint and, 54
  and Cucumber Salad, 28
  -Mustard Sauce, Smoked Salmon with, 4
Domaine de la Ponche, 217
Doutre-Roussel, Chloé, 272
Dressings:
  Basil-Lemon, 297
  Basil-Lemon, Spring Onion, Cucumber, and
    Basil Salad with, 31
  Basil-Lemon, Spring Onion, Tomato,
    Avocado, and Basil Salad with, 32
  Buttermilk-Thyme, 298
  Buttermilk-Thyme, Steamed Eggplant with,
    182
  Creamy Lemon-Chive, 299
  Creamy Lemon-Chive, Zucchini Spaghetti
    with, 213

Duck Breast, Seared, with Espelette Pepper
Jelly, 111–12
Durand, Roland, 58

L'Ecailler du Bistrot, Paris, 78
Eggplant:
-Cumin Spread, Chunky, 12
Daube, 179
Johannes's Picnic, 183
Roasted, and Rustic Tomato Sauce, Cumin-
Scented Chickpeas with, 152
Roasted, Towers with Tomato Sauce, Fresh
Cheese, and Basil, 177–78
Steamed, with Buttermilk-Thyme Dressing,
182
Tomato, Basil, and Cheese Timbales, 175–76
and Tomatoes from the Velleron Market, 181
Eggs:
Poached, Creamy Polenta with, 239–40
Poached, Watercress Salad with Creamy
Bacon and, Bistrot Paul Bert's, 22–23
Potato and Chive Omelet, 238
Victor Emmanuel's Salad, 39
Des Épinards, Rien de Plus!, 203
Escoffier, Georges-Auguste, 295
Espelette Pepper, 112
Individual Chocolate Custards with, 272
Jelly, 307
Jelly, Seared Duck Breast with, 111–12
Red Peppers, Tomatoes, Onions, and Cumin,
200
Salt, 311
Tuna Strips with, 99

Fava Beans, Penne with Basil Purée, Parmesan
and, 138
Fennel:
in L'Angle's Vegetable Salad, 41–42
and Fig Salami for Blue Cheese, 242
Sautéed Quail with Mustard and, 113–14
Shaved, and Parsley Salad with Sheep's Milk
Cheese, 38
Fig(s):
and Fennel Salami for Blue Cheese, 242
Fresh, on Rosemary Skewers, 244
Fish and Shellfish, 76–105
Cod, Six-Minute Fresh, Steamed on a Bed of
Rosemary, 76
Crab, and Avocado "Ravioli," 80
Crabmeat, Fresh, Celeriac Salad with, 78
Monkfish with Savoy Cabbage and Spanish
Ham, Susan's, 103–5

Mussels with Chorizo and Cilantro, 81
Mussels with Swiss Chard and Saffron
Cream, 82–83
Oysters, Warm, with Spinach and Spicy
Cream Sauce, 84
Salmon Wrapped in Spinach Leaves with
Caper, Lemon, and Olive Sauce, 86–87
Sardines, Quick-Cured, with Shallots on Rye
Bread, 88
Sardines in Parchment with Tomatoes and
Onions, 89–90
Sea Scallops on a Bed of Leeks, 91–93
Skate, Poached, with Sauce Gribiche, La
Cagouille's, 94–95
Smoked Salmon, Potato-Chive Waffles with
Capers, Crème Fraîche and, 228
Smoked Salmon with Dill-Mustard Sauce, 4
Squid, Baby, Salad with Garlic, Olives,
Tomatoes, and Parsley, 97
Squid, Baby, Seared, with Parsley and Garlic,
96
Squid Squares Stewed in Tomatoes and
White Wine, 8
Tuna, Chive, and Shallot Tartare, Le Kaiku's,
102
Tuna Confit with Tomatoes, Capers, and
White Wine, 100–101
Tuna Strips with Espelette Pepper, 99
Flan, Pumpkin, with Lemon Sauce, 287–88
Flan de Potimarron, Sauce Citron, 287–88
Fleur de Sel, 310
Fleurs de Courgettes Farcies, 216
Fond de Volaille Maison, 294–95
Fougasse au Citron et au Romarin, 264–65
Frauenknecht, Madeleine, 217
"Frites" de Patates Douces, 204
Fruits, Seasonal, Roasted with Honey-Lemon
Sauce and Fresh Lemon Verbena, 290
Fruits d'Eté au Four à la Verveine Odorante, 290

Gagnaire, Pierre, 71
Galette(s):
Potato, Boulevard Raspail, 230
Rosemary-Apple-Cranberry, 268
Galette Fine aux Pommes, Airelles et Romarin,
268
Galettes de Pommes de Terre du Boulevard Raspail,
230
Garlic:
Baby Squid Salad with Olives, Tomatoes,
Parsley and, 97
green "germ" of, 55

Mayonnaise, Spicy, 304
-Rich, Seven-Hour Leg of Lamb, 126
Roasted Fresh, 184
Sautéed Brussels Sprouts with Olive Oil and,
169
Seared Baby Squid with Parsley and, 96
Gaspacho, 55
de Betterave, 58
à la Fraise, 10
de Légumes d'Été à la Coriandre, 51
Gâteaux:
aux Amandes et Carottes, Sorbet Thym-Citron,
284–85
aux Noisettes et Miel de Bruyère, 276
Pistache-Cerises, Sorbet aux Cerises, 279–80
aux Poires et Amandes, Sucre Amande, 273–74
Gaufres de Pommes de Terre au Saumon Fumé,
228
Gazpacho:
Chilled Beet, 58
Tomato, 55
Tomato and Strawberry, 10
Gelée de Piment d'Espelette, 307
Germain, Thierry, 90
Germon, George, 225
Gigot d'Agneau en Chemise de Menthe et de Miel,
122–23
Gigot de Sept Heures à l'Ail, 126
Goat Cheese:
Cucumber, and Spring Onion Salad Le Cinq
Mars, 26
"Oreos" with Truffles, 234
and Savory Mixed Herb Sorbet, 6
Warm, and Artichoke Cannelloni the
Lancaster, 136–37
Zucchini Blossoms Stuffed with Basil and,
216
Good Gardener, The, 176
Les Gourmandines, Provence, 65
Graines de Courge Grillées, 2
Grains, 140–44
Couscous, and Chickpeas, 149
Great: Quinoa, Spelt, Rice, Millet, and
Sesame, 153
Rice Pilaf, Golden Cauliflower and, 144
Risotto, Pea and Mint, 140–41
Risotto, Pumpkin and Sage, 142–43
Le Grand Pré, Roaix, 184
Gras, Yves, 83, 120, 183
Gratins:
Parmesan, Pine Nut, and Truffle, 235–36
Potato, from the Savoy, 222

Pumpkin, with Pistachios and Pistachio Oil, 202

Swiss Chard Rib, with Pine Nuts and Parmesan, Yannick Alléno's, 206–7

Gratins:

de Bettes de Yannick Alléno, 206–7

de Potiron à la Pistache, 202

Savoyard, 222

Gray, Patience, 301

Green Beans with Summer Savory, 164

Grenadine, Rhubarb-Berry Compote in, 289

Ham:

Smoked, Asparagus with Gruyère and, 159

Spanish, Monkfish with Savoy Cabbage and, Susan's, 103–5

Haricots Verts à la Sarriette, 164

Hazelnut:

and Heather Honey Cake, 276

Oil, Jerusalem Artichoke Soup with, 71

Herbs:

Savory Mixed, and Goat Cheese Sorbet, 6

on storing fresh, 123

see also specific herbs

Hernandez, Antoine, 77

Honey:

Heather, and Hazelnut Cake, 276

-Lemon Sauce and Fresh Lemon Verbena, Seasonal Fruits Roasted with, 290

and Mint Crust, Roast Leg of Lamb with, 122–23

Hotel Meurice, Paris, 206

Huile:

de Basilic, 312

de Truffe, 313

Huitres Chaudes aux Épinards, Sauce Epicée, 84

"Ice Saints," 166

Jalapeño-Polenta Bread, 258

"Jardin de Curé," 151

Jefford, Andrew, 118, 129

Jelly, Espelette Pepper, 307

Seared Duck Breast with, 111–12

Jerusalem Artichoke(s):

Minted, Salad with Mâche, 44

Soup, with Hazelnut Oil, 71

in Winter (Vegetable) Kaleidoscope, 196–97

Jo and George's Potato Crispies, 225

Johannes's Picnic Eggplant, 183

"Julia's Kitchen," 178

Julien, Guy, 190, 205, 272

Julien, Tina, 190

Jus de Tomates Vertes, 5

Le Kaiku's Tuna, Chive, and Shallot Tartare, 102

Killeen, Johanne, 225

Lamb:

Couscous with Chickpeas and Zucchini, 124–25

Leg of, Garlic-Rich Seven-Hour, 126

Roast Leg of, with Honey and Mint Crust, 122–23

Lamb, Charles, 163

Lamb's Lettuce (Mâche):

Minted Jerusalem Artichoke Salad with, 44

Purée, 186

Lamy, Hubert, 118

The Lancaster, Warm Goat Cheese and Artichoke Cannelloni, 136–37

Langlois, Fabrice, 120, 182, 240

Lanières de Thon au Piment d'Espelette, 99

Lapin:

aux Artichauts et au Pistou, 117–18

au Vin Rouge et aux Olives Noires, 115–16

Lebanese Flatbread with Feta and Mint, 262–63

Leeks:

Sea Scallops on a Bed of, 91–93

Steamed, in Mustard and Caper Vinaigrette, 188

Lemon(s):

and Artichokes, Grilled, with Spicy Garlic Mayonnaise, 158

-Basil Dressing, 297

-Basil Dressing, Spring Onion, Cucumber, and Basil Salad with, 31

-Basil Dressing, Spring Onion, Tomato, Avocado, and Basil Salad with, 32

Caper, and Olive Sauce, Salmon Wrapped in Spinach Leaves with, 86–87

-Chive Dressing, Creamy, 299

-Chive Dressing, Creamy, Zucchini Spaghetti with, 213

-Honey Sauce and Fresh Lemon Verbena, Seasonal Fruits Roasted with, 290

Parsley, Mint, and Orange Flatbread, 261

-Roasted Potatoes with Bay Leaves, 231

and Rosemary Flatbread, 264–65

Sauce, Pumpkin Flan with, 287–88

Zest Sorbet, 278

Zesty, Salt, 310

Lemon Thyme:

Sorbet, 286

Zucchini Carpaccio with Avocado, Pistachio Oil and, 214

Lemon-Verbena, Fresh, Seasonal Fruits Roasted with Honey-Lemon Sauce and, 290

Lentil, Chickpea, and Swiss Chard Stew, Curried, 63–64

Loomis, Susan Hermann, 103

Louis XIV, King, 141, 176

Macarons aux Amandes, Sorbet Amande-Lait Fermenté, 282

Magrets de Canard à la Gelée de Piment d'Espelette, 111–12

Maïs á la Coriandre, 174

Mayonnaise, Spicy Garlic, 304

Meats, 115–33

Beef, Braised, with Carrots, 119–20

Lamb, Garlic-Rich Seven-Hour Leg of, 126

Lamb, Roast Leg of, with Honey and Mint Crust, 122–23

Lamb Couscous with Chickpeas and Zucchini, 124–25

Pork Sausage with Potatoes and Red Wine Vinaigrette, 128–29

Rabbit, Braised, with Black Olives, Red Wine, and Pine Nuts, 115–16

Rabbit with Artichokes and Pistou, 117–18

Veal, Sauté of, with Fresh Tarragon, 132

Veal and Cabbage Rolls with Parmesan, 130–31

Mélange de Légumes Thaï, 212

Méli-Mélo:

de Graines et Céréales, 153

d'Herbes et de Légumes, 37

de Légumes d'Hiver, 196–97

Meyssonnier, Antoine, 196

Millet, in Great Grains, 153

Mini-Toasts au Chèvre et à la Truffe, 234

Mint(ed):

Baby Spinach, and Radish Salad, 34

Broccoli Purée with a Hint of, 167

Chicken Breasts with, Capers, White Wine and, 110

Fresh, Chilled Cucumber and Yogurt Soup with Dill and, 54

Fresh, Spaghetti with Green Olives, Garlic and, 139

Fresh Peas with Spring Onions and, 198

and Honey Crust, Roast Leg of Lamb with, 122–23

Mint(ed) (continued)
    Jerusalem Artichoke Salad with Mâche, 44
    Lebanese Flatbread with Feta and, 262–63
    Parsley, Lemon, and Orange Flatbread, 261
    and Pea Risotto, 140–41
    Potatoes in Chicken Stock with Butter and, 226
    Potato Salad with Spring Onions, Capers and, 227
    Tomato Coulis with Asparagus and, Guy Savoy's, 56
    Wild, Wild Mushrooms in Parchment with, 194
Monkfish with Savoy Cabbage and Spanish Ham, Susan's, 103–5
Morels:
    in Cream, Fresh White Bean Soup with, 65–66
    Wild, in Cream, 189
Morilles à la Crème, 189
Moules:
    aux Blettes en Crème Safranée, 82–83
    au Chorizo et Coriandre, 81
Mushrooms, 195
    Roasted Chickpeas, Artichokes, Tomatoes and, 146
    Wild, Autumn Vegetable Ragout with, 190–93
    Wild, in Parchment with Wild Mint, 194
    see also Morels
Mussels:
    with Chorizo and Cilantro, 81
    with Swiss Chard and Saffron Cream, 82–83
Mustard:
    Beet Tartare with Capers, Shallots and, 14
    and Caper Vinaigrette, Steamed Leeks in, 188
    -Dill Sauce, Smoked Salmon with, 4
    Sautéed Quail with Fennel and, 113–14

Oils:
    Basil, 312
    Hazelnuts, Jerusalem Artichoke Soup with, 71
    Pistachio, Pumpkin Gratin with Pistachios and, 202
    Pistachio, Zucchini Carpaccio with Avocado, Lemon Thyme and, 214
    Truffle, 313
    see also Olive Oil
Olive(s):
    Baby Squid with Garlic, Tomatoes, and Parsley, 97

Black, Braised Rabbit with Red Wine, Pine Nuts and, 115–16
Black, and Cherry Tomato Salad, 30
Green, Spaghetti with Garlic, Fresh Mint and, 139
Lemon, and Caper Sauce, Salmon Wrapped in Spinach Leaves with, 86–87
Olive Oil:
    Oven-Roasted Red Peppers in, 199
    Sautéed Brussels Sprouts with Garlic and, 169
Omelette de Pommes de Terre et à la Ciboulette, 238
O'Neill, Catherine, 224
Onimus, Jean-Pierre, 217
Onions:
    in L'Angle's Vegetable Salad, 41–42
    Red Peppers, Tomatoes, Cumin, and Espelette Pepper, 200
    Sardines in Parchment with Tomatoes and, 89–90
    see also Spring Onion(s)
Orange, Parsley, Mint, and Lemon Flatbread, 261
Oysters:
    and Rye Bread, 85
    Warm, with Spinach and Spicy Cream Sauce, 84

Pain:
    Arabe à la Feta et à le Menthe, 262–63
    Arabe aux Parfums d'Agrumes, 261
    aux Dattes et aux Noix, 248
    aux Noix, 250
    à la Polenta Epicée, 258
    de Quinoa à la Tomate, 256–57
Pannequets de Chou au Parmesan, 130–31
Pantry, 294–316
    Basil-Lemon Dressing, 297
    Basil Oil, 312
    Basil Purée, Light, 301
    Buttermilk-Thyme Dressing, 298
    Chicken Stock, Homemade, 294–95
    Cilantro Sauce, Fresh, 302
    Curry Paste, Thai, 309
    Curry Powder, 308
    Espelette Pepper Jelly, 307
    Espelette Pepper Salt, 311
    Garlic Mayonnaise, Spicy, 304
    Lemon-Chive Dressing, Creamy, 299
    Lemon Salt, Zesty, 310
    Shallot Vinaigrette, 300
    Tomato Sauce, Chunky Fresh, 305

Tomato Sauce, Rustic Oven-Roasted, 306
Truffle Butter, 314
Truffle Cream, 313
Truffle Oil, 313
Vinaigrette, Classic, 296
Watercress Pesto, 303
Paré, Ambroise, 96
Parker, Robert, 125
Parmesan, 73
    and Artichoke Soup, 48
    Autumn Celeriac, Celery, and Chestnut Soup with Rosemary and, 70
    Baby Artichokes with Avocado, Pine Nuts and, 156–57
    Cabbage and Veal Rolls with, 130–31
    Penne with Fava Beans, Basil Purée and, 138
    Pine Nut, and Truffle Gratins, 235–36
    Swiss Chard Rib Gratin with Pine Nuts and, Yannick Alléno's, 206–7
Parsley:
    Baby Squid with Garlic, Olives, Tomatoes and, 97
    Couscous Salad with Spinach, Spring Onions and, 150
    Mint, Lemon, and Orange Flatbread, 261
    Seared Baby Squid with Garlic and, 96
    and Shaved Fennel Salad with Sheep's Milk Cheese, 38
Passiflore, Paris, 58
Pasta, 136–39
    Cannelloni, Warm Goat Cheese and Artichoke, the Lancaster, 136–37
    Penne with Fava Beans, Basil Purée, and Parmesan, 138
    Spaghetti with Green Olives, Garlic, and Fresh Mint, 139
Pastry, Light, Flaky Whole Wheat, 270
Pâte:
    Brisée Légère, 270
    à Curry Thaï, 309
Pea(s):
    Fresh, with Mint and Spring Onions, 198
    and Mint Risotto, 140–41
Pear(s):
    -Almond Cake, Crunchy, 273–74
    Saffron, and Prune Compote for Cheese, 241
Penne aux Fèves, 138
Peppers:
    Perfect Roasted, 69
    Red, Oven-Roasted, in Olive Oil, 199
    Red, Tomatoes, Onions, Cumin, and Espelette Pepper, 200

Roasted Orange, Soup, 68–69
  see also Espelette Pepper
Pesto, Watercress, 303
Pesto au Cresson, 303
Petit Pots de Crème au Chocolat au Piment
  d'Espelette, 272
Petits Artichauts aux Pignons et au Parmesan,
  156–57
Petits Pois à la Menthe et Oignons Nouveaux, 198
Piment d'Espelette, 112
Pine Nuts:
  Baby Artichokes with Avocado, Parmesan
    and, 156–57
  Braised Rabbit with Black Olives, Red Wine
    and, 115–16
  Parmesan, and Truffle Gratins, 235–36
  Swiss Chard Rib Gratin with Parmesan and,
    Yannick Alléno's, 206–7
Pistachio(s):
  -Cherry Cake with Cherry Sorbet, 279–80
  and Pistachio Oil, Pumpkin Gratin with, 202
Pistou:
  Rabbit with Artichokes and, 117–18
  Winter Root Vegetable, 72–73
Pistou aux Légumes d'Hiver, 72–73
Pizza, Quick Whole Wheat, with Artichokes,
  Capers, and Fresh Tomatoes, 259–60
Pizza de Blé Complet aux Artichauts, Câpres et
  Tomates, 259–60
Poilâne, Lionel, 85
Poireaux Vinaigrette, 188
Pois Chiches:
  et Aubergine au Cumin en Sauce Tomate, 152
  Champignons, Tomates, et Artichauts au Four, 146
Poivrons Rouges:
  au Four, 199
  et Tomates au Piment d'Espelette, 200
Polenta:
  -Cheese Crackers, Spicy, 7
  Creamy, with a Poached Egg, 239–40
  -Jalapeño Bread, 258
  Wedges, Creamy, 148
Polenta Poêlée, 148
Pommes de Terre:
  au Bouillon de Menthe, 226
  au Four, 224
  au Four au Citron et au Laurier, 231
  Gaufres de, au Saumon Fumé, 228
Pork Sausage with Potatoes and Red Wine
  Vinaigrette, 128–29
Potage de Tomates aux Asperges et à la Menthe de
  Guy Savoy, 56

Potato(es), 222–31
  in Chicken Stock with Mint and Butter, 226
  and Chive Omelet, 238
  -Chive Waffles with Smoked Salmon,
    Capers, and Crème Fraîche, 228
  Crispies, Jo and George's, 225
  Galettes, Boulevard Raspail, 230
  Golden Roasted, with Gruyère, Smoked
    Bacon, and Chives, 224
  Gratin from the Savoy, 222
  History of, 129
  Lemon-Roasted, with Bay Leaves, 231
  Pork Sausage with Red Wine Vinaigrette
    and, 128–29
  Salad with Spring Onions, Capers, and Mint,
    227
  Spicy, in Thai Medley, 212
Poudre de Curry, 308
Poulet en Crapaudine à la Vinaigrette d'Échalote,
  108–9
Poultry, 108–14
  Chicken, Grilled, with Shallot Vinaigrette,
    108–9
  Chicken Breasts with Mint, Capers, and
    White Wine, 110
  Duck Breast, Seared, with Espelette Pepper
    Jelly, 111–12
  Quail, Sautéed, with Mustard and Fennel,
    113–14
Le Pré Catelan, Paris, 29, 303
Prune, Saffron, and Pear Compote for Cheese,
  241
Pumpkin(s):
  Bread with Toasted, Seeds, 254–55
  Flan with Lemon Sauce, 287–88
  Gratin with Pistachios and Pistachio Oil, 202
  Purée, 62
  and Sage Risotto, 142–43
  Seeds, Toasted, Seasoned, 2–3
Purées:
  d'Artichaut et de Haricots Blancs, 19
  de Brocoli à la Menthe, 167
  de Chou-fleur, 172
  de Courgettes, 219
  de Feuilles de Bettes au Bacon de La
    Beaugravière, 205
  de Mâche, 186
  de Pois Chiches à la Coriandre, 18

Quail:
  How to Butterfly, 114
  Sautéed, with Mustard and Fennel, 113–14

Quénard, André and Michel, 110
Queues de Lotte au Chou Vert et au Bellota de
  Susan, 103–5
Quinoa:
  in Great Grains, 153
  -Tomato Bread, 256–57

Rabbit:
  with Artichokes and Pistou, 117–18
  Braised, with Black Olives, Red Wine, and
    Pine Nuts, 115–16
Radish(es):
  in L'Angle's Vegetable Salad, 41–42
  Baby Spinach, and Mint Salad, 34
  and Butter Lettuce Salad with Radish
    Sandwiches, 24
  in Winter (Vegetable) Kaleidoscope, 196–97
Ragout d'Automne aux Champignons, 190–93
"Raviole" d'Avocat au Crabe, 80
Red Wine:
  Braised Rabbit with Black Olives, Pine Nuts
    and, 115–16
  Vinaigrette, Pork Sausage with Potatoes and,
    128–29
Reichrath, Raoul, 184
Rémoulade de Céleri-rave au Crabe, 78
Rhubarb-Berry Compote in Grenadine, 289
Rice Pilaf, Golden Cauliflower and, 144
Risotto:
  Pea and Mint, 140–41
  Pumpkin and Sage, 142–43
Risotto:
  aux Petits Pois et à la Menthe, 140–41
  au Potiron et à la Sauge, 142–43
Riz Pilaf au Chou-Fleur et aux Épices, 144
Romero, André and Frédéric, 242
Rondelles de Courgettes en Sauce Tomate, 218
Rosemary:
  -Apple-Cranberry Galette, 268
  Autumn Celeriac, Celery, and Chestnut Soup
    with Parmesan and, 70
  Fresh, Asparagus Braised with Bay Leaves
    and, 160
  and Lemon Flatbread, 264–65
  -Scented Whole Wheat Brioche, 251–53
  Six-Minute Fresh Cod Steamed on a Bed of,
    76
  Skewers, Fresh Figs on, 244
Rothfeld, Steven, 14, 230
Rye Bread:
  Oysters and, 85
  Quick-Cured Sardines with Shallots on, 88

Saffron:
    Cream, Mussels with Swiss Chard and, 82–83
    Pear, and Prune Compote for Cheese, 241
Sage and Pumpkin Risotto, 142–43
Sailer, Johannes, 49, 82, 183
Salades:
    de Betterave: Le Rouge et l'Or, 40
    de Chou, Carottes et Céleri Râpés, 36
    de Ciboule, Concombre et Basilic, 31
    de Ciboule, Tomates-Cerises, Avocat et Basilic, 32
    de Concombre à l'Aneth, 28
    de Concombre au Chèvre Frais du Cinq-Mars, 26
    de Cresson du Bistrot Paul Bert, 22–23
    de Doucette aux Topinambours et à la Menthe, 44
    de Fenouil au Fromage de Brebis, 38
    aux Jeunes Pousses d'Épinard, Radis, et Menthe, 34
    de Laitue et Radis, Accompagnée de Canapés aux Radis, 24
    aux Légumes d'Hiver de l'Angle du Faubourg, 41–42
    de Petits Calmars à la Provençale, 97
    de Pommes de Terre, Sauce Printanière, 227
    de Tomates-Cerises et Olives Noires, 30
    de Tomates de Frédéric Anton, 29
    Tricolore, 39
Salads, 22–44
    Baby Spinach, Radish, and Mint, 34
    Baby Squid, with Garlic, Olives, Tomatoes, and Parsley, 97
    Cabbage, Carrots, and Celery, Grated, 36
    Carrots, Fennel, Radishes, Beets, and Onions: L'Angle's Vegetable, 41–42
    Celeriac, with Fresh Crabmeat, 78
    Cherry Tomato and Black Olive, 30
    Coleslaw, Tangy, 35
    Couscous, with Spinach, Parsley, and Spring Onions, 150
    Cucumber, Spring Onion, and Goat Cheese, Le Cinq-Mars, 26
    Cucumber and Dill, 28
    Grated Beet: The Red and the Gold, 40
    Heirloom Tomato, Frédéric Anton's, 29
    Jerusalem Artichoke, Minted, with Mâche, 44
    Potato, with Spring Onions, Capers, and Mint, 227
    Radish and Butter Lettuce, with Radish Sandwiches, 24
    Shaved Fennel and Parsley, with Sheep's Milk Cheese, 38
    Shaved Vegetable, 37
    Spring Onion, Cucumber, and Basil, with Basil-Lemon Dressing, 31
    Spring Onion, Tomato, Avocado, and Basil, with Basil-Lemon Dressing, 32
    Victor Emmanuel's, 39
    Watercress, with Creamy Bacon and Poached Egg, Bistrot Paul Bert's, 22–23
Salami de Figues aux Graines de Fenouil, 242
Salmon:
    Smoked, with Dill-Mustard Sauce, 4
    Smoked, Potato-Chive Waffles with Capers, Crème Fraîche and, 228
    Wrapped in Spinach Leaves with Caper, Lemon, and Olive Sauce, 86–87
Salt:
    Espelette Pepper, 311
    Fleur de Sel, 310
    Zesty Lemon, 310
Sanchez, Juan, 96, 127, 139
Sardines:
    in Parchment with Tomatoes and Onions, 89–90
    Quick-Cured, with Shallots on Rye Bread, 88
Sardines:
    Marinées aux Échalotes sur Toast de Seigle, 88
    en Papillote aux Tomates et Oignons, 89–90
Sauces:
    Caper, Lemon, and Olive, Salmon Wrapped in Spinach Leaves with, 86–87
    Chunky Fresh Tomato, 305
    Curdling of, 299
    Dill-Mustard, Smoked Salmon with, 4
    Fresh Cilantro, 302
    Gribiche, Poached Skate with, La Cagouille's, 94–95
    Honey-Lemon, Seasonal Fruits Roasted with Fresh Lemon Verbena and, 290
    Lemon, Pumpkin Flan with, 287–88
    Spicy Cream, Warm Oysters with Spinach and, 84
    Tomato, Rustic Oven-Roasted, 306
    Tomato, Zucchini Coins in, 218
Sauces:
    Basilic-Citron, 297
    Basilic Légère, 301
    au Citron et à la Ciboulette, 299
    à la Coriandre, 302
    au Lait Fermenté au Thym, 298
    aux Tomates Cuites au Four, 306
    aux Tomates du Jardin, 305
Saumon:
    en Chemise d'Épinards, Sauce aux Olives, 86–87
    Fumé, Sauce Moutarde à la Menthe, 4
Sauté de Veau à l'Estragon, 132
Savoy, Guy, 48, 56
    Guy Savoy's Tomato Coulis with Asparagus and Mint, 56
Sea Scallops on a Bed of Leeks, 91–93
Sel:
    au Piment d'Espelette, 311
    au Zeste de Citron, 310
Sesame, in Great Grains, 153
Shallot(s):
    Beet Tartare with Capers, Mustard and, 14
    Quick-Cured Sardines with, on Rye Bread, 88
    Tuna, and Chive Tartare, Le Kaiku's, 102
Shallot Vinaigrette, 300
    Grilled Chicken with, 108–9
    Roasted Asparagus with Arugula and, 162
Sherry Vinegar and Thyme, Chorizo with, 9
Skate, Poached, with Sauce Gribiche, La Cagouille's, 94–95
Le Soleil, Paris, 167
Sorbets:
    Almond-Buttermilk, 283
    Buttermilk, 271
    Lemon Thyme, 286
    Lemon Zest, 278
    Savory Mixed Herb and Goat Cheese, 6
    Sheep's Milk Yogurt, 291
    Sweet Cherry, 281
    Tomato, 211
Sorbets:
    Amande-Lait Fermenté, 283
    aux Cerises, 281
    au Chèvre Frais et aux Herbes Aromatiques, 6
    au Lait Fermenté, 271
    au Thym-Citron, 286
    à la Tomate, 211
    au Yaourt de Brebis, 291
    au Zeste de Citron, 278
Soupes:
    d'Artichauts au Parmesan, 48
    d'Automne au Céleri-Rave, Céleri et Marrons, 70
    de Betterave au Curry, 59–60
    de Courge Musquée au Curry, 61–62
    de Maïs à la Coriandre et au Paprika Espagnol, 52
    de Pois Chiches, Lentilles et Blettes, 63–64
Soupions à l'Ail et au Persil, 96

Soups, 48–73
    Artichoke and Parmesan, 48
    Beet, Curried, 59–60
    Beet Gazpacho, Chilled, 58
    Butternut Squash, Spicy, 61–62
    Celeriac, Celery, and Chestnut, Autumn, with Parmesan and Rosemary, 70
    Chickpea, Lentil, and Swiss Chard Stew, Curried, 63–64
    Corn, with Cilantro and Smoked Spanish Paprika, Chunky, 52
    Cucumber and Yogurt, with Dill and Fresh Mint, Chilled, 54
    Heirloom Tomato, Corn, and Cucumber, Chilled, with Fresh Cilantro, 51
    Heirloom Tomato, Marinated, 49
    Heirloom Tomato Broth with Tarragon, 50
    Jerusalem Artichoke, with Hazelnut Oil, 71
    Orange Pepper, Roasted, 68–69
    Tomato Coulis with Asparagus and Mint, Guy Savoy's, 56
    Tomato Gazpacho, 55
    White Bean, Fresh, with Morels in Cream, 65–66
    Winter Root Vegetable Pistou, 72
Spaghetti aux Olives Vertes et à la Menthe, 139
Spaghettis de Courgettes, 213
Spaghetti with Green Olives, Garlic, and Fresh Mint, 139
Spahn, Ruth, 217
Spanish Paprika, Smoked, Chunky Corn Soup with Cilantro and, 52
Spelt, in Great Grains, 153
Spinach:
    Baby, Radish, and Mint Salad, 34
    Couscous Salad with Parsley, Spring Onions and, 150
    Just Spinach!, 203
    Leaves, Salmon Wrapped in, with Caper, Lemon, and Olive Sauce, 86–87
    and Spicy Cream Sauce, Warm Oysters with, 84
Spring Onion(s):
    Couscous Salad with Spinach, Parsley and, 150
    Cucumber, and Basil Salad with Basil-Lemon Dressing, 31
    Cucumber, and Goat Cheese Salad Le Cinq-Mars, 26
    Fresh Peas with Mint and, 198

    Potato Salad with Capers, Mint and, 227
    Tomato, Avocado, and Basil Salad with Basil-Lemon Dressing, 32
Squash Purée, 62
Squid:
    Baby, Salad with Garlic, Olives, Tomatoes, and Parsley, 97
    Baby, Seared, with Parsley and Garlic, 96
    Squares Stewed in Tomatoes and White Wine, 8
Stock:
    Homemade Chicken, 294–95
    Making of, 295
Strawberry and Tomato Gazpacho, 10
Summer Savory, Green Beans with, 164
Susan's Monkfish with Savoy Cabbage and Spanish Ham, 103–5
Sweet Potato "Fries," Spicy, 204
Swiss Chard:
    Chickpea, and Lentil Stew, Curried, 63–64
    Leaf Purée with Bacon La Beaugravière, 205
    Mussels with Saffron Cream and, 82–83
    Rib Gratin with Pine Nuts and Parmesan, Yannick Alléno's, 206–7

Taboulé aux Épinards, 150
Tarragon:
    Fresh, Sauté of Veal with, 132
    Heirloom Tomato Broth with, 50
Tartare:
    de Betterave aux Câpres, Moutarde et Échalotes, 14
    de Thon à la Ciboulette Le Kaiku, 102
Tartinade de Pois Chiches au Basilic, 16
Têtes d'Ail au Four, 184
Thai Curry Paste, 309
Thiebault, Joël, 40, 167, 196
Thyme:
    -Buttermilk Dressing, 298
    Chorizo with Sherry Vinegar and, 9
Timbales d'Aubergines, Tomates et Basilic, 175–76
Le Timbre, Paris, 59
Tomates:
    au Four à la Purée de Basilic, 209
    Tartare, 210
Tomato(es):
    Baby Squid with Garlic, Olives, Parsley and, 97
    Cherry, and Black Olive Salad, 30
    Cherry, Oven-Roasted, 208

    Coulis with Asparagus and Mint, Guy Savoy's, 56
    Eggplant, Basil, and Cheese Timbales, 175–76
    and Eggplant from the Velleron Market, 181
    Evergreen, Cooler, 5
    Fresh, Quick Whole Wheat Pizza with Artichokes, Capers and, 259–60
    Gazpacho, 55
    Heirloom, Broth with Tarragon, 50
    Heirloom, Corn, and Cucumber Soup, Chilled, with Fresh Cilantro, 51
    Heirloom, Salad, Frédéric Anton's, 29
    Heirloom, Soup, Marinated, 49
    Provençal Roast, with Light Basil Purée, 209
    -Quinoa Bread, 256–57
    Red Peppers, Onions, Cumin, and Espelette Pepper, 200
    Roasted Chickpeas, Mushrooms, Artichokes and, 146
    Sardines in Parchment with Onions and, 89–90
    Sauce, Chunky Fresh, 305
    Sauce, Rustic Oven-Roasted, 306
    Sauce, Zucchini Coins in, 218
    Sorbet, 211
    Spring Onion, Avocado, and Basil Salad with Basil-Lemon Dressing, 32
    and Strawberry Gazpacho, 10
    Tartare, 210
    Tuna Confit with Capers, White Wine and, 100–101
    and White Wine, Squid Squares Stewed in, 8
Troisgros, Michel, 136
Truffes aux Pignons de Pin et Parmesan, 235–36
Truffle(s), Truffled:
    Butter, 314
    Chaource, 237
    Cream, 313
    Goat Cheese "Oreos" with, 234
    Oil, 313
    Parmesan, and Pine Nut Gratins, 235–36
Tuna:
    Chive, and Shallot Tartare, Le Kaiku's, 102
    Confit with Tomatoes, Capers, and White Wine, 100–101
    Strips with Espelette Pepper, 99
Turnips:
    Spicy, in Thai Medley, 212
    in Winter (Vegetable) Kaleidoscope, 196–97
    in Winter Root Vegetable Pistou, 72–73

Vanucci, Louis-Jacques, 167
Veal:
    and Cabbage Rolls with Parmesan, 130–31
    Sauté of, with Fresh Tarragon, 132
Vegetable(s), 156–219
    Artichokes and Lemons, Grilled, with Spicy
        Garlic Mayonnaise, 158
    Asparagus, Roasted, with Arugula and
        Shallot Vinaigrette, 162
    Asparagus Braised with Fresh Rosemary and
        Bay Leaves, 160
    Asparagus with Gruyère and Smoked Ham,
        159
    Autumn, Ragout with Wild Mushrooms,
        190–93
    Baby Artichokes with Avocado, Pine Nuts,
        and Parmesan, 156–57
    Broccoli Purée with a Hint of Mint, 167
    Brussels Sprouts, Sautéed, with Garlic and
        Olive Oil, 169
    Brussels Sprouts, Steamed, with Bacon and
        Cream, 170
    Cabbage, Steamed, Creamy, 171
    Cauliflower Purée, 172
    Corn Kernels, Butter-Warmed, with Fresh
        Cilantro Leaves, 174
    Eggplant, Johannes's Picnic, 183
    Eggplant, Roasted, Towers with Tomato
        Sauce, Fresh Cheese, and Basil, 177–78
    Eggplant, Steamed, with Buttermilk-Thyme
        Dressing, 182
    Eggplant, Tomato, Basil, and Cheese
        Timbales, 175–76
    Eggplant and Tomatoes from the Velleron
        Market, 181
    Eggplant Daube, 179
    Garlic, Roasted Fresh, 184
    Green Beans with Summer Savory, 164
    Just Spinach!, 203
    Lamb's Lettuce Purée, 186
    Leeks, Steamed, in Mustard and Caper
        Vinaigrette, 188
    Morel Mushrooms, Wild, in Cream, 189

Mushrooms, Wild, in Parchment with Wild
    Mint, 194
Peas, Fresh, with Mint and Spring Onions,
    198
Pumpkin Gratin with Pistachios and
    Pistachio Oil, 202
Red Peppers, Oven-Roasted, in Olive Oil, 199
Red Peppers, Tomatoes, Onions, Cumin, and
    Espelette Pepper, 200
Salad, Shaved, 37
Sweet Potato "Fries," Spicy, 204
Swiss Chard Leaf Purée with Bacon La
    Beaugravière, 205
Swiss Chard Rib Gratin with Pine Nuts and
    Parmesan, Yannick Alléno's, 206–7
Thai Medley: Spicy Turnips, Squash,
    Carrots, and Potatoes, 212
Tomatoes, Oven-Roasted Cherry, 208
Tomatoes, Provençal Roast, with Light Basil
    Purée, 209
Tomato Sorbet, 211
Tomato Tartare, 210
Winter Kaleidoscope: Carrots, Jerusalem
    Artichokes, Turnips, and Radishes, 196–97
Winter Root Vegetable Pistou, 72–73
Zucchini Blossoms Stuffed with Goat Cheese
    and Basil, 216
Zucchini Carpaccio with Avocado, Lemon
    Thyme, and Pistachio Oil, 214
Zucchini Coins in Tomato Sauce, 218
Zucchini La Ponche, 217
Zucchini Purée, 219
Zucchini Spaghetti with Creamy Lemon-
    Chive Dressing, 213
see also Potato(es)
Velouté de Haricots Blancs, Morilles à Crème, 65–66
Versini, Dominique, 117
Vinaigrettes:
    Classic, 296
    Mustard and Caper, Steamed Leeks in, 188
    Red Wine, Pork Sausage with Potatoes and,
        128–29
    Shallot, 300

Shallot, Grilled Chicken with, 108–9
Shallot, Roasted Asparagus with Arugula
    and, 162
Vinaigrettes:
    Classique, 296
    aux Echalotes, 300

Walnut(s):
    Bread, Quick, 250
    and Date Bread, 248
Watercress:
    Pesto, 303
    Salad with Creamy Bacon and Poached Egg,
        22–23
Wells, Walter, 119, 179, 196, 203, 264
White Bean(s):
    and Artichoke Dip, 19
    Fresh, Soup with Morels in Cream, 65–66
White Wine:
    Chicken Breasts with Mint, Capers and, 110
    Squid Squares Stewed in Tomatoes and, 8
    Tuna Confit with Tomatoes, Capers and,
        100–101
Winter Kaleidoscope: Carrots, Jerusalem
    Artichokes, Turnips, and Radishes, 196–97
Winter Root Vegetable Pistou, 72–73

Yogurt:
    and Cucumber Soup, Chilled, with Dill and
        Fresh Mint, 54
    Sheep's Milk, Sorbet, 291

Zucchini:
    Blossoms Stuffed with Goat Cheese and
        Basil, 216
    Carpaccio with Avocado, Lemon Thyme,
        and Pistachio Oil, 214
    Coins in Tomato Sauce, 218
    Lamb Couscous with Chickpeas and, 124–25
    La Ponche, 217
    Purée, 219
    Spaghetti with Creamy Lemon-Chive
        Dressing, 213